CLASSICAL SAMARITAN POETRY

Classical Samaritan Poetry

LAURA SUZANNE LIEBER

EISENBRAUNS | University Park, Pennsylvania

Library of Congress Cataloging-in-Publication Data

Names: Lieber, Laura Suzanne, author, translator.
Title: Classical Samaritan poetry / Laura Suzanne Lieber.
Description: University Park, Pennsylvania : Eisenbrauns, [2022] | Includes biblio-
    graphical references and index.
Summary: "An anthology of annotated English translations of fifty-five Classical
    Samaritan poems"—Provided by publisher.
Identifiers: LCCN 2021056813 | ISBN 9781646021826 (hardback) | ISBN
    9781646022977 (paper)
Subjects: LCSH: Samaritan religious poetry—Translations into English. | Hymns,
    Samaritan Aramaic—Translations into English.
Classification: LCC BM960 .L54 2022 | DDC 892/.29—dc23/eng/20220111
LC record available at https://lccn.loc.gov/2021056813

Eisenbrauns is an imprint of The Pennsylvania State University Press.

The Pennsylvania State University Press is a member of the Association of University
Presses.

It is the policy of The Pennsylvania State University Press to use acid-free paper. Pub-
lications on uncoated stock satisfy the minimum requirements of American National
Standard for Information Sciences—Permanence of Paper for Printed Library Material, ANSI z39.48-1992.

CONTENTS

ACKNOWLEDGMENTS

This book would not exist without the encouragement and support of my colleague and friend Steven Fine, who first brought this body of literature to my attention and who graciously invited me to participate in the Israelite Samaritans Project at Yeshiva University. I also owe sincerest thanks to Reinhard Pummer, whose work proved essential to this task and who proved himself, again and again, a generous reader of an autodidact's drafts, and to Moshe Florentin, who has shared of his work and time, even from afar. I am also grateful to Benyamim Tsedaka, cultural ambassador of the modern Samaritan community in Israel and, to my surprise and delight, a frequent visitor to North Carolina, owing to the hospitality of Margaret Wooten. I would also like to express my thanks to the participants in the "Old Testament Figures in Late Antique Poetry Workshop," hosted at the University of Waterloo, and the panelists and interlocutors at the European Association for Biblical Studies in Krakow; insights, questions, and suggestions from both groups helped to refine the work presented here. Similarly, I am grateful to Rodney Werline, whose gatherings at Barton College have fostered a true community over the years and generated ongoing conversations of enduring importance. I also express my gratitude to the Research Centre "Dynamics of Jewish Ritual Practices in Pluralistic Contexts from Antiquity to the Present" at the Universität Erfurt, Max Weber Kolleg—particularly my hosts, Claudia Bergmann and Jörg Rüpke; my research fellowship in Erfurt enabled me to complete much of this manuscript.

The errors and infelicities in this text are all my responsibility; what elegance this work possesses reflects my debt to Gene McGarry, who brings both knowledge and skill to the task of editing, and to Alex Ramos and the editorial staff at Penn State University Press and Eisenbrauns. I am grateful to Patrick Alexander for his enthusiasm for this project from the beginning. Nor would this book exist without the continued support of friends and colleagues in my "home" department of religious studies, and my "home-away-from-home" departments of classical studies and German studies, as well as collaborators near and far. I owe a particular debt to the comparative-hymnography community created (with great energy and intentionality) by Georgia Frank, Susan Ashbrook Harvey, Derek Krueger, Michael Swartz, and Ophir Münz-Manor. I am also thankful for the gracious collegiality of the Medieval Hebrew Poetry Colloquium—particularly Elisabeth Hollender and Wout van Bekkum—where I was always welcomed in the kindest and warmest way to share these poems, works that are neither medieval nor in Hebrew.

I conclude these acknowledgments, as always, with an expression of love for and gratitude to my family. To mom and dad, who have always encouraged me; to my sister, Debbie, whom I treasure; to Norman, whose friendship and care have been unwavering; and to Julian and Daniel, who make me laugh and give each day meaning. But the person to whom I dedicate this volume is one who will not read his name here; this book is for my big brother, Kenneth Andrew Lieber. I miss you every day.

ABBREVIATIONS

CAL	*Comprehensive Aramaic Lexicon* (http://cal.huc.edu)
D	Solomon Brown. "A Critical Edition and Translation of the Ancient Samaritan *Defter* (i.e., Liturgy) and a Comparison of It with Early Jewish Liturgy." PhD thesis, University of Leeds, 1955.
DeutR	Deuteronomy Rabbah
DSA	Abraham Tal. *A Dictionary of Samaritan Aramaic*. 2 vols. Leiden: Brill, 2000.
ExodR	Exodus Rabbah
GenR	Genesis Rabbah
JPA	Jewish Palestinian Aramaic
LamR	Lamentations Rabbati
m.	Mishnah
MidPs	Midrash on Psalms
MS(S)	manuscript(s)
MT	Masoretic Text
PdRK	Pesiqta de Rab Kahana
RPH	Ze'ev Ben-Hayyim. *The Recitation of Prayers and Hymns* [in Hebrew]. Vol. 3, part 2, of *The Literary and Oral Tradition of Hebrew and Aramaic Amongst the Samaritans*. Jerusalem: Academy of the Hebrew Language, 1967.
RSV	Revised Standard Version
SamP	Samaritan Pentateuch. Abraham Tal, ed. *The Samaritan Pentateuch, Edited According to MS 6 (C) of the Shekhem Synagogue*. Tel Aviv: Tel Aviv University Press, 1994.
SamT	Samaritan Targum. Abraham Tal, ed. *The Samaritan Targum of the Pentateuch: A Critical Edition*. 3 vols. Tel Aviv: Tel Aviv University Press, 1980–83.

SAP   A. S. Rodrigues Pereira. *Studies in Aramaic Poetry (c. 100 B.C.E.–
            c. 600 C.E.): Selected Jewish, Christian and Samaritan Poems.*
            Leiden: Brill, 1997.
SL   Arthur E. Cowley. *The Samaritan Liturgy.* 2 vols. Oxford: Claren-
            don, 1909.
SongR   Song of Songs Rabbah
TM   Ze'ev Ben-Hayyim. *Tibat Marqe: A Collection of Samaritan
            Midrashim* [Hebrew]. Jerusalem: Israel Academy of Sciences and
            Humanities, 1988.

Introduction

THE BOUNDARIES OF THE PERIOD known as late antiquity are often defined along religious lines: it can be said to begin with Constantine and the Christianization of the Roman Empire and to end with the birth of Islam.[1] And yet, while to some extent religious affiliations were aligned with imperial borderlines and power structures—Christians on one side, Zoroastrians and later Muslims on the other—such broad generalizations obscure the multiplicity of religious communities that textured the landscape of the Mediterranean world and the Levant, from Spain to Persia. Indeed, the chief legacy of late antiquity may very well be the religious dynamism that endured in this region long after the seventh century, into the present day, as religious traditions both established and nascent, indigenous and influenced from afar, emerged from and encountered one another. These communities concretized distinctive practices, beliefs, and worldviews in diverse literary works, monuments, and artifacts, even as they also retained roots in a larger and shared cultural matrix we call, as a shorthand, late antiquity.

Between the third and seventh centuries CE, the eastern Mediterranean world sustained a multitude of diverse, and diversifying, ethnic-religious communities. Most notably, this epoch witnessed the fierce and expressive final flourishing of Greco-Roman polytheism, with all its political and philosophical richness; the resurgence of a dynamic and vital Judaism, expressed in its monumental architecture and literary output; and the emergence of an assertive and diverse imperial Christianity in both East and West. The literary, material, and visual remains of this period testify to the vibrancy and creativity of all these communities as they encountered, resisted, coexisted with, and responded to one another. The most familiar religions of the modern West—Judaism, Christianity, and Islam, in all their fraught and entangled complexity—constitute enduring legacies of this formative, and transformative, period.

1. For a thorough discussion of this contentious periodization, see Marcone, "Long Late Antiquity?"

Reading antiquity through the lens of the present, however, can lead to distortions and oversights, particularly in regard to populations, cultures, and ideologies that today seem quite marginal or even exotic but were important, if perhaps localized, realities in the ancient world. One such case would be Zoroastrianism, the religion of the political elites of the Achaemenid Empire and its Parthian and Sassanian successors, and a familiar presence in the literature of both early Syriac-speaking Christians and the Jews of Babylonia. Today, there is a small but clearly identifiable contemporary Zoroastrian diaspora that proudly recalls its millennia of imperial history.[2] Another long-lived community—far smaller in antiquity than the Persian Zoroastrians, and less powerful, yet hardly marginal—is that of the Samaritans: the faithful "guardians" (*shomerim*, a play on the Hebrew form of their name) of their Torah and traditions, who have a history as long as that of the Jews. The Samaritans of late antiquity, and particularly their religious self-expression as preserved in the poetry of their "classical" age, are the subject of the present volume.

A full overview of Samaritan history, culture, and traditions far exceeds the scope of this work, and so the present introduction serves primarily to sketch the broad outlines of the subject, with an eye toward contextualizing classical Samaritan poetry and providing bibliographic sources for readers who wish to delve deeper into any given topic. As will become clear, one recurring challenge is the paucity of information from late antiquity; the poems in this volume constitute one of the most robust sources of knowledge we have for concepts and traditions that are otherwise articulated, and more fully developed, only in the medieval and even early modern period. The dates of key figures—for instance, the great reformer Baba Rabbah (lit., "the great gate")—are modern hypotheses, and I have attempted to flag uncertainties and debates among scholars. Just as with Jewish *piyyut* (liturgical poetry), where the chronology is relative, enabling periodization but not dating, the only truly inarguable statements one can make about most of these poems are that they are written in an authentic Aramaic from late antiquity (as discussed below) and that they are revered by the Samaritan community to this day.

A Starting Point

Like the Zoroastrians, the Samaritans have maintained their distinctive identity into the present: a population of around eight hundred individuals is split

---

2. On Zoroastrianism, especially in the modern world, see the essays collected in Williams, Stewart, and Hintze, *Zoroastrian Flame*, and Stausberg, Vevaina, and Tessmann, *Wiley Blackwell Companion to Zoroastrianism*.

between the city of Holon, outside Tel Aviv in the modern state of Israel, and the vicinity of Mount Gerizim, their holiest site, located in the West Bank near Nablus (Neopolis), known in the Bible as Shechem.[3] Historically, the Samaritans have generally lived in close proximity to Shechem, but literary and material sources indicate that small but noteworthy Samaritan diasporas did exist throughout the ancient world.[4] Between the fourth century BCE and the nineteenth century CE, Samaritan communities are attested in Egypt, Greece, Italy, Asia Minor, the Levant, and the Arabian Peninsula. These exile communities were often conflated with nearby Jewish communities by their Christian and Muslim contemporaries because overt cultural markers shared by the two groups—including iconography, architecture, language, and names—are more conspicuous to outsiders than the theological and ideological differences that separate them.

Today, for the most part, outside of modern Israel, Samaritans are known not on their own terms, as a modern religious and ethnic community with their own religious traditions and historical integrity, but rather through the lenses of others. In the Anglophone world, familiarity with Samaritans comes almost exclusively through the New Testament parable of the good Samaritan (Luke 10:30–37) and the institutions that derive their names from that story, such as Good Samaritan hospitals and the Samaritan's Purse charity organization. Other passages, such as the Samaritan woman at the well (John 4:4–26), may also come to mind.[5] The problematic nature of such perceptions hardly needs articulation;

3. Several essays treating the modern Samaritan community can be found in Dušek, *Samaritans*. On the self-understanding of the history and population of Samaritans in Israel and Palestine over the last century, see Israelite Samaritan Information Institute, "Population." The ancient capital of Samaria, Shechem, now lies in the Palestinian territories. While it is now common to equate Shechem with Neapolis (modern Nablus), biblical Shechem occupied the site now known as Tell Balāṭa; Neapolis was founded as a Roman city in 72 CE by the emperor Vespasian. See Campbell, "Shechem—Tel Balâtah."

4. For a summary of the evidence for Samaritan diaspora settlements, see Zsengellér, "Samaritan Diaspora in Antiquity." As Zsengellér notes, it can often be very difficult to distinguish Samaritan communities from Jewish communities. See also Crown, "Samaritan Diaspora"; Pummer, *Samaritans*, 180–87; Rutgers, *Hidden Heritage*, 84–85, 276–77. For a time, modern Samaritans rejected the idea of a Samaritan diaspora; see A. B. Institute of Samaritan Studies, *Samaritan Survival*. This pamphlet categorically denies the existence of a Samaritan diaspora, stating that "diasporas were never established outside the Land of Israel" (1). More recently, however, the community's leaders have revised their position; see Tsedaka, *Understanding the Israelite-Samaritans*, 8.

5. John 4:4–26 describes Jesus's encounter with the Samaritan woman (v. 9), who expresses surprise that Jesus, a Jew, would request a drink from her; she subsequently testifies on Jesus's behalf to her village. Samaritans appear elsewhere in the New Testament too, often in contexts where they are foils for other groups, either Gentiles or Jews; see Matt 10:5 (where Jesus instructs his disciples to avoid the towns of Gentiles and Samaritans and seek out "the lost sheep of Israel"), John 8:48 (where the Jews accuse Jesus of being a Samaritan and of being possessed by a devil), Luke 17:16 (which describes the healing of a leper who is also a Samaritan), and Acts 8 (which describes Phillip's successful mission to Samaria and the figure of Simon Magus).

it is as if we knew Jews only through the New Testament. The popular usage of the term "good Samaritan" itself often obscures the stereotyping that gave the Christian parable its power: a story about a figure whose compassion for a Jewish wayfarer was noteworthy precisely because of the poor reputation of Samaritans among Luke's audience. Even a quick survey of ancient sources, however, reveals a far more documented, if complex and even contradictory, history than modern colloquial familiarity would suggest.

Samaritans in Antiquity Through the Eyes of Others

Searching for the origins of the Samaritans tends to lead down an array of ideological rabbit holes. Although a diverse array of sources is available, they tend to be deeply or at least implicitly polemical, and often stock characters—"the Samaritan" and "the Jew"—serve as foils for the identity-creation process of other parties. A brief survey of several key moments and sources will illustrate how others have seen Samaritans, as well as how Samaritans have seen themselves.

The classical Samaritan writings presented in this volume were likely composed—and committed to memory and, eventually, to writing—in the late third and fourth centuries CE, but the Samaritan community is much older. As with the other Abrahamic traditions, Samaritan cultural history forms a complex nexus of canon, languages, liturgy and rituals, and traditions of exegesis. Thus, while Samaritanism acquired its still-recognizable contours in the third and fourth centuries—through its textual production, liturgical creativity, political engagement, and so forth—its roots stretch back into the same ancient soil from which Judaism and Christianity emerged, the Torah.[6]

Samaritans, like Jews, identify as Israelites; indeed, they regard themselves as the true keepers of Israelite tradition and Jews as wayward sectarians.[7] Samaritans share much with the Jews, including a reverence for the Torah, but other texts considered biblical by Jews—the Prophets and the Writings of the Jewish Tanakh

6. There are obvious parallels with early Christianity and Islam, as well—traditions that likewise trace their origins to texts and traditions arising from ancient Israel. The affinity—however ambivalent it may be—between Jews and Samaritans, however, is arguably closer than that between other groups, as evident in antiquity and even in the legal status of Samaritans in modern Israeli law (where identity cards and passports of Samaritans label the bearer as a *yehudi shomroni*, "Samaritan Jew"). See Schreiber, *Comfort of Kin*, especially 52–68, where the intervention of Yitzhak Ben-Zvi on behalf of the Samaritans is described.

7. Medieval Samaritan chronicles trace the origin of the schism between Jews and Samaritans to the actions of Eli (1 Sam 1–4), who arrogated the high priesthood to himself and set up a schismatic temple in Shiloh; this temple is the direct ancestor of the schismatic temple in Jerusalem. See Kartveit, "Origin of the Jews and Samaritans."

(the Christian Old Testament)—do not constitute part of Samaritan scriptures. Nor do the Samaritans hold as sacred any works outside the Pentateuch. It is not that the Samaritans were unaware of the Prophets and the Writings; it seems that in the wake of their schism with the Jewish community in the Hasmonean period, they specifically repudiated these other works, most likely because of the central role that Jerusalem (rather than Mount Gerizim) played in them.[8] Indeed, within Samaritan tradition, the name "Samaritans," or in Hebrew *Shomronim*, does not primarily imply an affiliation with the geographical region of Samaria (*Shomron*), the seat of the kingdom of Israel in the north. Rather, they embrace their role as *shomerim*—"keepers" or "guardians"—who maintain fidelity to what they understand to be the pure Israelite tradition that they alone keep, including the Torah-only tradition.[9] The complicated relations of the Samaritan community with other religious communities in antiquity make the appearance of parallels between Samaritan and Jewish or Christian traditions particularly intriguing, as such resonances can be attributed to common traditions centuries in the past or explained as independent, unrelated developments, or as developments in one community transmitted to another through recurring contact. In general, as the poems translated in this volume reveal, Samaritan communities (like Jews, and also like Christians) were part of a larger common culture in late antiquity on which they impressed their own distinct inflection.

As a consequence of their loyalty to an austere Pentateuchal canon, the Samaritans do not accept as scriptural the Jewish and Christian works in which Samaritans as such are first depicted. We may not be surprised that polemical works such as Ezra and Nehemiah found no welcome in the Samaritan Bible; other works, such as Psalms, while less overtly problematic, were likely regarded as alien because they bear a strong stamp of Judahite tradition and a history of connection to worship in the Jerusalem Temple (as opposed to Mount Gerizim).[10] Just as importantly, the Samaritan Pentateuch (SamP) itself

---

8. See the discussion in Beckwith, "Formation." As Beckwith notes, not all writings outside the Torah were explicitly problematic from a Samaritan perspective, but their unilateral rejection of most of the Jewish canon served as an unambiguous marker of their distinct religious identity.

9. Indeed, the modern Samaritans maintain a careful distinction between their identity as "guardians" and those who are simply from the geographic region of Samaria (*shomronim*, or "Samarians"), although the identities in practice can overlap. The Samaritans' self-understanding as "keepers of tradition" can be found in sources as early as the church fathers; see Pummer, *Early Christian Authors on Samaritans*. Also central to Samaritan identity is their reverence for Mount Gerizim as the chosen locus of the temple; they reject the Jewish identification of Mount Zion as the Temple Mount.

10. As Beckwith notes, "The rejection of the Prophets and Hagiographa would have left the Samaritans without any account of the history of their forbearers between the death of Moses and recent times. In due time they made good this lack by producing chronicles, which drew upon the Jewish scriptures and upon traditions of their own which gave them a more distinguished past" ("Formation," 86).

differs from the Jewish Masoretic Text (MT) in key ways, notably its affirmations of the importance of the Samaritan holy site, Mount Gerizim, over against Jewish attachment to Mount Zion.

The complicated (and ultimately irretrievable) origins of the Samaritan community, and by extension the Samaritan Torah and liturgy, are bound up in its long entanglement with Judeans and thus Jews. One key moment in this history was the fall of the Northern Kingdom (which included Samaria) to the Assyrians in 722 BCE. When the Kingdom of Israel fell, at least some refugees from the north presumably fled south, bringing with them any number of texts, traditions, and understandings, including perhaps the kernel of what would become the Deuteronomistic tradition. (It is worth noting that Jerusalem and Zion are never mentioned in Deuteronomy, even in the MT; SamP Deut 27:4, however, describes Moses commanding that stones from the Jordan be used to build an altar on Mount Gerizim. This altar anticipates the temple to come.) Later, when Nebuchadnezzar II's soldiers deported the political and intellectual elites of Judah to Babylonia in the sixth century BCE, they left behind any number of faithful, if impoverished, Israelites (including some who no doubt yearned for a return to Samaria) among the Judahites.[11]

Already in the Hebrew Bible, in the postexilic books of Ezra and Nehemiah, Samaritans are portrayed as antagonists of the community of returning Judean exiles. Their hostility reflects the rift between the cultural elites (embodied by Ezra and Nehemiah) who had been deported to Babylonia and returned to resume control of Judean society under Persian protection, on the one hand, and those who had never left the Land and had faithfully kept ancestral traditions and thus viewed themselves as "the keepers" (*ha-shomerim*, i.e., the Samaritans), on the other. The historical text of 2 Kgs 17, however, names this population "Cutheans" (*Kutim*), a derogatory term that distances them from Judeans.[12]

The origins of the Samaritan community lie in the tension between, on the one hand, a synthesis of these northern traditions from Samaria with closely related traditions from the Southern Kingdom and, on the other, divisions among communities that were exacerbated by the experience of the Babylonian

<hr/>

11. For a discussion of the early history of the Samaritans, from the Assyrian period to the late Roman period (and thus including early Christianity as well as early Judaism), see Knoppers, *Jews and Samaritans*. Concise and useful summaries of Jewish and Christian traditions of Samaritan origins can be found in Pummer, *Samaritans*, 10–25. Also important are the essays in Zsengellér, *Samaria, Samarians, Samaritans*; Hjelm, "Samaritans," is especially helpful in articulating the challenges in writing about Samaritans as a distinctive group.

12. The term *Kutim*/"Cutheans" derives from 2 Kgs 17:24, 30, where "Kuthites" are among the deportees resettled in Samaria by the Assyrians. This association of Samaritans with Cutheans is polemical, as it assigns the Samaritans an origin outside the land of Israel; essentially, the rabbis use this nomenclature to reciprocate the Samaritan denial of the Judean "authenticity" of the returnees from Babylonian exile.

destruction of Judah. In this period, "keepers of tradition" can refer to those who retained an ancestral attachment to Samaria and its variants of Israelite sacred history and traditions, alongside those who were similarly faithful to the Judean versions of the same. Thus, the Samaritans with whom Ezra and Nehemiah clash in the period of Persian restoration should not be understood as "pagans" or aliens, although that is how texts such as 2 Kgs 17 depict them; instead, they are Israelites (with roots in the Kingdom of Israel) whose history does not include the experience of Babylonian exile, but who nonetheless experienced displacement (from the north), subjugation, and occupation. This gulf in terms of religious outlook represents an early "parting of the ways" between Jewish (Judean) Israelites and their Samaritan Israelite kin. Ezekiel vividly describes the Jewish idea that God abandoned Jerusalem and Judah to dwell with the Jewish (Judean) Israelites in Babylon, while those left behind believed they were the ones keeping the faith alive in its true form on its native soil. Furthermore, in the eyes of those Judeans who returned from Babylonian exile, the very traditions so faithfully kept by those who were never exiled preserved not divine ideals but rather the wayward practices that resulted in the exile in the first place. Faithfulness was regarded as wayward stubbornness. But for the Samaritans, who in their medieval chronicles refer to Jews as "the erroneous ones," "rebels," "heretics," and "people of error," it is clear that the same response of rejection ran in the other direction, as well.[13]

These communal fissures and recombinations suggest the complexity of the relationship between these two communities, two populations that shared so much (including nearly identical Torahs) but also repeatedly sought to distinguish themselves from each other. But it bears remembering that in antiquity the Samaritans played an ongoing role in negotiations of Jewish identity and its boundaries precisely because of their own identity as "Israelites" who were emphatically not "Judeans/Jews." Jewish historical experience was shaped by the experience of surviving exile, while Samaritan identity emerged from the experience of conquests and occupations by parties at times alien and in other cases kin. The differences between Samaritan and Judean Israelites were subsequently amplified by theological differences that likely emerged over time as ways of asserting boundaries through rival claims concerning whose customs of worship were correct and, eventually, whose Torah was correct.

Over the centuries, these differences widened into an unbridgeable breach. The gulf between the two communities is symbolized to this day by disagreement over the location of God's chosen site of worship: Mount Zion for the Jews but Mount Gerizim (near modern Nablus, ancient Shechem) for the Samaritans. Furthermore, while the Jews and Samaritans share a reverence for the

---

13. Stenhouse, "Chronicle of Abu 'l-Fatḥ."

Torah, which is venerated as a scroll in the synagogues of both communities, the Samaritan text is written in a distinctive alphabet (a form of the old Hebrew alphabet, in contradistinction to the "Assyrian"—Aramaic—square letters of postexilic Jewish writing).[14] In terms of differences between the Samaritan text and the MT, the Samaritan offers fewer anthropomorphic descriptions of God, employs slightly more decorous language in some instances, includes passages that are paralleled elsewhere in the Torah but not in the MT, and (most significantly) posits Mount Gerizim as the place where sacrifices should be offered when the Israelites enter Canaan (SamP Deut 27:4). When the differences are few, they bear even more cultural weight. Thus, while it can be difficult for archaeologists to distinguish between Jewish and Samaritan settlements and synagogues, we can assume that those who lived there knew who they were— and what spaces they considered sacred, whom they could marry, and what authorities they could trust.

According to Jewish biblical sources, Samaritan gestures toward reunification in the period of Ezra and Nehemiah were rebuffed, and distrust and disagreement hardened into mutual animosity by the time of the Second Temple. The parable of the good Samaritan in the New Testament hinges on the surprising idea that a Samaritan would become the benefactor of a Jerusalemite. In the passage, Jesus offers the parable in response to the question "And who is my neighbor?"

> Jesus replied, "A man was going down from Jerusalem to Jericho, and he fell among robbers, who stripped him and beat him, and departed, leaving him half dead. Now by chance a priest was going down that road; and when he saw him he passed by on the other side. So likewise a Levite, when he came to the place and saw him, passed by on the other side. But a Samaritan, as he journeyed, came to where he was; and when he saw him, he had compassion, and went to him and bound up his wounds, pouring on oil and wine; then he set him on his own beast and brought him to an inn, and took care of him. And the next day he took out two *denarii* and gave them to the innkeeper, saying, 'Take care of him; and whatever more you spend, I will repay you when I come back.' Which of these three, do you think, proved neighbor to the man who fell among the robbers?" He said, "The one who showed mercy on him." And Jesus said to him, "Go and do likewise." (Luke 10:30–37, RSV, adapted)

The parable turns on the assumption that the man's presumed kin—the priest and the Levite—do not act as his "fellows," while the Samaritan, who is expected to shun the wounded Jew, acts with tremendous compassion. Community and

---

14. For references to writing in "Assyrian" characters, see m. Megillah 1:8; 2:2; m. Yadayim 4:5.

fellowship are matters of choice rather than kinship, of behavior rather than blood. This parable demonstrates the creation of community by demonstrating that even a Samaritan can act in a way that joins him to the fellowship.[15]

Given the ethnic, ritual, and theological affinities of Samaritans and Jews for each other, Samaritans seem to have challenged the boundaries of Judaism in a way that Christians did not. We see Jewish engagement with Samaritans in Jewish sources, where Samaritans appear in both narrative and legal contexts in ways that allow the rabbinic authors to discuss boundary definitions: Where are the lines between "in" and "out"? Just as Jews served as literary foils for the creation and articulation of Christian self-understanding in the New Testament and patristic writings, rabbinic sources deploy Samaritans, often as stock characters (akin to the Gentile philosopher, emperor, and matron), in their own literary works—and they do so more often and in more complicated ways, given the vast quantity and temporal span of this body of writing.[16] One passage from Genesis Rabbah, the early and influential collection of rabbinic interpretations of Genesis, highlights the subtle and nuanced relationship to Samaritans that typifies rabbinic understandings—polemical and otherwise—of these (estranged or accepted) kin. The text depicts an argument over the relative merits of Mount Zion and Mount Gerizim (a motif also invoked in John 4:20).

Rabbi Jonathan was going up to pray in Jerusalem, when he reached that Palatinus[17] and saw there a certain Samaritan (חד שמריי).[18] He asked him, "Where are you going?" He (Rabbi Jonathan) replied to him, "To pray in Jerusalem." "And would it not be better to pray at this holy mountain than at that dunghill of a house?" he (the Samaritan) asked. "In what way is it blessed?" he (Rabbi Jonathan) inquired. (The Samaritan responded:) "Because it was not submerged by the waters of the Flood."
  Now the *halakhah* (on the subject) was forgotten[19] for a moment by Rabbi Jonathan, but his ass-driver said to him, "Rabbi! If you will permit

---

15. The story of the Samaritan woman at the well (John 4:4–42) likewise uses a Samaritan as a foil for the Jews. This story, which recalls betrothal scenes from the Hebrew Bible, recounts a conversation between a Samaritan woman and Jesus, whom she addresses as a Jew. The exchange is intellectually robust and concludes with the woman recognizing Jesus as the messiah—showing that she sees the truth more clearly than the Jews whom she expected to antagonize her.

16. For a recent essay that summarizes the evolution of "Cutheans" from wayward kin to (functional) non-Jewish outsiders, see Lehnardt, "If a Cuthean Comes."

17. The term פלאטנוס (lit., "palace") refers to a royal residence and here indicates specifically "that palace"—Mount Gerizim, the house of the King of Kings (that is, the deity) in Samaritan tradition.

18. The parallel version in SongR 4:3 (25a) reads "a certain Cuthean" (חד כותי), a term that suggests greater distancing from the community; it also inserts the same term later in this passage, when the ass-driver responds to the Samaritan.

19. Lit., "hidden from the eyes of." The parallel in SongR reads, "The matter was hidden."

me, I will answer him." "Do so," he said. He responded: "If (this mountain is) among the high mountains, then it is written, 'And all the high mountains were covered' (Gen 7:19). Or if (this mountains is) among the low ones, the verse ignored it."[20]

Rabbi Jonathan immediately dismounted from his ass and made him (the driver) ride three miles (in his place), and he applied three verses to him: "There shall be no barren males or females among you or your cattle" (Deut 7:14)—i.e., even among your cattle drivers;[21] "Your forehead (*rakkatekh*) is like a pomegranate split open" (Song 4:3)—i.e., even the emptiest (*rekanim*) among you are as full of answers as a pomegranate [is full of seeds]; and thus it is written, "No weapon that is fashioned against you shall prevail; and any tongue that contends with you in dispute, you shall defeat" (Isa 54:17).[22]

This passage displays an awareness of Samaritan beliefs concerning the chosenness of their sacred mountain, alongside the assumption of a polemic against Jewish veneration of Mount Zion, even after the destruction of their temple (one to which Jews would need a ready response). The passage does not assume that their manner of worship is different, only the preferred location: the Samaritan even proposes that the Jew worship on Mount Gerizim instead of Mount Zion. The Samaritan is depicted as offering a distinctly Samaritan reading of Genesis—invoking the biblical text to argue for the superiority of Mount Gerizim in the context of sacred, universal history. Perhaps most intriguingly, the Samaritan's argument leaves the rabbi speechless, and it is his ass-driver who keeps his wits and is able to reply. The Samaritan is, in short, a potentially persuasive, albeit estranged, kinsman.

The Samaritans do not figure only in rabbinic exegesis, however. They are even more prominent in halakhic writings. In early rabbinic legal writings—the Mishnah and Tosefta—the Samaritans (often derogated as *Kutim/* "Cutheans") occupy an explicitly marginal place: not precisely Jewish, but not precisely not-Jewish. In m. Berakhot 7:1, a Samaritan is counted in the quorum needed for the recitation of grace after meals (a right denied to a *nokhri*, a non-Jew), in m. Demai 3:4, a Samaritan miller is equated with a boorish (but Jewish) miller, and in m. Demai 7:4, Jews are permitted to consume Samaritan wine. At the same

20. SongR 4:3 (25a) adds, "With that reply, that Cuthean was silenced, and he could not find a response." The ass-driver's response to the Samaritan's assertion argues that Mount Gerizim was indeed covered by the Flood, for if it were truly a high mountain, then Gen 7:19 would have applied to it, and otherwise, we can assume it was covered because scripture did not even see fit to mention it. The gist is that Samaritan tradition, and Samaritan pride in Mount Gerizim, is in error.

21. "Barren" here is understood as "devoid of learning." A learned response is one's "offspring."

22. GenR 32:10, in Theodor and Albeck, *Midrash Bereshit Rabbah*, 1:296–97; the parallel in SongR 4:3 (25a) is later and somewhat more expansive.

time, a tradition in m. Rosh Hashanah 2:2 recalls how Samaritans interfered with the signal fires used to announce the new year, and m. Shevi'it 8:10 compares Samaritan bread, hyperbolically, to pork. While m. Berakhot 8:8 notes that one may say "Amen" after a blessing is recited by a Samaritan, it specifies that one may do so only after the Samaritan has concluded his prayer—presumably to ensure that he does not insert references to Mount Gerizim and, in essence, make his blessing sectarian. And m. Ketubbot 3:1 includes Samaritan maidens in a list of women of ambiguous status (in terms of whether they are owed damages in cases of rape), along with female proselytes and freed, converted slaves. Samaritans feature even more frequently in the Tosefta, although just as ambivalently. Ultimately, as Reinhard Pummer notes, "the early rabbis were not so much concerned with the Samaritans as such, but rather wanted to clarify their own identity by examining to whom, exactly, the halakhic rulings apply. The Samaritans emerge in the process as an 'interstitial' category, neither Jewish nor non-Jewish."[23] Although it is a question meriting serious additional study, we must also consider the fact that Jewish writings in Palestine, where there was a robust, historical Samaritan community, would reflect a relationship with Samaritans different from what is found in sources arising in Babylonia, where there may have been a small Samaritan diaspora community but where Samaritans may have functioned more as figural, imaginary antagonists.[24]

Samaritans are also the primary topic of the minor, extracanonical talmudic tractate Kutim—that is, "Cutheans."[25] The final text of Kutim dates to after the closing of the Palestinian Talmud (ca. late fourth century CE), at the earliest.[26] While this text contains early traditions contemporary with the Mishnah and Tosefta, those earlier sources were reworked in late antiquity in order to create or more forcefully articulate boundaries between Samaritans and Jews. A comparison of tractate Kutim with earlier rabbinic sources reveals an increasing estrangement between Jews and Samaritans: practices that are permitted in the Mishnah and Tosefta, such as drinking Samaritan wine, are prohibited in Kutim. The tractate effectively makes the Samaritans "less Jewish" than they appear in earlier rabbinic sources. Even the term *kutim*, as opposed to *shomronim*, suggests the increasing estrangement between the groups.

23. Pummer, *Samaritans*, 68. See also Lightstone, "My Rival, My Fellow"; Schiffman, "Samaritans in Tannaitic Halakhah."

24. Babylonian rhetorical use of Samaritans may, when viewed this way, recall the uses of "rhetorical Jews" in some early Christian writings; see Shepardson, *Anti-Judaism and Christian Orthodoxy*.

25. There is no parallel tractate for other religious groups, who are, broadly speaking, understood to be addressed by the tractate Avodah Zarah (idol worship). The existence of tractate Kutim highlights the insider–outsider marginality of the Samaritans in Jewish antiquity.

26. On tractate Kutim, see Lehnardt, "Die Taube auf dem Garizim" and "Samaritans (*Kutim*)." Steven Fine of Yeshiva University is preparing a new edition of this important work.

Samaritans also feature prominently in early Christian writings, which do not contain any systematic treatments of Samaritans parallel to tractate Kutim but which nonetheless touch on a variety of subjects: the origins of the Samaritans and their identity as heretics or idolaters, the Samaritan Torah, Mount Gerizim, Samaritan theology and messianism, and Samaritan political involvement.[27] These Christian sources are often contradictory, because they are using Samaritans for rhetorical purposes (as foils for the pious or heretical), or because the ethnic term "Samaritan" is being used interchangeably with the geographical adjective "Samarian" (specifically in discussions of whether Simon Magus, "from Samaria," was a Samaritan), or simply because Samaritan traditions changed over time. Nevertheless, by charting agreements between early rabbinic and early Christian sources, it becomes possible to reconstruct, however tentatively, a reality—or perceived reality—of Samaritans in antiquity. Even as early Jewish and Christian sources deploy these estranged kin and fractious neighbors as rhetorical foils for issues of internal identity politics, they offer oblique insights into the place and perception of Samaritans within the larger world of late antique society.[28]

For many modern, nonspecialist readers, knowledge of the Samaritans begins and ends with their own sacred texts, which are emphatically not Samaritan works and which approach Samaritans from the role they can play in shaping Jewish and Christian identity. In short, popular understanding of the Samaritans is wholly dependent on Christian and Jewish sources, and not works authored by the Samaritans themselves.

We are lucky, however, to have a number of Samaritan works from the late third and fourth centuries CE in hand, alongside various material artifacts.[29] We thus can work to reconstruct the richness of Samaritan society not only from without but also from within.[30] These texts and the traditions they contain, along with inscriptions and objects uncovered by archaeologists, illuminate the Samaritan world from within, countering the ancient sources that regard them as categorically "other." If we had only literature *about* Samaritans, our understanding of their vigorous creativity in this momentous time period would be woefully incomplete.

27. See Pummer, *Early Christian Authors.*

28. Jews play a similar boundary-defining role in Christianity in this period; for an analysis that highlights this particular rhetorical use of one religious tradition as a foil, and boundary definer, for another, see Shepardson, *Anti-Judaism and Christian Orthodoxy.*

29. On Samaritan material culture, see the essays in Crown, *Samaritans,* especially the following chapters: Pummer, "Samaritan Material Remains"; Pummer, "Inscriptions"; Sixdenier, "Elements of Samaritan Numismatics." For a summary of the status of Samaritan archaeology overall, see Dar, "Archaeological Aspects." Also note the discussion of synagogues below.

30. The sources from late antiquity do not parallel all the genres we have from Jewish and Christian sources; in particular, Samaritan legal (halakhic) writings are not preserved until the medieval period.

For Samaritans, by Samaritans

Samaritan writings from late antiquity are largely "inward" in orientation. They were written for use in religious worship and study, and unlike the rabbinic sources examined above, they are less interested in issues such as boundary delineation. Even so, the texts reveal a great deal about the communities in which they were created and preserved. The use of Hebrew and Aramaic by Samaritans reveals the close kinship between Samaritans and Jews in particular, as well as cultural affinities with Palestinian Christians in late antiquity. On the other hand, even though the Samaritan Torah and the Jewish Torah are essentially identical in content, they are radically different in appearance: Samaritan Torah scrolls, and Samaritan writings in general, are written in a distinctive ornamented script that closely resembles preexilic (Paleo-Hebrew) writing, in contradistinction to the square "Assyrian" (Aramaic) letters used in most contexts by Jews in the postexilic period. The very choice of script thus becomes a marker of Samaritan difference from Jews.

The core of the Samaritan literary canon is unquestionably the Torah, both in the Hebrew original (SamP) and its Aramaic translation, the Samaritan Targum (SamT). The Torah is not the only sacred text of the Samaritans, however. The classical, nonscriptural literary canon of the community appears to have originated within a single, late third- and early fourth-century CE lineage: Amram Dare (Amram the Elder, who was also known as Tute [Titus]); his son, Marqe; and Marqe's son, Ninna. According to tradition, Amram participated actively in the Samaritan reforms of the revolutionary Baba Rabbah, and he is also the first Samaritan *payyetan* (liturgical poet) whose works survive. His son Marqe (Marcus, in Latin) authored the central exegetical work of Samaritan tradition, *Tibat Marqe* (Ark [i.e., anthology] of Marqe)—also known as *Memar Marqe* (Speech of Marqe).[31] While that prose work remains his most-studied literary product, he also wrote numerous *piyyutim* (liturgical poems; plural form of *piyyut*), many of which remain in the Samaritan prayer service. Marqe's son, Ninna (Nonnus), was also a poet, although only one major composition by him survives, alongside one or two shorter works of dubious attribution. The hymns of these three poets constitute core components of the Samaritan liturgy down to the present day.

Largely because of the transformations that the Samaritan community underwent during the fourth century CE—including changes in ritual and exegesis shaped by Amram and Marqe within the larger context of Baba Rabbah's "reformation"—this period can be seen as the classical era of Samaritan literature.

---

31. Citations of *Tibat Marqe* in this work follow the critical edition by Ben-Hayyim, *Tibat Marqe* (*TM*).

The writings of Amram, Marqe, and Ninna shaped the Samaritan liturgy as it existed throughout the Middle Ages and into the present. While their poetry has garnered less prestige (and less scholarly attention) than Samaritan writings in prose—notably the exegetical compilation *Tibat Marqe*, the historical chronicles, and legal (halakhic) works—these poems constitute a significant component of the Samaritan religious experience. Indeed, these poems demonstrate that the Samaritan community participated fully in the "poetic renaissance" of late antiquity, when liturgical poetry became a central part of religious ritual throughout the Roman Empire among Christians, Jews, and Samaritans alike.

The body of classical Samaritan poetry—the poetry of the late third and fourth centuries CE, written by Amram, Marqe, and Ninna—is gemlike: small but precious, easily obscured yet quick to sparkle. In this study, a selection of these poems will be lifted out of the shadows and held up to the light, so that all may gain a better sense of these treasures.

Aside from the Torah (written in Hebrew but using a preexilic style of script), the texts composed by the Samaritans in late antiquity were written in Samaritan Aramaic, a form of Palestinian Aramaic closely akin to Jewish Palestinian Aramaic. Samaritan Aramaic was the vernacular of the Samaritan community until about the tenth through twelfth centuries CE, when it was supplanted by Samaritan Palestinian Arabic.[32] The liturgical poetry of Amram, Marqe, and Ninna, as well as the SamT, were all written in Samaritan Aramaic; postclassical Samaritan poetry, by contrast, contains much more Hebrew.[33] In terms of both liturgical and daily language, Samaritans were no different from their neighbors in the land of Israel in late antiquity. Certainly in terms of their oral and auditory lives—whether speaking in the synagogue or in the street—Jews, Samaritans, and Christians would have found one another mutually comprehensible.

Although the liturgy of the Samaritan synagogue in late antiquity cannot be reconstructed precisely, we do know that the Torah occupied the place of pride. In general, the liturgy consisted of the recitation of a Torah passage framed by the reading of hymns and prayers. In order to permit more of the Torah to be included in the service, anthologies of Torah verses called *qatafim* (קטפים, "gleanings") were read. *Qatafim* appear to be some of the earliest elements of Samaritan liturgy, and they were prepared for each of the five books of the Torah (serving as condensed or abbreviated versions of each book); other *qatafim* were compiled for specific Sabbaths, holy days, and life-cycle events, or to draw together teachings from the Torah on specific themes. The various readings,

---

32. Kaufman, "Dialectology." The *Comprehensive Aramaic Lexicon* (*CAL*) classifies Samaritan Aramaic, along with Jewish Palestinian Aramaic and Christian Palestinian Aramaic, as forms of "Palestinian Aramaic."

33. Florentin, *Late Samaritan Hebrew.*

hymns, and prayers were assembled into a prayer book known as the *Defter*; two-thirds of the hymns in the *Defter* were composed by Amram, Marqe, and Ninna. In practice, however, we can assume that the liturgy was a product of oral literacy: while the prayer leader may have had written texts or cues available, most of the community would have participated by reciting memorized passages or by repeating portions of a text read aloud.

Just as classical Samaritan texts and practices reveal an obvious, if complex and mutable, kinship with late antique Jewish modes of writing and living, given the importance of exegesis among both Jews and Christians in this period, we should not be surprised that Samaritans in antiquity produced a tradition of haggadic scriptural interpretation that is comparable to those bodies of writing, although it is neither as voluminous nor as diffuse. The SamT, rather like the rabbinic Targum Onqelos (and the Greek versions of the Torah, known collectively as the Septuagint), lacks haggadic expansions; the major exegetical work—*Tibat Marqe*—consists of six relatively brief chapters, two of which date (at least in large part) to roughly the fourth century CE (i.e., the time of Marqe) and three of which are later.[34] Samaritan ritual systems likewise reveal overt similarities with rabbinic practice—including nomenclature, such as the use of "synagogues" and the composition of *piyyutim*—even as they reveal commonalities with early Christian modes of piety too. Indeed, even more than language, scriptural versions, and exegetical traditions, a shared love of liturgical poetry may be most revealing of the deep cultural affinities linking these three entangled religious traditions.

Samaritan Liturgy and Poetry: The Scholarly Context

As distinct from discussion of Samaritans in the context of the Hebrew Bible and the New Testament, the modern study of Samaritan culture, history, liturgy, and literature in late antiquity began in the early twentieth century.[35] The liturgical poetry of this community was a key resource for scholars early on. The two most important early scholars were Moses Gaster, whose history of the Samaritans relied largely on their own historical chronicles and his communications with contemporary Samaritans, and A. E. Cowley, whose 1909 edition of the Samaritan liturgy remained the standard edition of their prayer texts (in Hebrew, Aramaic, and Arabic) for over half a century.[36] Indeed, Cowley's edition was supplanted only in the mid-twentieth century by linguistic expert

34. It is telling that Ben-Hayyim describes *TM* as a "midrash" in his edition.
35. By far the most useful tool for gaining an overview of scholarly work on the Samaritans (spanning the biblical period to the modern) is Pummer, "Samaria/Samaritans."
36. Gaster, *Samaritans*; Cowley, *Samaritan Liturgy*. Brown's "Critical Edition of the Ancient Samaritan *Defter*" is less well known but contains translations of portions of Cowley's text.

Ze'ev Ben-Hayyim's five-volume compendium, which offers the best editions presently available.[37] Ben-Hayyim's edition of *Tibat Marqe* likewise replaced John Macdonald's edition, although the latter remains popular for the accessibility of its English.[38] Abraham Tal's critical editions of both the Samaritan Aramaic translation of the Torah—the Samaritan Targum—and the Samaritan Pentateuch itself marked a foundational step in the study of Samaritan culture; Tal provided scholars with essential texts and, through his lexicon of Samaritan Aramaic, a tool with which to read them.[39] Much of the broader cultural and contextual work has been undertaken by Pummer and Alan D. Crown. Since the 1980s, they and their students have helped bring the study of Samaritan texts, traditions, and practices from antiquity to the present into the larger discourse of religious studies.[40]

In recent decades, building on the foundation of twentieth-century scholarship, Samaritan studies has begun to blossom into a full-fledged discipline. Steven Fine has drawn attention to the archaeology and material culture of the Samaritans in antiquity, while Moshe Florentin's work has highlighted the richness of medieval Samaritan poetry.[41] A. S. Rodrigues Pereira included works by Marqe in his volume on Aramaic poetry, a project that stands out for its ambition to bring linguistically related works together across religious divisions.[42] In step with these scholarly developments, the Samaritan community in Israel has in recent years become newly engaged in "outreach" under the leadership of Benyamim Tsedakah, whose work has included a volume containing English translations of the Samaritan Torah and the Masoretic Torah in parallel format.[43]

Collectively, these scholars have articulated the diverse facets of Samaritan culture in late antiquity—what we might call early Samaritanism, on the model

37. Ben-Hayyim, *Literary and Oral Tradition*.

38. MacDonald's *Memar Marqah* is based on an inferior MS, the eighteenth-century British Museum 7923, but his edition is still widely used in Anglophone scholarship. Ben-Hayyim's *TM* provides editions of two earlier MSS that represent two different recensions: a complete sixteenth-century manuscript from Shechem and an earlier fragmentary manuscript. The sixteenth-century manuscript is the basis for the electronic edition available through *CAL*. Ben-Hayyim translated the Aramaic portions of *TM* into Modern Hebrew.

39. For the Samaritan Aramaic translation of the Torah, see Tal, *Samaritan Targum*. For the Pentateuch, see Tal, *Samaritan Pentateuch*. For the lexicon, see Tal, *Dictionary of Samaritan Aramaic*. Schorch's *Leviticus* is the first volume of a projected six-volume critical edition of the Samaritan Pentateuch, overseen by Schorch.

40. The bibliography of writings by Crown and Pummer is extensive, and many of the most important works are listed in Pummer, "Samaria/Samaritans"; this is in many ways an update of Crown and Pummer, *Bibliography of the Samaritans*. Particularly useful as a comprehensive overview is Pummer, *Samaritans*.

41. Fine, "For This Schoolhouse Is Beautiful"; Florentin, *Samaritan Elegies*. See also the very useful survey in Dar, "Archaeological Aspects of Samaritan Research." For a reading of the Samaritan material in a more general context, see Patrich, "Urban Space in Caesarea Maritima."

42. Rodrigues Pereira, *Studies in Aramaic Poetry*.

43. Tsedaka and Sullivan, *Israelite Samaritan Version of the Torah*.

of early Judaism and early Christianity—when all three religious traditions took forms still recognizable today. What remains to be done, however, is to study classical Samaritan sources with the same sophisticated methods that have been applied to the analogous material from early Christianity and, as is increasingly the case, early Judaism. That is, the philological study of Samaritan texts needs to be supplemented by the theoretical models and tools of literary, ritual, and performative studies in order to elucidate not only the rich content of Samaritan culture but also the ways in which that culture was fully embedded in and integrated with late antique society more generally.

Samaritan Liturgy and Poetry: The Samaritan Context

Much of Samaritan history from late antiquity, including the history of Samaritan culture, remains unknown and, likely, unknowable. But we do possess a rich body of liturgical poetry from this period, along with the early portions of *Tibat Marqe* and the SamT. These works indicate the broad contours of the contexts in which classical Samaritan liturgical poetry emerged. Samaritans shed light on a variety of late antique phenomena: they were actively engaged in internal reform movements and anti-imperial rebellions; their literature, as noted above, was varied, even if the corpus was small; and as poetry, these works must be studied as part of the poetic renaissance of late antiquity. Each of these three contexts—social, exegetical, and literary—will be explored in brief here, with an eye toward contextualizing the discussions of individual poems in this anthology.

The Social and Geopolitical Context

The earliest examples of Samaritan poetry date to the late third or early fourth century, shortly after the likely date of the reforms of Baba Rabbah. According to Samaritan tradition, Baba Rabbah was the firstborn son of the Samaritan high priest Nathaniel; he instituted his religious reforms in response to a period of persecution by the Roman authorities in the third century CE (perhaps during the rule of Severus Alexander [222–35] or slightly earlier, under Caracalla [211–17]). Initially, rather than encouraging his community to participate in anti-imperial rebellions, he directed their energies inward, toward pietistic practices. He reopened synagogues and dispatched deputies—four lay Israelites and three priests (seven men in all)—to lead the Samaritan communities in prayer and Torah study.[44] (Legend also credits Baba Rabbah with waging war against the

44. At the time of Baba Rabbah (ca. third century CE), there were robust Samaritan settlements along the coast of Palestine, as well as in Egypt, Carthage, and Rome, among other locations. Given

Romans, and with evading Jewish assassination plots.) According to the Samaritan chronicles, one of these seven "sages" (*khakima*) was the priest Amram Dare, the earliest of the classical Samaritan liturgical poets and the father of Marqe. The Samaritan historical tradition, then, suggests a connection between the rise of Samaritan liturgical poetry and a period of broad—indeed, legendary—religious reformation.[45] The fourth century was a momentous period for the Roman Empire as a whole and a transformative one for the Samaritans as well.

Initially, the Christian emperors of Rome did not attempt to exert control over their non-Christian subjects. Only with the emperor Honorius in 404 CE did the early Byzantine rulers begin to issue decrees against Jews, Samaritans, and "idolaters" in the land of Israel—with questionable and at best uneven enforcement.[46] The Theodosian (438) and Justinian (529–34) codes imposed restrictions on Samaritans as well as Jews, and these prohibitions serve as indicators of non-Christians' activities. Eventually, oppression led to active unrest and a series of Samaritan uprisings. Two of these revolts attracted Jewish participants: the so-called Gallus revolt of 351 and the second, more impressive revolt of 614, when the Jews and Samaritans assisted the Persians in their brief conquest of Jerusalem. The first Samaritan uprising, however, dates to 484, during the reign of the emperor Zeno, who replaced the synagogue on Mount Gerizim with a church dedicated to Mary Theotokos after the rebellion was put down.[47] A minor revolt followed during the reign of Zeno's successor, Anastasius I (r. 491–518), and a second major uprising occurred in 529.

While preceded and followed by spasms of imperial persecution and popular resistance, the fourth century CE seems to have been a period of relative peace and stability for the Samaritans.[48] It was in this period that the Samaritan community restored its holy precincts on Mount Gerizim, and there is evidence of interference from Jews, Christians, or polytheists.[49] It will be especially significant below in the current study that, in this period, the Samaritans also began to build impressive synagogues in Samaria and beyond, repurposing stones from

---

the legendary nature of the Baba Rabbah material, however, it is impossible to assign concrete locations to the places where his deputies might have served.

45. Pummer, *Samaritans*, 131–34.

46. For the wider context of this moment from the perspective of the Byzantine empire, see Doyle, *Honorius*.

47. For descriptions of the Samaritan rebellions as recalled (with some discrepancies among them) by John Malalas, Procopius of Caesarea, Choricius of Gaza, and Cyril of Scythopolis, see Pummer, *Early Christian Authors on Samaritans*.

48. On the Samaritan revolts in late antiquity in the Galilee region, see Di Segni, "Samaritan Revolts"; Sivan, *Palestine in Late Antiquity*. Also note Lieber, "You Have Been Skirting," which addresses the Samaritan revolts from the Jewish perspective.

49. Di Segni, "Church of Mary Theotokos."

destroyed Roman buildings and temples.[50] The poetry of Amram Dare, Marqe, and Ninna arose during this century of tranquility, on the heels of and in concert with Baba Rabbah's reformation, prior to the wave of imperial persecutions and concomitant revolts. Indeed, Samaritanism as we now know it took shape during this remarkable epoch, and it was this form of Samaritanism that was able to endure through the subsequent centuries of trauma and that has persisted, despite external pressures, to the present day. Although many Samaritan communities were destroyed during the uprisings of the sixth century, both literary sources and archaeological finds indicate the endurance and even renewal of Samaritan villages later in the same century.[51]

The theology and philosophy of the classical Samaritan writings are imprinted with the concerns of the late antique intellectual world. In particular, Marqe's later writings reveal a specifically Samaritan understanding of the idea of the Logos as a kind of personified or active law, although he develops this idea in two very different ways. In his prose work *Tibat Marqe*, he describes Moses in terms that are distinctly Logos-like: he existed incorporeally prior to creation and he understands the very mind of God.[52] In his poetry, however, Marqe treats the Torah itself as a kind of incarnation, a tangible manifestation of the divine, as is especially visible in several of the poems included in this volume where the Torah acts, possesses agency, and is not practically distinguished from its divine author.[53] The tension between these treatments of Moses and the Torah may reflect the life-setting of each work. In *Tibat Marqe*, composed for a scholarly setting, Moses (the paragon of learning) acquires an aura of near-divinity, while in the poems intended for use in a liturgical setting, where the Torah scrolls manifest the divine connection to the community, it is the writing that is thus exalted. Indeed, throughout these poems, the boundaries between divine author, prophetic scribe, and revealed text can become difficult to discern.

Although the writings of Amram Dare, Marqe, and Ninna manifest a kind of organic Greco-Roman philosophy, their theology anticipates concerns that are even more fully developed in Islam. The language the Samaritan poems use to assert God's singularity sounds particularly striking to modern ears: insistent declarations that "there is no God but the one" recur throughout the compositions by Amram Dare, Marqe, and Ninna. Indeed, this phrase is just as much a liturgical cue as a line of poetry, and one that surely invited communal

50. For a concise summary of current understandings of Samaritan synagogues in antiquity (with particular attention to the vexing question of how they can be distinguished from Jewish synagogues), see Pummer, "Synagogues."
51. Di Segni, "Samaritan Revolts," 480; Magen, "Areas of Samaritan Settlement."
52. Broadie, *Samaritan Philosophy*, 73–87.
53. Lieber, "Scripture Personified."

participation. Even more evocative are litanies such as this one from Amram's corpus (Amram 1, ll. 17–21):

> There is no God but our master,
> And no book like his Torah,
> And no true prophet like Moses,
> And no complete faithfulness,
> Nor truth, except his.[54]

On the one hand, this language almost anticipates the popular Jewish Shabbat table-song "Ein Adir" (There is none so splendid), which catalogues qualities that unify God, Moses, the Torah, and the children of Israel.[55] That poem, however, most likely postdates Marqe by centuries and emerged in an entirely different context; the parallels simply reflect common concerns with articulating the uniqueness of God, scripture, community, and the prophet who signifies the bond among them and the desire to express such beliefs in an acrostic hymn. At the same time, these Marqan lines—along with the frequently repeated creedal phrase "There is no God but the one!"—echo what we now think of as the Islamic creed that "there is no God but God and Muhammed is his true prophet," but the Samaritan poetry predates Muhammed by centuries. The influence of Islamic culture on medieval and modern Samaritan language and liturgy is evident: Arabic became the vernacular of the Samaritan community after the seventh century CE, as well as the language in which the prayer-book corpus of liturgical poetry presents many of the explanatory glosses, transitions, and ligatures (the headnotes that stipulate the occasions on which each poem may be performed). But both the poetic assertions of monotheism and the liturgical "catch phrases" that conclude many of the poems are native to Samaritan literature.[56] It seems that Islam and Samaritanism share a deep, organic commitment to an articulated monotheism that stresses the singularity of God, of prophet, and of scripture. As with the resonances between Samaritan and Jewish texts, the correspondence of Samaritan and Muslim motifs arises from a common worldview rather than from influence.

The Samaritans were fully present, organically involved participants in the culture of the land of Israel in late antiquity. They resisted imperial power with notable vigor (if little success), they transformed their culture in lasting ways that

54. Note the very similar passage in Amram 4, ll. 29–34.

55. For the text of the hymn, see 2982א in Davidson, *Thesaurus of Mediaeval Hebrew Poetry*, 1:140. Davidson does not offer a hypothesis on its date but notes that it is a *hakafah* poem for the holy day of Simkhat Torah. It seems likely to be a Sephardic poem and is presumably medieval in origin. It is also known as *Mipi El* (From the mouth of God), based on its refrain.

56. On ligatures, see Anderson and Giles, *Tradition Kept*, 359–60.

reveal a sense of assertiveness and confidence in both architectural and literary achievements, and their manner of expression reflects an awareness of Hellenistic lines of thinking that resonate with trends in Jewish writing, even as they anticipated creedal statements that would become closely aligned with Islam.

The Samaritan Literary Context

While the Samaritan community was never large and its written legacy is modest when viewed against the quantity of works surviving from Jewish and Christian communities of late antiquity, the textual heritage of the Samaritans remains significant for modern scholars of religion. The most commonly referenced work is the SamP, as it bears directly on the critical study of the Hebrew Bible and links the Samaritan tradition to the shared literary tradition of Jews and Christians. Modern writers have generally focused on locating and analyzing those places where the Samaritan Pentateuch differs from the MT of the Torah (and how it relates to other ancient witnesses, such as the Septuagint and the Dead Sea Scrolls). Yet, compared to the Christian and Jewish scriptures, the Samaritan canon possesses a radical simplicity, limited as it is to the five books of the Pentateuch, unvocalized and written in an archaic Hebrew script.

The brevity of the Samaritan canon, on the one hand, and its centrality to the liturgy on the other, shaped Samaritan poetry. Jewish and Christian liturgical poetry is richly intertextual, with every stanza and phrase marked by quotations of or allusions to verses and traditions from elsewhere in their scriptures. Samaritan poetry, by contrast, revolves around the key themes, episodes, and figures of the Torah—in particular the creation narratives of Gen 1–2 and the Sinai episode in Exod 19–20. Indeed, whereas Jewish poetry in particular often resembles a mosaic woven out of phrases from throughout the Hebrew Bible, the Samaritan poems focus on theological and theoretical matters, perhaps because the canon itself was already present in the liturgy through the recitation of the *qatafim*. The Samaritan poetry does not renarrate scriptural episodes in any linear way but rather explores them in an almost imagistic way, exhibiting a potent ritual function.

In general, while the Samaritan poetry by Amram, Marqe, and Ninna displays significant reliance on scriptural traditions, it is substantially independent of Samaritan exegetical traditions. Yose ben Yose and Ephrem the Syrian, from the Jewish and Christian traditions, respectively, both engage in complex but robust ways with traditions of biblical exegesis in their poetry. By contrast, classical Samaritan poetry routinely differs from the SamT, although it emerged in the same time period, and even more conspicuously from *Tibat Marqe*, despite the fact that both the prose and the poetic texts were produced by the same family.

Despite the obvious independence of Samaritan *piyyutim* from other early Samaritan writings—these compositions are not simply poeticized targum or exegesis—it makes sense to read contemporary works together. Examining the Samaritan poems in the context of the SamT helps us to understand both bodies of writing more fully.[57] Much of the SamT dates to roughly the same period as the classical *piyyutim*: Tal dates the earliest stratum (BL Or. MS 7562) to the age of Baba Rabba and his reforms (which may coincide with the canonization of the SamT), while the later layers (MS Nablus 6[81] = MS 6 of the Shechem synagogue) may be dated several centuries later but still within late antiquity. The *piyyutim* often quote phrases from scripture in Aramaic (occasionally in Hebrew as well); rarely, however, do the quotations precisely align with the language preserved in the SamT. This lack of alignment itself suggests that scriptural translation was a fluid phenomenon in Samaritan antiquity—there was no "canonical" targum, and the text was freely "updated" over time. But variations in the Aramaic translation of the Hebrew text of the Torah probably did not hinder listeners from grasping allusions to scripture in Aramaic verse; they knew the Hebrew text well enough to discern and appreciate allusion even through the veil of translation. They could hear the scripture behind the Aramaic poetry without the aid of a targum.

While the SamT helps to illustrate the linguistic independence of the classical poets, a comparison of Samaritan *piyyut* to *Tibat Marqe*, the major exegetical work of Samaritan antiquity, highlights the exegetical creativity of both genres. *Tibat Marqe* in its entirety is attributed to Marqe, whose poetry is included here, and substantial portions of it can be reliably dated to roughly the same time period as the poems studied here. Parallels between *Tibat Marqe* and the poetry presented here are clearly discernible, especially their overlapping thematic interests, as both works display intense fascination with the exodus narrative, the Sinai narrative, and the figure of Moses. These resonances, which manifest themselves in narrative arcs, vivid imagery, and shared language, are noted in the commentaries. Alignments between *piyyutim* and *Tibat Marqe* are not as common as one might assume, however, even in the poems ascribed to the author of the midrash. Indeed, as the commentary in the translation highlights, the two bodies of writing often differ in subtle but important ways. Poetic rhetoric can also be more difficult to decipher because more ambiguous and elliptical than prose, more resonantly multivalent. Yet this does not mean that one should turn to *Tibat Marqe* for aid in interpreting Samaritan poetry. In fact, the opposite is true: reading *Tibat Marqe* in light of the poems explored here highlights robust liturgical and poetic elements in the midrash. These features of *Tibat*

---

57. Tal, *Samaritan Targum*; the introduction in vol. 3 is particularly useful as a resource for understanding the history of this work. See also Tal, "Samaritan Targum."

Marqe are more likely rhetorical than performative, however—particularly the liturgical elements that open and close each book of the compendium.

The poetry embedded in *Tibat Marqe* is lovely but strikingly different in form from the liturgical poetry. For example, toward the end of book I, there is an evocative lyric in which elements of the landscape anticipate the arrival of the Israelites as they cross over to freedom. The sea, the waters of Marah, the manna, the rocks, the valley, Sinai, the Jordan, Mount Gerizim, the hills, and the plains all beckon to the people, evocatively "calling to them silently" (כרז לון במשתוק).[58] It is a song of silence, and it is not included in the body of classical poetry but embedded within a prose text. The differences between liturgical *piyyut* and this "exegetical" poetry—in form, function, and rhetoric—merit study in their own right.

We are increasingly accustomed to examining the settings in which scriptural texts, translations, exegesis, and hymns were used and experienced by Jews and Christians as part of our attempt to understand the rich complexity of these works, and Samaritan *piyyutim* and their prescriptive ligatures benefit from the same consideration. In particular, it is essential to keep in mind that the poems were liturgical, meaning that they were performed as part of religious rituals, presumably in the presence of the Torah scroll. We should note that no passages were read directly from the scroll, nor does it seem that a targum was read as part of a Torah service, either as a living performance of translation that complemented a reading in Hebrew (e.g., like the Jewish targums in some synagogue practices and as presumed by the Mishnah) or as a substitute for the original-language text (as per the role of the Greek translation in Christianity).[59] While these practices are attested in synagogues and churches in antiquity, Samaritan ritual was distinctive. The physical presence of the scroll was central: *seeing* the scroll was the essential act, rather than *hearing* words read directly from it. While in Jewish worship the Torah scroll certainly has a symbolic function, it also has a very practical function in the Torah-reading ceremony; in the Samaritan synagogue, however, it is important almost exclusively as a symbol. The scroll's presence as tangible evidence of revelation and covenant reifies the theology of the poetry. While we have models of poetry that relies on the detailed narrative content of the portion of scripture read on a given day to construct what can be understood as a variety of liturgical exegesis (notably from the Jewish tradition), the Samaritan model indicates that the *idea*

---

58. Thus the Leningrad MS; the other MS employed by Ben-Hayyim has simply "calling out to them" (כרז לון). The text is in *TM* I §71 (א–ב51, pp. 97–99).

59. For a concise summary of the state of scholarship on rabbinics, see the review essay by Visotzky, "Leaning Literary, Reading Rabbinics." For a description of early Samaritan Sabbath observance—albeit one that relies heavily (of necessity) on medieval accounts—see Weiss, "Sabbath among the Samaritans."

of revelation—represented by the Torah scroll itself—can be just as conducive to literary creativity.

Indeed, comparing *Tibat Marqe* to Marqe's poetry underscores how genre and context shape the themes and motifs of literary works. *Tibat Marqe* is a strongly philosophical work, each of its constituent chapters focuses on a specific idea or episode, and the earliest materials (which likely date to the time of Marqe, whether or not the attribution to him is correct) include chapters covering the deliverance from Egyptian bondage ("The Book of Wonders"), the Song at the Sea (Exod 15), and the sins of Israel (as in Deut 27:9–27). *Tibat Marqe*'s emphases on Moses, revelation, redemption, and sin are shared with the classical Samaritan *piyyutim*, but the poetry is not simply *Tibat Marqe* set to song. The poetry is far more elliptical, less linear, less narrative, and less grounded in the biblical "story," although it assumes extensive familiarity with the content of scripture. The poetry seems far less didactic—it is certainly less explicatory—and appears to be more invested in creating an experience and setting a mood than in interpreting scripture.

Samaritan Piyyutim *in the Context of Late Antique Hymnography*

The classical Samaritan *piyyutim* did not emerge in isolation. They constitute part of a broad turn toward liturgical poetry among not only Jews but also Christians. Indeed, the late third and early fourth centuries CE witnessed the flourishing of distinctive poetic traditions in Hebrew, Jewish Palestinian Aramaic (JPA), and Syriac, as well as in Samaritan Aramaic, and these works presaged the emergence of hymnody in Greek by the sixth century CE.

The liturgical poems of each community are distinctive, and direct dependence of a given tradition on another is unlikely: the differences are both too distinctive and too organic, and the linguistic and geographic spread too great. Nevertheless, the apparently sudden emergence of liturgical poetry across traditions and languages suggests that Jews, Christians, and Samaritans alike were responding to elements of their common culture. None of the Samaritan *piyyutim* attempt to replicate the aesthetics of biblical poetry in the way that the Qumranic Hodayot do.[60] The very Hebrew/Aramaic term *piyyut*, borrowed from the Greek word *poesis* (and thus cognate with the English words "poet" and "poetry"), suggests an awareness among Jews and Samaritans alike that these compositions reflected something novel and innovative. The novelty of liturgical hymns was relatively universal, regardless of religious community, but the specific manifestations of this newness reflected the distinct liturgies and aesthetics of the particular traditions.

---

60. On the Hodayot, see Nitzan, *Qumran Prayer*; Nitzan, "Prayers for Peace."

Jewish, Christian, and Samaritan hymnographies do have some elements in common, however. For example, a number of poems by the Samaritan poet Marqe, the early Jewish poet Yose ben Yose, and the Syriac-speaking Christian poet Ephrem—three different traditions, three different languages—straddle the boundaries between poetry and prose. They are rhythmic but lack rhyme, and although they may be organized by alphabetical acrostics, they are not elaborate in form; they display regular strophic structure, perhaps with a refrain. Yose's Shofarot poems, and also some of his Avodah poems, share with some of Marqe's works (in particular) a kind of unhurried capaciousness created by long lines and expansive stanzas. These works are all undeniably poetic—rich with parallelism, rhythm, and consonance and assonance, and composed in stanzaic form—and yet they share a common aesthetic that sets them apart from the poetic forms that would come to dominate in Judaism and Christianity in the sixth and seventh centuries, and in medieval Samaritan poetry as well.

Whereas Yose and Ephrem share formal elements (broadly speaking) with Marqe, Marqe's language is essentially the same as that found in the corpus of JPA poetry. The JPA poems are themselves a diverse assemblage (spanning the fourth through seventh centuries), and the relationship of these poems to the emerging body of Hebrew poetry, also written by and for Jews, remains unclear. Nevertheless, the language of the JPA poems and of the poems by Amram, Marqe, and Ninna is essentially the same, and they would have been mutually comprehensible without mediation or translation.

The Performative Context

While it might help explain why liturgical poetry became so widespread across diverse ethnic, linguistic, and religious communities in late antiquity, the origin of these poems cannot be reconstructed. They navigate complicated social tensions: they innovate, but using language and imagery that is deeply traditional; they embody the practice of piety, but in ways as entertaining as edifying; they were written for a very contemporary audience but draw on phrases of hoary antiquity. These poems, in short, have no single origin, but they shed light on the communities in which they were performed, preserved, and transmitted.

These poems must have been just as significant components of worship in Samaritan synagogues as their congeners were in Jewish and Christian congregations, and their appeal lies in their synthesis of contemporary late antique culture with deeply compelling Samaritan traditions and stories, in settings that reinforced and resonated with both elements of the poems. We see this hybridity in several ways: the poems' frequent deployment of evocative images and concepts, including access to angelic liturgies and mystical knowledge; their use of rhetorical techniques familiar to their listeners from the worlds of theater and law; their resonance with the physicality of the liturgy, such as in their appeals to the sensory stimuli that would have surrounded the worshippers in antiquity; and their dynamic relationship with the architecture and materiality of early Samaritan synagogues.

Liturgical performance should not be separated from the larger context of rhetorical performance that surrounded the Samaritan community and formed a consensus on what constituted effective communication, regardless of setting, in late antiquity. We can examine these poems through the lens of the rhetorical handbooks (*progymnasmata*) that reflect the training of ancient orators and shed light on both public speaking and the closely aligned practices of theatrical actors (mimes and pantomime) of late antiquity. Samaritan *payyetanim* may have employed the same techniques as these other public communicators. Furthermore, an appreciation of these rhetorical techniques makes it possible to identify deeper aesthetic preoccupations shared by liturgical poems and *Tibat Marqe*—similarities that go beyond parallel motifs or theological assertions and include a common delight in *ethopoeia* (speech-in-character) and *enargeia* (vividness).

Social norms of public speech also help us to understand the role of acclamation in congregational participation. Acclamation—the practice of communal or congregational shouting or chanting in a public venue—was ubiquitous in antiquity. In the case of the Samaritans, the practice resonated with the scriptural precedent of the antiphonal chanting of blessings and curses from Mount Gerizim and Mount Ebal (Deut 11 and 27). In *Tibat Marqe*, we find vivid recreations of acclamatory chanting set in the biblical period and staged on the shore of the Sea of Reeds:

> The great prophet Moses was singing this Song (i.e., Exod 15, the Song at the Sea), section by section. At the conclusion of each section, he would fall silent, and the elders and all Israel would say in a loud voice: "Sing to the Lord, for he has triumphed gloriously; the horse and his rider he has cast into the sea!" (Exod 15:1).
>
> All Israel would respond to the voice of the elders and would say in a loud voice, from the least and to the greatest, from the youngest to the eldest, in unison: "[He is] my strength and my song, and he is my salvation: this is my God and I will glorify Him, my father's God, and I will exalt Him! YHWH is a hero in war, YHWH is His name!" (Exod 15:2–3). After this utterance, they would fall silent, until they heard the voice of the prophet Moses, who would say another section; then all the elders would respond and say in a loud voice: "Sing . . !" and they (the Israelites) would sing. When they were done with the words of the Song, they set

out after Moses and the (divine) Glory: stars walking on the earth, the sun and the moon traveling, Moses and the Glory.[61]

This passage describes a complicated yet putatively spontaneous antiphonal performance, with Moses, the elders, and the community reciting their assigned lines in a particular order. The author here appears to be imagining the performance of Exod 15 as if it were a liturgical performance from his own period. His restaging of the biblical scene was plausible precisely because it projected contemporary practices back into the past.[62]

These lenses—rhetorical and performative—help us to see both performer and audience more clearly, to articulate their roles, and to recover their own sense of the meaningfulness of the performative act. This form of analysis has already been fruitfully applied to Jewish and Christian hymns from antiquity, and in this volume it will help us to identify essential features of Samaritan poetry as well. We can hardly grasp these performative norms, however, without considering the physical setting of the hymns themselves: the concrete space of the synagogue, and the emotional space created by religious ritual.

The synagogue, not the temple, was the locus of religious ritual in Samaritan antiquity, although as in the case of their Jewish counterparts who lamented the destruction of Zion, Samaritans' memory of and longing for a temple on Mount Gerizim was of central importance.[63] Of the Samaritan synagogues that have been excavated, several date from roughly the same time period as the hymns examined in this volume (ca. fourth century CE) and reflect the transformation of Samaritan culture under Baba Rabba, which included the reorganization of the leadership and the transformation of the liturgy.[64] In short, the synagogues seem to complement the literary evidence with physical evidence of a transformation, or perhaps institutionalization, of Samaritan worship in the fourth

---

61. *TM* 2 §54 (103ב–104ב, p. 153), trans. MacDonald, *Memar Marqah*, 2:80 (adapted). This passage, it bears noting, is in Hebrew and likely dates from a later period than that of Marqe himself, but given the ubiquity of acclamation throughout the ancient Mediterranean world, it seems plausible that the scene described here would resonate with liturgical practices familiar to readers and was perhaps based on the performance of *piyyutim*.

62. On liturgical acclamation in the land of Israel during the period when Marqe lived, see Lieber, "With One Voice."

63. For a history of material culture on Mount Gerizim, see Magen, *Mount Gerizim Excavations*.

64. Levine discusses the flurry of Samaritan synagogue construction under Baba Rabbah (including a synagogue on Mount Gerizim opposite the site of the destroyed sanctuary) and makes the following observation: "If this last suggestion [of dating the reformations of Baba Rabba to the mid third century] is accepted, then Samaritan synagogue building would constitute an interesting chronological parallel to the appearance of the mid third-century Jewish synagogues, and the two may even be related in some way" (*Ancient Synagogue*, 190–91). See also Magen, "Samaritan Synagogues."

century. The Samaritan synagogue was an organization of sacred space strongly colored by the memory of the temple that once stood on Mount Gerizim and would, it was believed, stand again.

Samaritan synagogues in late antiquity were located both inside and outside the territory of Samaria within the Land of Israel, as well as in the Samaritan diaspora. Unlike Samaritan synagogues built in later centuries, however, the late antique structures are not consistently oriented toward Mount Gerizim, whereas Jewish synagogues of the same period are usually—although not universally— oriented toward Jerusalem.[65] Common motifs in late ancient Samaritan syna- gogue mosaics include the altar, the Torah shrine, and the tabernacle and related items (menorahs, incense shovels, shofars), similar to what we find in contem- porary Jewish synagogues.[66] There are visual differences, however, such as the tendency (according to present evidence) for Samaritan synagogues to avoid depictions of animals and humans. It is particularly striking that, while multiple Jewish synagogue mosaics portray birds in cages, the Samaritan synagogue in Khirbet Samara contains a depiction of an empty cage.[67] While Jewish syna- gogues became increasingly comfortable with depictions of animals, humans, and heavenly figures in late antiquity, the consistent Samaritan aesthetic prefer- ences militated against such visuals, perhaps reflecting a more stringent under- standing of the Torah's prohibition on images.[68]

In the Samaritan context, mosaic depictions of ritual items may reflect both a memory of temple ritual (expressing both nostalgia and a concern for the authenticity of religious expression) and hopes centered on the narrative of the prophetic-messianic figure known as the Taheb ("he who returns/restores"). In this, they resemble Jewish depictions of similar items that display longing for suspended religious practices and also aspirations for their restoration, as well as

---

65. On the challenges of distinguishing Jewish and Samaritan synagogues, see Pummer, "Samaritan Synagogues and Jewish Synagogues"; Magen, *Samaritans*, 117–80. Pummer provides an excellent summary that takes the most recent scholarship into account (*Samaritans*, 91–112).

66. Until recently, the absence of depictions of the lulav and etrog—two of the four species that are employed ritually in the Jewish observance of the Festival of Booths—were considered evidence of a synagogue's identity as Samaritan rather than Jewish. The absence of this imagery was assumed to reflect the distinct Samaritan interpretations of the Torah's commandments concerning these items. Whereas Jews symbolically wave bundles of the four species, Samaritans use palm fronds to construct the roofs of their sukkahs and decorate them with fruits. See Jacoby, "Four Species." However, this common understanding has recently come into question; see Pummer, "Synagogues," and Lieber, "Shabbat in the Garden of Eden."

67. See Magen, "Samaritan Synagogues"; Pummer, *Samaritans*, 91–112.

68. Aesthetic preferences are complicated and reflect a variety of sources, including religious values but also local norms and histories. Visuals can reflect acceptance of broader societal trends or their explicit rejection, but oversimplification in analysis must be avoided. It is, however, worth noting how Samaritan aesthetic preferences anticipate similar preferences among the Muslims who would later become the majority population in Samaria.

their enaction through artistic representation. [69] The Samaritan temple on Mount Gerizim was razed by John Hyrcanus in 110 BCE, and in the aftermath of this trauma, a Samaritan version of a more widespread tradition emerged concerning the concealment of the cult vessels and implements from the wilderness period in an undisclosed and subsequently forgotten location.[70] The identity of the original concealer varies but is most commonly either Eli or Uzzi; Josephus, however, identifies him as Moses, which is at the very least a resonant association.[71] According to popular Samaritan belief, the Taheb—who seems to represent a new Moses—would restore these items to use after recovering them from their hiding place. The early origin of this tradition is underscored by Josephus's reference to it in his *Antiquities*, where he describes how a man "catered to the (Samaritan) mob, rallied them, bidding them to go in a body with him to Mount Gerizim. . . . He assured them that on their arrival he would show them the sacred vessels which were buried there, where Moses had deposited them. . . . But before they could ascend, Pilate blocked their projected route up to the mountain."[72] The fact that Josephus identifies Moses as the one who originally concealed the implements may reflect some awareness that the eventual recoverer will be a second Moses: "the returning one" will restore the people to their shrine and the holy vessels to the people. It is a message of both hope and authenticity.

By the time of Baba Rabba's reformation (or restoration), it is likely that Samaritans were denied any kind of regular access to their sacred mountaintop. Control of Mount Gerizim constituted a flash point in relations between Samaritans and ruling powers. In the second century CE, the emperor Antoninus Pius built a temple to Jupiter on the northern ridge of Mount Gerizim, Tell er-Ras (which is not the same peak on which the Samaritan temple stood); near the end of the fifth century, the church of Mary Theotokos was constructed on the Samaritan holy site.[73] The national-political symbolism of the sacred

69. The Jewish synagogue in Huqoq, currently being excavated by Jodi Magness, seems to reflect a particularly messianic visual program. Of particular interest is a mosaic that depicts the beasts from Dan 7, about which Magness says, "The Daniel panel is interesting because it points to eschatological, or end of day, expectations among this congregation" ("Newly-Discovered").

70. Anderson, "Mount Gerizim"; Hall, "From John Hyrcanus to Baba Rabbah." On the hidden temple vessels, including parallel legends in Hellenistic and rabbinic Jewish sources, see Collins, "Hidden Vessels," and Kalimi and Purvis, "Hiding of the Temple Vessels." Note the New Testament passage in which a Samaritan woman speaks of a messiah who will come and "show us all things" (John 4:25), perhaps including the location of these concealed items.

71. Eli rejected the authority of Uzzi and founded a schismatic shrine at Shiloh, according to Samaritan traditions paralleling those in 1 Sam 1–4. See Kartveit, *Origins of the Samaritans*, 26–39; Pummer, *Samaritans*, 9–14.

72. Josephus, *Antiquities* 18.85–87; translation adapted from *Jewish Antiquities* (trans. Feldman), 7:61–64. Also note Bowman, "Early Samaritan Eschatology."

73. Medieval Samaritan tradition credits the emperor Hadrian with construction of the Roman temple, but archaeological excavations indicate that Antoninus Pius was likely responsible for the

mountaintop precincts on Gerizim and Zion and the religious centrality of the image of the shrine in Samaritan and Jewish synagogues suggest a common orientation and experience shared by Samaritans and Jews in late antiquity.

Synagogue space—Jewish or Samaritan—differs from other spaces. The spatial configuration and adornment of synagogues indicate that they were built for a specific set of uses. The images used to decorate synagogues look to the past and anticipate future restoration, even as the physical structures serve to orient those within the building toward eternal sacred space. To step into a synagogue is to step into a slightly different time-stream, or perhaps it is more accurate to say that one steps out of the mundane flow of time altogether. Synagogue space is liturgical space, and synagogue time is liturgical time. As the stories of sacred tradition are brought to life through the reading of holy words in a hallowed space, the distant past becomes more proximate and the gulf between heaven and earth narrows. In some ways, the space—physical and temporal—created by liturgy and ritual exists apart from secular space and time, or rather represents a truer, more profoundly real manifestation of it. It is a creative and imaginative space, conjured by force of will and shaped by sounds, images, words, and symbols. The physical similarities between Jewish and Samaritan synagogues underline how the structures are distinguished by their respective liturgical texts and ritual practices.

Walls and words existed in a dynamic with each other. Only through the rituals that unfolded within it did the Samaritan synagogue become a sanctuary—a holy place. The presence of the Torah scroll in its niche represented the ongoing durability of revelation, the preservation of a sacred heritage; the recitation of verses extracted from the Torah (*qatafim*) gave voice to that inheritance; and the performance of *piyyutim* recreated key aspects of sacred history and experience, transforming the hoary past into intimate memory and bringing the mortal congregation into existential proximity with the heavenly hosts. All of these elements worked in concert, reinforcing and shaping each other. The *piyyutim*, for their part, respond to the sanctity of space and occasion, amplifying and even generating a sense of holiness and wonder in the moment.

Key Themes and Effects in Classical Samaritan *Piyyut*

At first glance, the body of classical Samaritan hymns may seem relatively uniform. Formally, this is certainly the case: while there are shorter works (especially the twenty-two hymns in the subset of Amram's poems known as the

---

first phase of Roman building on the site. See Magen, "Gerizim, Mount." On the location of the Roman temple, see Bull, "Ras, Tell er-."

Durran) and longer works (as exemplified in some of Marqe's more expansive compositions), within each poem the stanzas are of fixed length, and most
works are structured as acrostics. But this structural simplicity belies significant thematic complexity and imagistic creativity within the corpus. There is
rarely a simple narrative structure to the poems or a single festival setting that
might shape audience expectations, and as a result the distribution of motifs and
images may appear disorganized, leading casual readers to regard these works as
a diffuse mix of themes and ideas. But Samaritan *piyyutim* cannot be skimmed;
they are best appreciated when read slowly and closely. Patient examination dis-
closes not only striking contrasts between Samaritan *piyyut* and Jewish poetry
from late antiquity (the closest analogue to these works, particularly in the case
of JPA poetry, which is written in a very similar language and likewise favors
relatively simple structures[74]) but also potent insights into the religious world
of the Samaritan community at this pivotal time in its history.

   To be sure, the common aesthetic and performative sensibility of Samaritan
piyyutim differs from that found in contemporary Jewish and Christian liturgical poetry, where biblical and liturgical themes play a much more overt role in
the composition and utilization of hymns. But close reading reveals the unique
texture of each of the former, both within the corpus of the poetry and within the
context of Samaritan writings. Each poet, furthermore, favors certain themes.
The brief essays that introduce each poem translated in this volume highlight
some of the distinctive features of each composition. The following paragraphs
describe certain recurring figures, images, themes, and motifs that emerge as
particularly significant throughout the whole corpus.

   Each poet displays a slightly different relationship to time. Amram's poems
often entwine three critical temporal moments: the creation story (often exemplified by the Sabbath), the revelation of Torah at Sinai (and the Torah itself),
and the anticipated future, or "time of favor" (*rakhuta*), which is a restoration of
a past idyllic time. This future age is sometimes framed in terms of the redemptive coming of the Moses-like Taheb, whose arrival will put an end to the "time
of disfavor" or "turning away" (*fanuta*). Amram does not delineate when the
time of disfavor began or what initiated it, but he believed that it described
his present.[75] The poet's temporal focus shifts from poem to poem, and often
the chronological registers of creation, revelation, and restoration collapse into

---

74. Lieber, "No Translation Needed."

75. According to some medieval and modern Samaritan traditions, the time of favor came to an
end and the time of disfavor began when the priest Eli attempted to arrogate the high priesthood to
himself and set up a schismatic temple at Shiloh (see 1 Sam 1–4 in the MT). The earliest Samaritan
chronicle (the *Tulida*) offers a different account, however, and states that, in the time of the high
priest Uzzi, God hid the tabernacle built by Bezalel (Exod 31:1–11); see Florentin, *Tulida*, 76. For
a summary of the history and theology of this concept, see Pummer, *Samaritans*, 10–13; Dexinger,
"Samaritan Eschatology," esp. 276–77; Kartveit, "Origin of the Jews and Samaritans."

each other, with the Torah encoding the story of creation and the commands of the Sabbath and its hero Moses providing the prototype of the prophet-yet-to-come, or the Sabbath providing a taste of both the idyllic lost past and the eagerly anticipated future. At times, the Sabbath can even be interchangeable with the Torah (e.g., Amram 17). In place of strong narrative structures and chronologies, the poems juxtapose images and phrases to which they return with some elliptical repetition. This way of writing helps underscore points of contact across time and space: the ancestors who experienced the exodus and the present community, Moses and the Taheb, Sinai and the current service. One consequence of this blurring of past into present is that the time of favor—otherwise a vague, dreamlike past-future so different from the present it seems inherently remote—becomes almost tangibly immanent, if only through the experience of the present Sabbath. Nothing is far off, neither the triumphs and traumas of the past nor the promised rescue of the future.

Marqe, by contrast, dwells on the present almost exclusively. The time of disfavor (Marqe 1, l. 113) and the time of favor (Marqe 5, l. 87) are each mentioned just once, and the second Moses—the Taheb—is never mentioned (with the possible exception of Marqe 21, l. 97*). Marqe's poetry instead focuses on the opportunities, experiences, and failures of his own listeners. Torah is to be studied and revered, the Sabbath is to be kept, sins are to be regretted, and mercy is to be hoped for. It is not that Marqe ignores the past or the future, but rather that he seems to find the present moment urgent and compelling. In his compositions, Ninna conjures a vivid sense of the Sabbath—linking it with creation and with revelation, to be sure—and emphasizes the cyclical nature of time. Just as this Sabbath will depart, another will come.

Ninna left us only one or two poems—perhaps three, if Marqe 18 is included—and they all address a specific liturgical moment, the conclusion of the Sabbath. This focus lends Ninna's poetry a clear orientation in time: they are firmly anchored in the present, in that specific liminal moment when sanctified time returns to the workaday world. Ninna never mentions the Taheb, or the time of favor (or disfavor). Instead, he looks to the past for comfort, strength, and inspiration—to God as Creator, and to the legacy of his ancestors—while remaining focused on the current moment, so that he may help his community savor its joys, appreciate its gifts, and continue to hope that God will remain merciful and that the covenant with God's people will endure.

God, unsurprisingly, is almost always either the subject or object of the hymns. Throughout the poems, the poets speak about God to their congregations, sharing with them insights into God's nature, history, and qualities—a rhetorical tactic that can be understood as serving to remind God, indirectly, of precisely those same things. The poems also assume that God is an attentive listener who awaits prayer and finds it moving; the poets frequently address

God directly and in intimate terms (as in Amram 2 and Marqe 4, for example). These works often speak of and to God by invoking divine attributes—qualities that the poets can assure their communities that God possesses while reminding God to express them (see, for example, Amram 22 and Marqe 11 and 12). These are frequently listed and catalogued: God is merciful, good, and loyal; powerful, mighty, and mindful. He is a God who creates and rescues, who is just and fair but also anxious to forgive, and throughout it all, deserving of praise from both humans and angels. The poems do not develop God as a "personality"; God is defined more by attributes than by actions but is consistently understood as attentive and unwaveringly present. And, as is underscored by the liturgical phrase that concludes many of these hymns and is repeated within many of their stanzas, God is radically one. Singularity is the quintessence of the divine.

While God is praised as the Creator, revealer, and rescuer, the poets also develop distinctive interpretations of creation, revelation, and redemption, and the Torah provides them with a locus where these motifs intersect. Revelation is the source of our poets' knowledge of God's nature and actions, the Sabbath and its laws, and the promises that constitute a future redemption modeled on the past, in the person of the Taheb, the returning Moses. The Torah also represents the link between heaven and earth, between God and God's people, the essence of the covenant at the heart of Samaritan theology. In turn, Moses—the recipient and transmitter of scripture—constitutes an object of enduring fascination. Indeed, text and tradent are so deeply intertwined that they are, at times, indistinguishable (see, for example, Marqe 20). Yet the emphasis on Torah is striking: particularly in the works of Marqe, Torah becomes a character in its own right, and Moses is the hero of *Tibat Marqe*. Perhaps the liturgical poems underscore the importance of scripture, as revealed and received, precisely because of the fact that, as hymns, they embellish the liturgy and enrich the religious lives of the community: Torah links the people to God and to the sacred past and future. Moses, for all the mythic knowledge and power credited to him, is dead, the temple has been razed, and the Taheb has not yet come to initiate the time of favor. It is Torah that endures and is visible in the people's midst.[76]

Influenced by the aesthetics of the poetic line, which prizes parallelism and contrast, these poems make frequent use of antonymous word pairs. This rhetorical structure is not simply an aesthetic element of the compositions; the word pairs function as merisms, or markers of extremes, and gesture toward paradox: sin–forgiveness, angels–mortals, and revealed–concealed are particularly common, and suggest some of the different concerns of these poems (see, for example, Amram 17 and 25; Marqe 1, 2, and 9). Sin and forgiveness speak to the relational nature of Samaritan theology, in which people transgress but

---

76. See Lieber, "Scripture Personified."

God forgives. Such is the nature of each party, and this is one key aspect of the covenantal relationship. (The similar pair "to sin" and "to repent" obviously bespeaks an internal process familiar to the individuals at prayer.) The binary of angels (קעימין) and mortals (מאתין), by contrast, constitutes a merism that contains within it the entire created order, personifying the cosmos from heaven to earth; these two terms also hint at the contrast between "the living" and "the dead," an opposition that spans "this world" and "the world to come," to borrow rabbinic parlance. Finally, the pairing of "revealed" (גלי) and "concealed" (כסי) provides the poets with a way of articulating the miraculous paradox of contact between God and humanity. "Revelation" names that moment when the invisible becomes visible, when something that existed but was unknowable becomes manifest and known.

Finally, beyond those motifs and themes developed in the bodies of the hymns—the images and phrases that create a unity of texture and conceptual world across these poems—the cumulative effect of refrains and fixed phrases should also be noted. While recurring phrases, figures, and word pairs embellish individual stanzas throughout these works, refrains provide a means by which the community could participate in the performance of the hymns, internalizing them not only through passive listening but also by actively speaking some of the lines.[77] The refrain may be brief and frequently repeated, as in Marqe 16 ("Forever, let it be said!") and Marqe 20 ("And there is no writing as great as you!"), where the refrain follows every stanza, or it may be as long as a stanza, as in Amram 5, a short hymn in which the refrain occurs only twice:

We cry out unto him in secret, "Help!"
Perhaps he will help us?
O God of Abraham and Isaac and Jacob
Hear our voices, O our master,
And have mercy upon us in your mercifulness!

The refrain in Marqe 16, "Forever, let it be said," acts as an affirmation of the stanza that it concludes—a kind of drawn-out "Amen." The refrain in Marqe 20, "And there is no writing as great as you," has a different rhetorical function, turning the community into a chorus of praise that speaks directly to the personified Torah. The long refrain from Amram 5, by contrast, speaks to God from an explicitly communal perspective: "*We* appeal to *your* mercifulness." It expresses both uncertainty and hope, enacting the "crying out" that it describes and striving for confidence in the divine qualities it asserts. In its few lines, it deploys

77. On the power of refrains as a mode of participation, albeit in reference to Jewish liturgical poems, see Lieber, "Rhetoric of Participation."

a number of key words from the corpus as a whole: the worshippers' cry is (paradoxically) "concealed," while God is a source of help and characterized by mercy. Common elements of the corpus as a whole are given voice in this refrain.

Often, the themes, ideas, and images in these poems can be cryptic or unclear in isolation; the references in *Tibat Marqe* are rarely more fulsome, in part perhaps because the richly poetic rhetoric of Marqe's exegetical work has not been recognized.[78] Fuller articulations of key concepts—the nature and function of the Taheb, the origins of the time of disfavor, doctrines of the Sabbath and Torah—can be found in later works. And yet, while those later works may be responding in some fashion to a desire to elucidate these poems, it seems likewise clear that our poets presumed communal competency in and familiarity with the terms and ideas they reference. These ideas, thus, cannot be regarded as medieval inventions, but constitute an organic component of the worldview of these classical poets.

A Note on Texts and Translations

Over a decade ago, I published an article in which I explicated a Hebrew poem from the sixth century CE composed by the Jewish *payyetan* Yannai in light of the geopolitics of his time, including the urge that Jews may have felt to join with their Samaritan compatriots in rebelling against the Christian emperors.[79] That essay was about Samaritan history, but it included no Samaritan texts or voices. Samaritan liturgical poetry was simply not yet something of which I was aware. I had some familiarity with *Tibat Marqe*, the primary "midrash" of Samaritans in late antiquity, but the body of classical Samaritan poetry was beyond my ken. It would be several more years before a passing comment from Steven Fine would nudge me toward Samaritan *piyyut*.

Hymnography itself is a young and growing field, and comparative work is essential to knitting together the various discrete textual corpora, including Jewish material (in Hebrew and Aramaic) and Christian writings (in Syriac and Greek, as well as in Latin). The body of Samaritan poetry, while smaller than either the surviving Jewish or Christian corpora, offers an important counterpoint to the other two. The Samaritan experience, entwined with the history of Jews and Christians in the land of Israel, helps to illuminate points of commonality among the diverse corpora of liturgical hymns, as well as to highlight distinctive elements of each. For example, the simple structure of many

---

78. For example, on the Taheb, see *TM* 1 §64 (422, p. 89) and 2 §39 (902-א, p. 139).
79. Lieber, "You Have Been Skirting."

Samaritan poems—alphabetical acrostics structuring uniform stanzas, perhaps
with a refrain—is shared by the poetry of Yose ben Yose (ca. fourth century
CE), but the two are easily distinguished by differences in content. Similarly,
the language of the Samaritan poems is essentially the same as that of the JPA
corpus, but whereas the JPA poems lack any clear sense of liturgical setting, the
Samaritan poems were obviously composed for use in worship rituals. Essential to comparative study, however, has been the creation of sound critical editions of texts and, along with those resources, translations that allow scholars
in diverse areas and a range of disciplines to access original source materials.
This volume is a modest contribution intended to facilitate and encourage this
larger scholarly conversation.

The translations in this volume are based on the texts published in Ben-
Hayyim's five volumes, supplemented in some instances by the earlier work of
Cowley. I have included all of the works conventionally attributed to the three
classical Samaritan *payyetanim*—Amram Dare, Marqe, and Ninna—although
I have indicated when the attribution is dubious or mistaken, as is the case with
Marqe 18, which Ben-Hayyim notes is probably to be ascribed to Ninna. While
the creation of new critical editions (along with apparatuses such as digitized
manuscripts and acoustic recordings of Samaritan pronunciation traditions)
remains a desideratum, the editions of Ben-Hayyim and Cowley remain the
standards in the field and are quite accessible.[80]

In translating these poems, I have striven to balance clarity in English with
a loose fidelity to the rhythm and resonances of the Aramaic original. The stichometry typically follows that of Ben-Hayyim, at least insofar as it can be
maintained without compromising the fluency of the English text. Acrostics,
when present, are indicated in the margins; the reader will notice that acrostics
often use the letter *'ayin* (ע) where one would expect an *'aleph* (א), or a *heh* (ה)
in place of a *khet* (ח); these substitutions are a sign of the weakening of gutturals typical of Samaritan Aramaic (and of JPA as well).[81] Each hymn is preceded by the ligature indicating its traditional liturgical function. The footnotes
highlight particularly challenging or ambiguous words and phrases and also
serve to clarify allusions, quotations, and other subtle resonances, particularly
those that are difficult to reproduce in translation. The subtlety is amplified by
the fact that, in more than a few cases, the layers of translation are manifold:
in some instances, the English represents an Aramaic version of a scriptural

80. The text in Ben-Hayyim, *Recitation of Prayers and Hymns* [*RPH*], provides the basis for the
electronic version available through *CAL*. The *CAL* website also provides access to the best edition
of the SamT, courtesy of Avraham Tal.

81. On the weakening of gutturals in Aramaic in late antiquity, see Kutscher, *Studies in Galilean
Aramaic*, 67–96. In Samaritan Aramaic, the gutturals ח, ה, א, and ע are frequently heard as interchangeable; the uvular fricative ר (*resh*), however, is not subject to this confusion.

Hebrew original. Key Samaritan concepts—theological, historical, and exegetical—are also clarified in the notes. Within the poems themselves, refrains are italicized and boldface type indicates words and phrases that appear in Hebrew in the original Aramaic text. Brackets indicate English words that have been supplied to ensure a fluent translation. Ben-Hayyim's line numbering is preserved throughout; in the three poems where his text is incomplete (Marqe 15, 16, and 21), line numbers followed by asterisks are assigned to passages drawn from Cowley's edition.

The content and orientation of the annotations to these poems differ significantly from similar annotations in translations of Jewish and Christian liturgical poetry, in that the intertextual framework of these poems is distinctly Samaritan. The substantial majority of biblical allusions in these poems come from the Torah, the only text accepted as canonical by the Samaritan Israelites. Samaritan *piyyut* lacks the densely textured allusions to Psalms, Proverbs, and the Prophets that characterize Jewish and Christian hymnography. At the same time, these poems display significant independence from Samaritan texts with which we might expect them to resonate. For example, they do not often allude to the interpretative lore in *Tibat Marqe* in the way that Jewish poetry reflects the midrashic traditions alongside which it developed (even Marqe's poetry is relatively devoid of such allusions), nor do the Aramaic translations of scriptural passages always agree with the SamT, which dates to the same period. The lack of overlap between Samaritan *piyyut* and Samaritan exegesis or biblical translation suggests the independence with which these traditions emerged: Marqe's poetry is not simply his prose exegesis cast in a more rhythmic form,[82] and translation of scripture may have remained a dynamic practice, just as it did in Palestinian Jewish synagogues. The disjunction between Samaritan *piyyut* and Samaritan midrash and targums may also, however, draw our attention to the fact that, while these literary works—liturgical, exegetical, and pedagogical—were written for and preserved within the Samaritan community, the works themselves served different functions and reflected distinctive communal and religious needs and audiences.

Each poem in this volume is prefaced by a brief analytical introduction that highlights one or two particularly compelling aspects of the poem. It may also draw attention to large-scale structural features such as refrains, to distinctive themes that texture the work as a whole, to motifs that recur across multiple works, or to singularly striking lines or images that benefit from closer attention.

---

82. Indeed, the poetry embedded in *TM* itself awaits further study in light of its relationship to the poems presented in this volume, as well as to the body of late antique hymnography more broadly. For some excellent preliminary observations on the rhetorical use of poetry in *TM*, see Novick, *Piyyut and Midrash*, 68–75, 187–89.

Distinctive contextual elements related to ritual, theology, and history may also be singled out if a given poem provides a way into a larger subject, whether it be messianism, the figure of Moses, or the role of the Torah. The analysis of Samaritan *piyyutim* in the commentaries will draw attention to the variety of ways in which context—historical, exegetical, theological, performative, and ritual—can deepen our awareness of the complexity of *piyyutim*. No single poem will resonate with every potential aspect of context, but each poem will illustrate at least some component of contextual richness. Out of this analytical mosaic, the complex beauty and dynamism of classical Samaritan poetry will emerge. These miniature essays are, of course, far from exhaustive, and serve primarily to gesture toward the richness of this body of literature—a collection of poems that awaits sustained scholarly attention—and the kind of insights it can provide into Samaritan religiosity and late antique cultural expression more broadly.

Amram Dare (Amram the Elder)

AMRAM DARE IS THE EARLIEST Samaritan poet known by name, and the Aramaic poems ascribed to him are the earliest indication that the Samaritan community participated in the hymnographic revolution of late antiquity that transformed Jewish and Christian liturgical performance as well. He is the father of Samaritan poetry in both figurative and literal terms: not only are his works the earliest Samaritan *piyyutim*, but his son Marqe is recognized as the greatest classical Samaritan poet, and Marqe's own son, Ninna, is the last of the classical Aramaic poets of Samaritan tradition.

Much of Amram Dare's biography remains obscure. He is known in the tradition as "Amram the Elder" (perhaps to be identified with Amram ben Serad) as well as "Tuta" (his Latin name was evidently Titus). Amram Dare was a priest, a contemporary of the great Samaritan reformer Baba Rabbah, and an active participant in the renewal of Samaritan society in the late third and early fourth centuries CE. According to the Samaritan chronicles, Amram Dare was one of the seven sages whom Baba Rabbah sent out to minister to Samaritan communities after a period of Roman persecution in the early third century. Religious reformation and poetic innovation are embodied together in the person of Amram Dare.

Amram Dare's liturgical poems, the only writings attributed to him that have survived, remain a part of the Samaritan liturgy to the present day. Most of them are contained within a collection known as the *Durran* ("String of Pearls"), a name that apparently puns on the poet's honorific "Dare" (the elder). The twenty-two poems in the *Durran* (Amram Dare 1–22) share a common structure (or lack thereof): they are relatively brief hymns, unrhymed and variable in length, and are devoid of acrostics or other structuring devices. Nevertheless, the inclusion of just twenty-two of Amram Dare's hymns in the *Durran* lends the collection the aesthetic completeness of an acrostic; the fact that one of the twenty-two poems is of dubious authorship (Amram Dare 13) suggests that the compilers of the *Durran* were striving to meet that number. Six additional poems attributed to Amram Dare (23–28) are, however, longer and do contain acrostics.[1] All of these poems are composed in Samaritan Aramaic, a variant of Palestinian Aramaic and thus linguistically kin to the body of Jewish Palestinian Aramaic (JPA) poetry of the same approximate time and place.[2] All of the *piyyutim* attributed to Amram Dare can be found in the *Defter*, the Samaritan prayer book, in the section "Hymns [or: Liturgies (אמנות)] for the Sabbaths and Festivals."[3]

The twenty-two poems of the *Durran* lack a common form, but as noted above they share a basic brevity: the longest (Amram Dare 9) is forty-five lines and the shortest (Amram Dare 14) just fifteen lines. The lines themselves tend to be quite short and lack a fixed meter or rhythm. On the other hand, they are composed out of short (if irregular) phrases and feature a loose kind of parallelism, a style of composition that echoes to some extent the cadences of the Psalms. This literary echo is particularly intriguing because the Psalms appear in the Jewish Bible but not in the Samaritan canon. It may be that the general "sound-print" of the Psalms—which recurs, for example, in the Hebrew Hodayot hymns sung at Qumran and in Greek in the Wisdom of Solomon—may have resonated as "liturgical" within the Samaritan community. Psalmic patterning, whether in Hebrew, Greek, or Aramaic, can be easily mimicked and would perhaps have been received as a kind of "organic" liturgical sound by Amram Dare's community, given the centrality of the Psalms in Jewish and Christian worship in antiquity and the psalm-like cadences of the poetry within the Torah itself. At the same time, the difference in language between the Hebrew Psalms and the Aramaic poetry of Amram Dare, as well as the lack of Aramaic poetry prior to Amram Dare, may well indicate that the resonances reflect something more culturally diffuse, or an older, if unpreserved, tradition of Aramaic poetry among the Samaritans. By contrast, Amram Dare's longer *piyyutim* (23–28) are uniformly structured as alphabetical acrostics comprising twenty-two four-line stanzas composed of terse, short stichs. In their patterning, they recall the poems for the Shofar service composed by Amram Dare's Jewish contemporary, the

---

1. Ben-Hayyim includes in his edition of Amram's poetry a twenty-ninth poem that is univocally ascribed to him by Samaritan tradition, out of deference to its position in the *Defter*, but compared to Amram's other poems, it is exceptional for being composed in Hebrew and for its use of strong, regular rhyme. Ben-Hayyim tentatively attributed this poem to a much later Amram, a high priest who lived in Shechem in the thirteenth century (*RPH*, 12). It is not included in this volume.

2. On the classification of Samaritan Aramaic, see Kaufman, "Dialectology." For a critical edition of the Jewish Palestinian Aramaic [JPA] poetry, see Yahalom and Sokoloff, *Shirat Bene Maʿarava*; for an English translation of this body of poetry, see Lieber, *Jewish Palestinian Aramaic Poetry*.

3. The name of the prayer book was borrowed into Aramaic from the Greek διφθέρα, meaning "register" or simply "a hide prepared for writing."

payyetan Yose ben Yose (fourth century CE, Galilee); both Amram Dare and Yose seem to reflect a common aesthetic of liturgical poetry.

Although the two collections differ in terms of form, the poems of the *Durran* and the six acrostics present the poet in a variety of relationships to his audiences, God and the congregation. In both groups we find poems addressed directly to the deity (as "you," sg.) and poems that speak of God from a slight remove (as "he"), and in both groups, there are poems that feature the poet speaking as part of the community (as "we"), others in which he addresses them directly (as "you," pl.), and still others in which he speaks of them from a distance ("they"), either emotional or temporal. The poet's rhetorical stance vis-à-vis his listeners is generally stable within a single composition, but collectively Amram Dare's poetry creates a sense of the poet's own shifting intimacy: he is frequently proximate to his God and grounded within his community, yet able to distance himself from both.

Themes and motifs that are central to Amram Dare's verse include God's uniqueness, God's many attributes (particularly mercifulness), the sinfulness of the current generation, and the righteousness of the ancestors. The present moment is volatile: it is a time of punishment and oppression that has been earned (although a reprieve is possible), and yet, if the day is the Sabbath, it is a time of recovery and hope. The outlook is not particularly optimistic; the poet rarely makes excuses for the transgressions of the people, past or present, and rarely argues that relief has, in some way, been earned. Instead, Amram Dare's source of confidence in the future—or at least his source of hope—is God's compassionate nature.

These recurring themes are expressed through repeated vocabulary. The words associated with God's actions and inclinations include "love, mercy" (רחם), "compassion, favor, grace" (רתי), "goodness" (טוב), "to create, work" (עבד), "glory, splendor" (יקר), and "to help, save" (both דבק and ישע); those associated with people include "fear" (דחל) and "sin, transgression" (חיב), but also "hope, confidence" (סבר). One word associated with both God and people, however, is "steadfast, faithful" (אמן): God is reliable, even if that reliability means going against what is just in order to enact mercy, and the people can be relied upon not only to sin but also to regret and to cast themselves upon God's mercy, as their steadfast and reliable prophet, Moses, taught them. In general, while the clustering of themes and images varies from poem to poem, the rhetorical structures of the poems work through juxtaposition, with God and Israel in dynamic relationship with each other, pivoting around shared elements such as scripture or the Sabbath, or in tension over Israel's behavior and God's inclinations.

The figure of Moses occupies a particularly privileged place in Amram Dare's poetry, as the one who mediated between God and people—and in some sense continues to mediate through the Torah. Moses is unique, as God is; Moses is faithful, as God is; and what God uttered, Moses transcribed. Unlike God, however, Moses will not remain unique forever. Deuteronomy 18:15 depicts Moses as speaking of "a prophet like me," and in Deut 34:10, the Torah states that "there has not arisen since in Israel a prophet like Moses, whom the Lord knew face to face," which is understood in Samaritan tradition as a prophecy: while such a figure has not yet arisen, someday such a figure will come. This "second Moses" is referred to in classical Samaritan poetry and prose (including *Tibat Marqe*) as the Taheb (lit., "he who returns, restores"). The Taheb is not a messianic figure here—he is not a savior who will rescue the people (which is a divine, not mortal, task), nor is he a monarch (the Samaritans have no equivalent to a "Davidic line"), nor is he a priest (the office held by Moses's brother, Aaron). Instead, the Taheb is a figure of the renewal of prophecy and all that such an institution entails: direct communication with the deity and a restoration of harmonious intimacy between God and God's people.

Because Amram Dare's poems were composed for use in liturgy, Ben-Hayyim prefaces each translation with a headnote specifying the ritual occasions on which the poem is read.[4] There is, however, an inescapable anachronism in this framing, since we do not know what constituted the synagogue liturgy in Amram Dare's day, or even in the medieval period. Scholars hypothesize that the core of the Samaritan liturgy consisted of the reading of *qatafim*, anthologies of biblical verses that represent digests of entire books, together with selected hymns. Given the abundance of poems in the Samaritan liturgical tradition, one of the tasks of the priest overseeing the rituals for a given day would be to decide which of the available poems should be used to complement the scriptural readings.

Similarly, almost every poem here concludes with the liturgical phrase "May God be praised! There is no God but the one!" This phrase is not an organic part of the poems; rather, it enacts a transition from the poem back into the liturgical structure in which it is recited. That said, the phrase itself is often echoed within the poems and highlights the recurring theme of God's uniqueness that textures much of this corpus of poetry as a whole (including the works of Marqe and Ninna). As the poems of the *Durran* have no acrostic structure or other formal element to signal the end of the composition, this ritual cue is particularly important for practice, but it also serves to answer the rhetorical questions with which Amram Dare often closes his hymns. "Who is like God?" the poet asks,

4. See the discussion in *RPH*, 23–24; Ben-Hayyim's headings describe contemporary Samaritan use of the poems. On the cues in the liturgy, see Anderson and Giles, *Tradition Kept*, 359–60.

and the liturgy responds, no one! "May God be praised, there is no God but the one!"[5]

These lyrics can, at times, make a host of assumptions about concepts and traditions that register as at once familiar and strange to those acquainted with Jewish and Christian writings from antiquity. Often the difference lies in a matter of degree or a distinctive understanding of a widespread concept, such as the Sabbath or revelation. But read together, these poems offer a sense of a truly distinctive community, with its own concerns and aesthetics. They are, like the Samaritans themselves, clearly kin to the writings of Amram Dare's peers, including Yose ben Yose and Ephrem the Syrian, and yet the poetic affinities should not obscure the unique Samaritan-ness of these works.

1 "Since There Is No God but the One" (*SL*, 38–39; *RPH*, 41–43)

This hymn offers a lyrical celebration of God's unique power as manifest through his relationship with Moses, and through Moses, the rest of the people. Of particular note is Amram Dare's attention to spatiality: "world," "land," "camp," and "place" constitute settings for divine actions, while the references to Mount Horeb and the thorn bush invite listeners to imagine the wilderness revelation scenes of both Exod 3 and 19. God's actions, in turn, evoke movement within space: God bends himself downward so that he may interact with his prophet, and then raises his prophet to a heavenly realm accessible to no other mortal. While the spaces are not specifically visualized, the poet creates a sense of motion-in-space, leading the imagination up and down and depicting a scene of nearly cosmic breadth ("the world") that is simultaneously profoundly intimate ("beneath his hand").

Through the image of God sheltering creation beneath his hand, Amram Dare expands an image famously associated with Moses in Exod 33 to include everyone and everything. This phrase suggests the paradox that energizes much of the hymn: the relationship between a radically unique deity and a people that is exceptional only because God chose them to receive his revelation. The potential gulf between God and the mortal realm is navigated by a litany of other unique conduits that constitute a chain linking God to the congregation: God gives his unique Torah to his unique prophet Moses, which inspires a unique faith and fidelity among the people. When Moses asks, "What am I?" (l. 10), he stands in for the congregation, and when God promises that Moses shall see

---

5. The assertion of God's solitary, unique oneness appears in Samaritan epigraphy from an early date as well. See Tal, "Bilingual Greek-Samaritan Inscription."

his greatness (ll. 15–16), the poet suggests that the community of Moses is also unique. The presence of the Torah scroll in the community's midst attests to the bond between God and people.

The depiction of the Torah here, while brief and impressionistic, offers a vivid cluster of emphases that will be developed even more fully in the poetry of Marqe. While all creation shelters beneath the divine hand, only the community of Israel—the Samaritans—possesses God's handwriting, a document signed and sealed by God. The Torah is unlike any other kind of writing: it can never be erased, nor can the people and their faithfulness, manifest in the worship of God who bequeathed the Torah, be effaced. But the community's reverence for Torah and their worship of its giver does not benefit the community of the faithful alone; rather, their piety sustains the entire world. The intimacy of God's exchange with Moses has not only national but cosmic significance, as does the ritual of prayer in which this hymn itself is sung. Proper worship maintains creation, and the recitation of this hymn constitutes a key element of that sustaining and sacred task—an inescapable, instinctive response to the proximity of the holy.

> *Said on Sunday in the morning, on the first Sabbath of the month, the evening after Sabbath goes out* [motzei Shabbat] *on the Festival* (i.e., Passover), *on festivals, and on the Sabbaths that fall during festivals.*

> Since there is no God but the one,
> No world aside from his,
> And nothing worthy of worship[6] except his greatness,
> Whoever dwells in his camp[7]
> 5   Shall acclaim the master of the land.
> Indeed, all the children of [his] place
> Magnify him, for he himself is Lord.[8]

6. Lit., "and nothing shall be worshipped."

7. Lit., "dwells in His sojourning." This line is difficult, and Ben-Hayyim suggests that there is an error in the text (*RPH*, 41–42). The word בתותביי is clearly derived from the verb יתב ("to sit, dwell"); in his translation, Ben-Hayyim renders it as כתושב ("one who dwells like a sojourner"). *CAL* suggests "he who dwells in his residence(s) (or: among those who dwell with him?)" (s.v. *twtb*, *twtb'* I). The translation above follows Ben-Hayyim's suggestion to interpret בתותביי in light of the JPA lexeme תותבו ("dwelling place").

8. This translation understands ארכן as a loan from the Greek ἄρχων ("lord, magistrate"), as in *DSA*, 63, s.v. ארכון. Alternatively, the word ארכן could be derived from the root רכן ("to bend, incline") and interpreted as a description of God's lowering the divine self to the summit of Sinai and, in general, drawing near to the human congregation. That root, however, more conventionally describes religious prostration, suggesting that God's bending to speak to humanity inspires a human response of bending in worship.

And thus Moses did at Mount Horeb
When he stood before the thorn bush
10 And said to his master: "What am I?"
And his master placed him at a level[9]
That no [mortal] king can reach,
And God stood him upon that height
And assured him concerning the concealed world
15 When he said that "a prophet like Moses" [Deut 34:10][10]
Would see the like of his greatness.[11]
There is no God but our master,
And no book like his Torah,
And no true prophet like Moses,
20 And no complete faithfulness,
Nor truth except his,
And the world does not flourish entirely
Unless he is worshipped exclusively.
Lo, the heavens and earth bear witness[12]
25 That divinity belongs to the one, to his greatness,
For he made them and arrayed them.
And lo, these letters are the very handwriting of God,
And Moses was forever faithful.
And indeed, in you they will believe[13] forever.
30 Who is able to erase this?
God is one and all is under his hand,[14]
A signature[15] that can never be erased

May God be praised!
There is no God but the one!

---

9. The word דרג can mean literally "step" as well as the more metaphorical "rank, office, status." Tal translates ll. 11–12 as "and his Master placed him on a rank that no king is authorized to place" (*DSA*, 367, s.v. יתב).

10. This translation follows Ben-Hayyim, who prefers a MS that reads דנביא in place of הן נביא and sees the particle -ד as introducing direct speech (*RPH*, 42). Deut 34:10 states, "And there never arose in Israel another prophet like Moses, whom the Lord knew face to face."

11. An allusion to Moses being permitted to behold God's glory without dying; see Exod 33:23. Lines 14–16 together depict God as assuring Moses that no other prophet will see his presence ("the concealed world") in the same way that Moses did.

12. Lit., "are witnesses."

13. Reading the variant יימנון (or יהימנון) in place of אימנון, with Ben-Hayyim (who refers to the tradition of pronunciation that he recorded; *RPH*, 43).

14. The image of being "under the hand" primarily conveys a sense that the world is entirely under God's authority. It may secondarily evoke protection, as when God shelters Moses in the cleft of the rock in Exod 33:22.

15. Lit., "seal."

2 "Unto You Do We Pray, O Our Master" (*SL*, 39; *RPH*, 44–45)

Whereas the previous poem spoke *about* God, this poem speaks directly to him. Amram Dare, as he usually does, speaks consistently from a single perspective. Here it is that of the community: he uses the plural pronouns "we," "us," and "our" and addresses God as "you." The hymn is rich with vocative forms; the poet appeals to God's attributes of power, both in his essence ("master" [ll. 1, 17] and "great one" [l. 5]) and in his actions ("Creator" [l. 13] and "rescuer" [l. 2]). The rhetoric of the poem creates an intimate liturgical space in which this dialogue takes place—and it *is* a dialogue, even if only the poet's voice is heard. God's speech is recalled (l. 20: "I am that I am" [Exod 3:14]), and even more importantly, the poet possesses the right to speak because he is partner to an established relationship: as the refrain concludes, "Recall the covenant with those who love you" (ll. 12, 23). This apparent monologue takes place within an ongoing conversation. The poet conveys the deep intimacy he personally feels, as revealed when he abandons the communal first-person plural in the poem's penultimate stanza and speaks in his own voice, addressing God individually as "my master" (l. 17). He speaks to God for his community, but also explicitly for himself.

The community is drawn into the conversation not only through the power of rhetoric but also through the recitation of a refrain. The refrain is not pithy, and it is repeated only twice, but into its five lines (8–12) the poet packs four imperatives seeking God's mercy. He appeals to God's nature ("I am that I am"), his proclivities ("as you are accustomed"), his recognition of the people's need ("lest we be lost"), and the covenant of divine mercy that binds God to his people. The rapid rhythm of the lines lends the refrain an almost antiphonal, call-and-response quality, with the congregation's attention intensely focused on the deity: appeals to God frame the self-references ("our lives" and "pity us") in the interior of the stanza.[16] It is as if God's mercy buffers them even within the rhetoric of prayer. And if we assume that this stanza was in fact recited congregationally, then the community not only assents to the poet's words through its intent and emotional participation but also shares in the utterance of the words. The liturgy, in a sense, has no fourth wall, and through the refrain, the community steps into the sacred space of dialogue conjured by the poet's words.

---

16. In contemporary Samaritan practice, prayers are recited antiphonally. As Pummer writes, "The Samaritans chant their prayers by dividing the community into two choirs, one standing on the right side of the synagogue, the other on the left. The group on the right side, together with the priest, sings the first and then immediately the third verse; at the same time the group on the left begins to sing the second verse and so on" (*Samaritans*, 283–84). We cannot assume that twentieth- and twenty-first-century practices reflect customs of the third and fourth centuries CE, but contemporary custom reflects a sensitivity to the antiphonal nature of these compositions.

Said at daybreak on Monday, on the second Sabbath of the month,
on festivals, and on the Sabbaths that fall during festivals.

Unto you do we pray, O our master,
O rescuer of the oppressed;
Of you are we in awe,
O worker of all wonders,

5   O great one, you who admonish us
At all times, and incline us to learn,
Even if we are rebellious and inclined to ignorance.

    Rather, as is your inclination,[17] be merciful [רחם]*!*
    *O "**I am that I am**" [Exod 3:14], have compassion* [רתי]

10   *[Upon] our lives, in your great goodness!*
    Pity us in your mercy, lest we perish!
    Recall the covenant with those who love you![18]

Creator of all the world,
Have mercy upon us in your compassion;

15   See our oppression and do not ignore our distress.
Fathers and sons appeal to your sovereignty.
O my master, turn not your face from us;
We are unable to withstand your punishments!

    Rather, as is your inclination, be merciful!

20   *O "**I am that I am**," have compassion*
    [Upon] our lives, in your great goodness!
    Pity us in your mercy, lest we be lost!
    Recall the covenant with those who love you!

    May God be praised!
    There is no God but the one!

---

17. The translations "incline us to learn," "inclined to ignorance," and "inclination" in ll. 6–8 reflect an effort to render in English a single common root, "to learn, teach" (אלף). Literally, the phrases would be translated, "At all times, and instruct [מלף] us / even if we are rebellious and cannot learn [דלא נילף] / rather, as is your habit [אלוף] . . ."

18. See *DSA*, 506, s.v. נהר, which cites Ben-Hayyim's translation (*RPH*, 44). On the translation "covenant" for דכרון/דכרן, see Ben-Hayyim's note on the phrase (ibid.). A more literal translation might read, "Recall the memorandum/remembrance of those who love you," but "remembrance" here has a more formal connotation.

3 "O Steadfast One, Toward Whom Everything Bows" (*SL*, 39; *RPH*, 45–48)

In this poem, Amram Dare speaks to God on behalf of the community—includ-ing those whose actions constitute an affront to God. He describes his contem-poraries as occupying a fragile space delimited by time: the past offers nar-ratives of both glory and shame, and the future promises both judgment and forgiveness. The fate of Israel, now as always, rests with God, but the poet gently reminds the deity that for all his incomparable power, his nature will surely incline him to act with mercy.

Looking to the past, the poet evokes canonical episodes from the Torah's history: first the patriarchs of Genesis and the power of ancestral merit, as he appeals to God to rescue the children for the sake of their fathers, then the dra-matic events of the rest of the Torah, as he recalls the flight from Egypt, the parting of the sea, and the unexpected triumph of the journey through the wilder-ness. Each historical station is linked with divine actions: Egypt with miracles, the sea with victory, and the wilderness with triumph over foes. These acts are cast not as mere beneficence or as strict fairness, but as evidence of God's faith-fulness to his covenant with those who love him.

Israel, however, responded to divine kindness with transgression. Specifi-cally, the poet jarringly juxtaposes the image of "those who love you" with the act of setting "an idol at the summit of the temple" (ll. 26–27). In acts of hubris—apparently mistaking themselves for God—the people repaid God's steadfast kindness with betrayal, and the poet relies on vivid language to depict the consequences they earned: a divine lightning-sword destroyed both the idols and their devotees. The defiled Temple was destroyed, and so too will such sin be punished in the future.

In both cases, past is paradigm, and the anxiety of Amram Dare's community derives from the two distinct futures predicted by their past. Are they fated for more divine kindness, however unmerited it may be? Or will the demands of justice, however terrible, come to pass? The final lines of the poem urge God toward compassion, as the poet leads the community in an assertion of God's forgiving nature, and yet Amram Dare also concedes that God will do as God wishes.

Rhetorically, we can see how the poet begins from a position of near-neutrality: he addresses God directly, as "you," while he speaks about the people in the third person as "it" and "they." This mode of speaking puts the poet some-what closer to God than to the community. And yet, at the end of the poem, the poet joins the community: "But we say . . ." (l. 30). In the end, the poet does not separate himself from his community. He can adopt a perspective sympathetic to the divine, but he does so not to condemn his people but to make his vision of God's compassionate nature more persuasive and compelling. His case made, he steps back and rejoins the people, anxiously awaiting their fate.

> *Said on Monday in the morning, on festivals, and on the Sabbaths that fall during festivals.*

O steadfast one, toward whom everything bows,
Gaze upon the world in your mercy,
For it stands anxiously today![19]
Remember Abraham, Isaac, and Jacob
5   And rescue their children,
For they occupy an anxious place.[20]

You are accustomed to working wonders
On behalf of those who love you everywhere:
You manifested[21] triumphs for them
10 In Egypt, at the sea, and in the wilderness.
And you worked wonders and miracles,
And you manifested every triumph on their behalf,
And you made their enemies bow down before them,
And your goodness shall be recounted forever,
15 For you remember your covenant with those who love you.[22]

O source of every victory in battle,[23]
It suffices for you to forgive those who provoke your wrath,[24]
For they[25] [only] imagine[26] all the terrestrial[27] things   ·
Are theirs. The lightning is your sword,
20 Fated to burn every transgressor

---

19. Reading יומן (= יומה הן) in place of יומין, with Ben-Hayyim (*RPH*, 45).

20. Lit., "they are situated in anxiety."

21. On this meaning of the root גלי, with the sense of "create," see *DSA*, 145.

22. See Amram 2, l. 12.

23. The translation reflects the elliptical nature of the line; literally, it reads: "O victor, through whom there is (victory) in every battle." See the discussion in *RPH*, 46.

24. Lines 17–19 are (like the preceding l. 16) difficult and possibly corrupt, with more MS variants than typical. The poet seems to praise God for his (temporary) indulgence of the community's enemies. The word מיסתך can mean "it is enough for you, it suffices for you" or "it befits you."

25. I.e., the Roman-Byzantines; see l. 22.

26. Lit., "see, look," or even "expect." The translation "imagine" gestures toward the idea of "envisioning, seeing" in the word, as well as affirming the delusional nature of the belief held by God's enemies.

27. Understanding מכה as spatial (as does Ben-Hayyim, who translates it as למטה; *RPH*, 46) rather than existential (i.e., "lowly, humble").

At the moment when you draw it[28] in triumph
And burn their[29] [false] gods and their worshippers
Every time they are reverenced.

Your time of favor[30] and your truth sustain them,[31]
25 And your goodness suffices for them as consolation.[32]
The children of those who love you place[33]
An idol[34] at the summit of the temple,
And all that great holiness
Is stripped from it by the hand of the wicked.[35]

30 But we say: Great is the God who so forgives,[36]
And he is able to triumph howsoever he wishes,
And no one can refuse.

May God be praised!
There is no God but the one!

4 "O Good One, Who Eternally Does Good" (*SL*, 40; *RPH*, 48–50)

In this composition, Amram Dare offers his community a doxological hymn. The entire poem speaks directly to the deity; the community is addressed indirectly, with worshippers described in the third-person singular ("he") rather than in the communal "we," after the introductory lines. The poet has thus positioned himself between God and the individual worshipper: he mediates the relationship while standing at a slight remove from it, becoming an intimate of God who can share with him some insights on the experience of mortals, even as his words remind his listeners of God's unique attributes.

28. God's lightning sword.
29. I.e., the transgressors of ll. 17 and 20.
30. רחותה is interchangeable with רעותה.
31. I.e., the Samaritans.
32. I.e., both as comfort and forgiveness.
33. For this meaning of מתקנין, see *DSA*, 961, s.v. תקן.
34. Lit., "impure thing."
35. These lines describe the desecration of Mount Gerizim and the coercion or complicity of Samaritans in the act. The Jerusalem Talmud may preserve a similar tradition: according to y. Avodah Zarah 44d, when Diocletian (r. 284–305 CE) came to the land of Israel, he decreed that all people except the Jews must offer him libations; the Samaritans obeyed the edict and thereafter their wine was deemed pagan and forbidden for Jewish consumption.
36. While מסובר may look like a passive participial form, it is the active participle of the reflexive conjugation (*מסתובר).

The language of the poem recalls that of royal psalms found in the Jewish Bible, although those poems do not constitute part of the Samaritan canon. As a paean to God's omnipresence, fidelity, intransience, and power, this hymn casts God as a beneficent ruler whose merits exceed anything a mortal ruler could hope to offer. It is only logical that humans worship such a king: he steadies his people when they tremble, and he never sleeps (l. 21; echoing Ps 121:3–4), he is victorious in battle (ll. 23–24; cf. Ps 98:1), and he is everywhere (l. 12; cf. Ps 139). The sense of intertextual richness becomes inescapable when the poet quotes from Exod 15 (l. 26), recreating the moment of divine recognition when the Israelites at the shore of the sea ask, "Who is like you?" (v. 11). The relationship the poet describes here has the timeless quality of the psalms, and the confidence of one secure in the bond between God and people. The poet does not speak here of sin and transgression, of human flaw and divine forgiveness; rather, he assumes a functioning and functional relationship of harmony.

For all of God's unique and universal potency, he is not a universal deity: he has a specific relationship with a specific community. The relationship is not based on Israel's intrinsic merit—as Amram Dare states, "we are unworthy" (l. 2)—nonetheless, it is utterly secure and the poet can speak of it with confidence. The poet concludes this hymn with a litany of specifics: God is unique, his Torah is unique, worship of him is the only true worship, and that worship must take place on Mount Gerizim. That locus is, as Amram Dare reminds his listeners in the hymn's final lines (33–34), "the house of God, / The chosen, the holy, the choicest spot of dry land!" With this language, the poet asserts unequivocally the merit of Samaritan claims. Until that point, the text is consonant with the beliefs of Jews and Christians, but those final two lines lend the poem utter specificity. God, our poet says, is a world-creating and universal God of truth, but true worship of God can be performed in only one place.

Said at daybreak on Tuesday, on the third Sabbath of the month, on festivals and on Sabbaths that fall during festivals.

O good one, who eternally does good,[37]
Act compassionately toward us, though we are unworthy.
We trust only in you;
All who were trusted have fallen and faded away.
5   All the kings have passed away,
But you are a king who does not pass away,
And a trusted one who does not fall—
Steadfast in greatness that is limitless

---

37. Or, "does good for the world."

And authority that is boundless,

10   And a glory that cannot be measured.[38]

Clasping close[39] those who love you, both far and near,

For you, O God, can be found in all places

And need not wander to a[nother] place;

Happy are his worshippers, who devote themselves

15   To you with complete faith.

And he who is devoted to you faithfully breathes free,

For you are with him in every place

Clasping him close, for thus he is pleasing to you,[40]

[You who are] keeping watch, day and night,

20   And in his sleep, he trembles[41] not

And he breathes freely, he whom you protect, for you do not sleep.

And no king can stand against you,

And no warfare can frighten you

Yours is the only triumph!

25   Let all the mouths say to you:

"Who is like you among the gods?" [Exod 15:11].[42]

Your name awes the world;

And what is any of this compared to your great might?[43]

Forever, there is no God but the one,

30   No prophet like Moses his prophet,

No writing like the holy Torah,

And no worship except of YHWH

In the presence of Mount Gerizim: the house of God,

The chosen,[44] the holy, the choicest spot of dry land!

---

38. From the root שום, "to evaluate" (see *DSA*, 882, and the discussion in *RPH*, 49).

39. The root דבק connotes physical proximity and, outside Samaritan poetry, most often reflects human piety in the act of "clinging" to a deity and that deity's ways; it is a particularly Deuteronomistic formulation (e.g., Deut 4:4; Josh 22:5; 1 Kgs 11:2). In classical Samaritan poetry, the term is often parallel to ישע, "to rescue" (see *DSA*, 165, s.v. דבק), but here the language (דבק ב-) and lack of parallelism suggests that simple clinging is the intended meaning.

40. Reading לך in place of לה. Alternatively, it is possible to read לה and translate as "for thus (you) favor him."

41. With Ben-Hayyim (*RPH*, 50), I take מתחנט to be an error and read here an *ethpeʿel* participle from the root נטט/נטנט (*DSA*, 519, s.v. נטט).

42. Cited in Aramaic translation.

43. Ben-Hayyim treats ll. 28–29 as a case of enjambment, reading the text of l. 28 plus the first word of l. 29, לעלם ("eternal, forever"), as a single unit: "And what is any of this compared to your great might / eternal? There is no God but the one" (*RPH*, 50). Enjambment, however, is rare in early Samaritan Aramaic poetry, and thus ll. 28 and 29 are treated as separate units in the translation here.

44. On the variant spelling בחורה (where we would expect בחירה), see *DSA*, 92, s.v. ביאר.

May God be praised!
There is no God but the one!

5 "The Almighty Is Powerfully Strong" (*SL*, 40; *RPH*, 51–53)

The theme of this poem is the desperate unworthiness of the Israelite people, both past and present: through the poem's words—both those spoken by the poet and those the congregation themselves recite—the worshippers acknowledge their unworthy actions and express desperation out of fear of their consequences. The poet creates a sense of the people as almost helpless. They cannot undo their transgressions, grievous as they are; instead, they throw themselves on God's mercy and rely on his love for their ancestors and his own compassionate nature.

The people are wicked, and although the poet does not catalogue their crimes, they seem to have offended through some form of idolatry, as Amram Dare quotes Exod 34:14, which prohibits worshipping other gods. The people do not sin out of ignorance; God has warned them, and the poet offers no excuses. Instead, the poet focuses his attention on the grief he and his people feel over their actions: he describes how the people "shout" for help and weep for themselves. They do not deserve God's compassion, but they hope for it nonetheless.

The repeated stanza—perhaps a kind of refrain (ll. 10–14)—offers an intriguing image of crying out (נצעק) for help "in secret" (בכסי; lit., "concealment"). In the first instance, this description of loud prayer follows immediately after an assertion that "we have no words" (l. 9), and it is in turn followed by a statement that "weeping fills the world" (l. 15). The second repetition is followed by a direct address to God, that he might accept our prayers "in your great kindness" (l. 29). In the first case, voices seem to have escaped the confines of the space that contained them; in the second, they strive to break through to God, to speak to God directly rather than in the third person. In the first, they are audible; in the second, they seek a hearing.

The tension within the phrase "cry out in secret" is tangible: the act of speaking loudly is jarring in the context of hiding. Loud sounds attract attention, whereas concealment demands silence. The phrase itself is not entirely clear. Perhaps it is God who is concealed and it is necessary to attract his attention so that he may notice the penitential regret of the people. But perhaps the community of the faithful understands itself as hidden away in its synagogues, sanctuaries that afford a safe space for earnest divine petition. In any case, the outpouring cannot be contained, and the cry pours forth until it fills the world. The question is whether the people's cries can breach the screen of heaven.

Either God is remote or the people are hidden, or perhaps both. In any case, a gulf separates the two parties, a space filled by the human voice and human tears, but also by a hope in divine proximity. For all their transgressions, the poet asserts that the people nonetheless trust in God and rely on him. Humans sin, but God forgives. The congregation piteously attempts to make itself heard. They hope that God, whose very nature is forgiveness, is listening.

> *Recited on Tuesday in the morning, on the Night of Atonement, and on "the day of the proclamation"* (also known as "the standing at Mount Sinai"—that is, the forty-sixth day of the counting of the omer).

The Almighty is powerfully strong,
He who dwells in the highest heavens,[45]
And he is found in every place.
[For[46] in] his goodness he agrees[47] [to all this],
5   To accept [the prayers of] those who incur
Transgressions, the one who forgives,[48] the good one.

Often do you warn[49] us, but we do not learn,
And the fate of the wicked approaches,
And we have no words before him.

10   *We cry out unto him in secret, "Help!"*
Perhaps[50] he will help us?
O God of Abraham and Isaac and Jacob,
Hear our voices, O our master,
And have mercy upon us in your mercifulness!

15   A great weeping fills the world:

45. Specifically, the poet uses מעונה (*maʿon*) to refer to heaven; in rabbinic literature, this is a specific level of heaven.

46. While most MSS read דארכן, Ben-Hayyim indicates that the version reading וארכן may be preferable (*RPH*, 51).

47. This is a difficult line. Ben-Hayyim (*RPH*, 51), based on the manuscript tradition, favors dropping the final two words: לכל חדה ("to all this"). The translation of (דארכן) as "to agree" is based on *DSA*, 63, s.v. ארכן; Tal understands it as a denominative verb from ארכן ("magistrate, leader," from the Greek ἄρχων), citing this passage in his entry. *CAL* (s.v. *ʾrkn*) cites *DSA* but prefers to translate this word as "to raise one's hand in an oath"; that said, *CAL* understands ארכן here to be a noun, "length." Ben-Hayyim translates, "his goodness agrees . . ." (*RPH*, 51).

48. Reading with Ben-Hayyim (*RPH*, 52); the text could also be translated as "the one who hopes, understands."

49. Or "bear witness against us."

50. For דמה as "perhaps," see *DSA*, 185, s.v. דמה.

We all weep for ourselves,
For lo, one who becomes arrogant[51] abolishes
The reward of all the righteous.
And the true writings[52] proclaim:

20 "You shall not bow down to another God" [Exod 34:14][53]
Cursed is the Hebrew who abandons
The faith of the upright.

We cry out unto him in secret, "Help!"
Perhaps he will help us?
25 *O God of Abraham and Isaac and Jacob,*
Hear our voices, O our master,
And have mercy upon us in your mercifulness!

And accept our prayers from us
In your great kindness!

May God be praised!
There is no God but the one!

6 "Great Is God, and None Like Him" (*SL*, 40–41; *RPH*, 53–55)

In this hymn, Amram Dare takes his listeners into the events of the book of
Exodus. For all its brevity, the poem divides into distinct units: an introductory
stanza that praises God, the people, and Moses as great and unique; a section
that recounts the revelation of Torah at Sinai; a section praising Yocheved as the
mother of Miriam, Aaron, and Moses; and a concluding petition that ancestral
merit may move God to rescue the present community.

In retelling the revelation of the Torah, the poet describes the event in the
present tense, narrating it to his community as a memory rather than history: "We assembled at Mount Sinai / On the day the writing descended"
(ll. 4–5).[54] The boundary between remote past and present is collapsed, and the

51. Lit., "one expanding (himself), making himself great"; Tal translates as "(a wicked one)
expanding abolishes the reward of the righteous" (*DSA*, 565, s.v. סגי). The lack of metathesis in the
word (i.e., מתסגי rather than מסתגי) leads Ben-Hayyim (*RPH*, 52) to suggest emending the text by
dividing the word into two: מת סכי מית or מת סכי מית סגי.

52. Ben-Hayyim (*RPH*, 52) translates as "letters" (of the alphabet).

53. Cited in Aramaic. The quotation is identical to SamT except for לאלה ("to God") where the
SamT has לאל.

54. This conflation of past and present can be traced back to the Torah. See, e.g., Exod 14:14
(in which the father is instructed to recount to his son how God brought "us" out of Egypt), Deut

congregation again bears witness to the wonder. The poet does not focus on the giving of the Torah, however, but on Moses, to whom God gave it. He stresses the intimacy of Moses's relationship with God: God summons Moses to heaven, dresses him with clouds, and bedecks his face with a beam of light. God, the divine king, waits on his servant, and the poet takes his listeners into the privy chamber. God, Moses, and people share a uniquely intimate space.

The poet then shifts his attention to Moses's own history and context. He praises Yocheved, the mother of Moses, as well as Moses's siblings, noting that the unique prophet came from a uniquely privileged line.[55] At the end of this unit, Moses's father—Amram—is also named, but while Moses and Aaron are praised, the poet's attention to women stands out. Yocheved is called a "pure and holy vine" (l. 18) who merits laudation, and Miriam is described in terms that explicitly place her on par with Moses. The hymn began by singling out Moses's uniqueness: no prophet like him will ever arise again (l. 3). In a striking passage as the poem concludes, Miriam is singled out in almost identical but feminized language: no prophetess like her shall arise again from Eve (ll. 29–30). This attentiveness to women—and particularly the honor accorded to Miriam—is unparalleled in classical Samaritan writings.

Praise of Amram and Yocheved, as parents of Moses, Aaron, and Miriam, leads the poet to conclude with an appeal to the power of ancestral merit: for their sake, if not ours, rescue us! The poet thus takes his listeners out of "historical" time—the world of Exodus—and into the present, a world more akin to Egyptian servitude. The emphatic reiteration of the uniqueness of the ancient prophets, male and female, underscores Amram Dare's point that redemption now must come directly from God. As praiseworthy and meritorious as the ancestors were, as vivid as their experiences remain, they constitute the past, and as the poet attends to the future, his appeal is to the deity. God, the prophet, and the congregation may all be great and unique, but the prophet has served his function, while God and the people remain in need of each other.

> *Said on Wednesday, on the fourth Sabbath of the month, on the festivals and on the Sabbaths that fall during festivals, and daily during the week of Shavuot.*

> Great is God, and none like him;
> Great is the community and none resembles it;

5:3 ("not with our ancestors did the Lord make this covenant but with us"), and Deut 29:14 ("with those who are standing here today . . . and those who are not here").

55. In *TM* 1 §27 (17א, p. 63), Amram and Yocheved are praised as the parents of "the sun and the moon" (Moses and Aaron).

Great is the prophet, and none like him has arisen!

We assembled at Mount Sinai

5 On the day the writing descended:
The shofar begins to sound,
And the prophet's voice grows strong
And the good one says: Let my prophet ascend!
And the prophet grows great and beautiful,
10 And he springs up[56] and reaches unto the heavens.[57]
Thus he is dressed[58] by the hand of he who is dressed [in a garment],
[But] since no king can be appointed to dress [another].[59]
Thus he covers him in a cloud,
And his face is bedecked with the beam of [divine] light,
15 So that all the nations might know
How Moses was the servant of God and his faithful one!

May Yocheved be remembered for good
The pure and holy vine
From whom these clusters of grapes[60] came forth:
20 One a prophetess, one a priest,
And one a god to the Egyptians.[61]
One walked within the fire,[62]
And one ate what remained from fire[-offerings]
And Miriam—when she sang at the sea,
25 The nations heard and were afraid.[63]
Their master said: Let them take their reward!

56. The root of יקלע is קלח, "to grow."

57. "Heavens" here renders ערפלה, a specific level of heaven in rabbinic cosmology.

58. See l. 28, in which Moses "puts on" (lit.; "dresses [himself]") in the divine title.

59. On the term מלו (lit., "qualified for, deserving of"), see *DSA*, 469, s.v. מלי; it is possibly related to the root מלא in the sense of "to ordain."

60. The term נכליה ("clusters of grapes") refers to notables in Samaritan Aramaic; see *DSA*, 525, s.v. אנכל.

61. I.e., Miriam (called a prophet in Exod 15:20), Aaron (the origin of the priestly line), and Moses (called by God to be a "god" to the Egyptians in Exod 4:16). The early stratum of *TM* (2 §33 [84ב, p. 135]) refers to Miriam as prophesying, but the language of this passage, according to Ben-Hayyim, is medieval. Similarly, the later tradition in *TM* 5 §23 (261ב, p. 321), depicts God speaking to Moses: "Far be it from you, O you who were called a god!"

62. The image of Moses walking in fire can be traced to Exod 19:18, which describes the fiery advent of God to Sinai. Later Samaritan tradition also stresses this image (e.g., *TM* 4 §102 [242ב, p. 297]: "Moses who trod the fire").

63. The language here echoes that of SamT Exod 15:14.

Let Aaron take my portion,[64]
Let Moses put on my title,[65]
And let Miriam be called a prophetess,
30 For no other like her arose[66] from [the line of] Eve!
May Amram and Yocheved be extolled:
Three holy ones
Arose from them.[67]

As their reward, O good one, rescue us
In your mercy.

May God be praised!
There is no God but the one!

7 "When You Rise Up at Daybreak" (*SL*, 41; *RPH*, 55–57)

This lovely lyric can be read as an early example of the genre that would come to be known as an *aubade*, or morning song. It celebrates the beauty and promise of the new day, and the routine wonder of the sunrise.

In this poem, Amram Dare speaks to the community directly (using the plural "you"), encouraging them to appreciate the beauty of morning and to recognize in it the providence of its Creator—and theirs. The wonder of the sun, its warmth and light, points to the even greater wonder of its maker. The sight of the sun becomes a reminder of the praise and thanks due to God.

Recited on Wednesday in the morning and on the Day of Atonement.

When you rise up
At daybreak[68]
And see the light dawning,
And it illumines the entire world,
5 Proclaim, one and all, and say:

May the radiant one be praised, he who kindles for the world,
A lamp that cannot be extinguished;

64. "Portion" refers to the priestly share in the offerings.
65. "Title" refers here to Moses being a "god" to the Egyptians, as noted above.
66. The poet applies language from Deut 34:10 (which describes Moses) to Miriam.
67. See *TM* 1 §27 (17א, p. 63), where Amram and Yocheved are compared to the sun and moon.
68. Lit., "the portion of the morning," meaning the moment when night cedes to day.

It traverses the firmament
And illumines the entire world,
10 Just as he, the master of all,
Kindles for the world a lamp that cannot be extinguished.
"In the beginning"[69] a treasure-room for lamps was made,
The heavens and the earth are a building that was not built;
The great light resembles its source.[70]

15 Day breaks forth every morning, opening up the world.
Dawn proclaims to humanity:[71]
"Rise up from your slumber,
And see the light, and praise its maker!"

May God be praised!
There is no God but the one!

8 "You Are the Glory, O God Concealed from All" (*SL*, 41–42; *RPH*, 57–59)

In this hymn of praise, Amram Dare focuses directly and exclusively on the deity, but from two perspectives. Each of the two stanzas offers a litany of divine attributes, constituting a doxology delineating God's power and majesty. The congregation enters the composition in the refrain, where they announce, "We will proclaim . . . and we will say . . ." (ll. 11–12); their statements then continue the praise of God as unique and singular.

Motion within the poem is cyclical. Each stanza follows a similar trajectory, from the transcendent to the immanent: it begins with praise of God in lofty terms and stresses God's incomparability, wondrous power, and loftiness, but as the stanza concludes, the poet pivots to divine mercy and accessibility. The first stanza ends with an appeal to the merciful nature of the life-giver, while the second describes how even the least of people is empowered to appeal to God. The motion in each stanza is a downward flow, from the heavenly realm to the world of men. The refrains then return the energy of the hymn upward: lifted by the praises of the community, God ascends. This stanza–refrain motion is underscored by a performative dynamic in which the poet speaks the divinely

---

69. The poet uses the Hebrew phrase בראשית (Gen 1:1).

70. Lit., "its root" (or "that which produces branches"); Tal translates as "the great light resembles a flame" (*DSA*, 869, s.v. שבשבה).

71. Lit., "the children of Adam" (*bene adam*).

oriented lines that describe the descent of the majestic deity toward the realm
of mortals and mercy, while the community, as if buoyed by the references to
God's compassion and responsiveness, responds with the words of the refrain.
While God never speaks in this poem—indeed, the only quotation in the poem
is in Israel's voice from the Song at the Sea (l. 23) and the communal voice
speaks in the refrain—the poet here creates a liturgical duet nonetheless, with
poet and congregation singing alternating parts to a divine audience.

The parts of the poem, stanzas and refrain, complement each other, but they
differ not only in voice and perspective but also in theology. The stanzas are
exclusively praise; the poet lists divine attributes, including God's glory and
power, his holiness and illimitable goodness. The stanzas speak with almost
breathless awe to the wondrous nature of God. The refrains, by contrast, empha-
size the element of interrelationship and reciprocity. Particularly intriguing is
the conditional phrasing: "If you accept us ... / We will proclaim ..." (ll. 10,
12). Amram Dare seems to suggest that God wants to hear the congregation's
prayers, that he descends to hear their words precisely in order that he may
ascend again upon those words. God's presence in the people's midst comes
as a response to the people themselves; their words drive the cycle of God's
descent and ascent. God's stunning power and magnificence make his responsiveness to prayer and praise that much more remarkable. Initially, it seems
that the motion of the poem derives from God, who actively moves in it, but
the refrain suggests that Israel shares equal responsibility. Although the poet
does not assert that Israel possesses any merit or any claim upon the deity and
presents prayer as the inevitable response to becoming aware of God's might
and goodness, he nonetheless bestows a certain kind of power upon the people.
God's greatness cannot go unrecognized. God's godhood is incomplete without
a people.

*Said at daybreak on Thursday, on the Night of Atonement, and on the
Day of Proclamation (also known as the day of "the standing at Mount
Sinai"—that is, the forty-sixth day of the omer).*

You are the glory, O God concealed from all;
But nothing, concealed or revealed, sees you.
Whose power compares to yours?
Or who understands the secrets of your glory?
5 Superior to all are you.
No one is your equal:
Creator and provider and supporter,
Life-giver, death-giver, sustainer

Of all, in your mercy.[72]

Unto you ascend praises from [every] heart and soul.

10   *If you accept us[73] in your great goodness,*
       We will proclaim before you with a great voice,
       And we will say to you: "Singular are you,
       O God, and none compares to you!
       Greatness is yours!"[74]

O awesome one, praised and exalted,

15   [You] who may do anything you wish,
       Your dwelling is at the summit of the world,
       But where you wish, you manifest
       In holiness and in glory and in greatness.
       All your works, who could equal?

20   Or the like of your wonders, who could create?
       Every mouth possessing power of speech,
       Let it proclaim and say to you,
       "Who is like you among the gods?" [Exod 15:11].[75]
       Lo, working so many wonders,

25   There is no end to your great goodness;
       He who is grand is obligated to you,
       And by the powerless[76] are you entreated.

       Unto you ascend praises from [every] heart and soul.
       If you accept us in your great goodness,

30   *We will proclaim before you with a great voice*
       And we will say to you: "Singular are you,
       O God, and none compares to you!
       Greatness is yours!"

       May God be praised!
       There is no God but the one!

---

72. Ben-Hayyim (*RPH*, 57) treats this line and the preceding one as a single line (l. 8).

73. I.e., accept our prayers.

74. Ben-Hayyim (*RPH*, 58) treats this line and the preceding one as a single line (l. 13).

75. This phrase translates the Hebrew of Exod 15:11 (מן כותך באלהיה); the SamT, in contrast, alters the Hebrew slightly (מן כבתך בחיוליה; lit., "who is like you among the powerful"), presumably to avoid the suggestion of multiple gods.

76. Lit., "small one."

9 "Imposing and Fearsome Fences" (*SL*, 42; *RPH*, 59–62)

In this unusual poem, Amram Dare expands on the idea of the righteous as intercessors. He focuses on figures from the Israelite past, offering a lineage from Adam through Caleb (thus from creation to the end of the exodus narrative, extending from the beginning of Genesis through the end of Deuteronomy and into the opening chapters of the book of Joshua, which is not included in the Samaritan canon). Moses remains the intercessor par excellence, and his efforts inspired the efficacious prayers of the other righteous. In turn, Moses is the paradigm for the Taheb ("he who returns"), the prophet "like Moses" who is destined to come in the future.

This poem offers an example of the rhetorical possibilities of early Samaritan *piyyut*. The poet's use of lists as a device is particularly in evidence here: first the catalogue of intercessory figures from the biblical past and, as the poem ends, the litany of actions that the Taheb will take upon his return. In each case, the list creates a strongly rhythmic effect—an upbeat cadence that on the one hand suggests inexorability and then, when the pattern is interrupted, concentrates attention on what follows, which in each case is praise. The list of ancestors is followed by two exclamations; the first (l. 32: "Happy are those who return!") speaks to the community, while the second (l. 36: "Happy is the world!") addresses the world. These two phrases conjure a sense of parity between the people who return and the Taheb, the "returning one" and redeemer, who complements or completes the congregation's actions.

Even more intriguing is Amram Dare's use of the rhetorical technique of *ethopoeia*, or "speech in character," in this poem. This technique, commonly used in the training of orators in antiquity, required students to compose declamations in the voice of characters from the classical tradition. Here, the poet employs the same technique to compose a stanza in the voice of a figure from biblical antiquity, Moses. Moses's words here are not reassembled out of biblical quotations, although certain phrases echo the Torah. Instead, Moses speaks the language of the community (Samaritan Aramaic) and his words resonate with the language Amram Dare uses in intercessory prayer in his own voice. Writing in Moses's voice is not merely a rhetorical flourish, however, or a clever theatrical technique to engage an audience. It makes Moses, the model intervener against divine wrath, a forerunner of Amram Dare himself and other contemporaries as they bridge the gap between Moses and the Taheb. Words such as those assigned to Moses in this poem are understood to have pleased God during the wilderness period; surely they are pleasing and efficacious in the present as well. The poet thereby imbues his prayer with Mosaic potency.

In the opening line of the poem, Amram Dare describes the righteous as "fences" or fence posts. They are upright, and when a sufficient number are assembled together, they serve a protective function. Even Moses, on his own, could not suffice; the Taheb, likewise, needs his hosts, and the poet relies on his community as well. The individual elements of a list, like the individual stakes constituting a fence, are hardly impressive, but the cumulative effect of the catalogue can be striking. Amram Dare knits the generations from Adam to Noah, Abraham, Moses, Caleb, and finally the Taheb into a single protective force that speaks with one voice: the voice of our poet, who we might infer understands himself to be yet another humble but upright post in the protective fence.

> *Recited on Thursday in the morning and on the fifth Sabbath of the month, on festivals, and on Sabbaths that fall during festivals.*

Imposing and fearsome[77] fences
Are the righteous of the world;[78]
The master of all deals mercifully
With all who tremble,[79] through their merit.[80]
5 Moses the prophet recalled[81] their merit
In the wilderness, until [his] wrath was turned aside
And his mercies were extended,
And rescue was discovered there.

He spoke a pleasing word:
10 "Life and death are in your power,
O you who are our concealed master![82]
If you see fit, in your righteousness,
Lift [your] wrath from upon us.
Spread your mercy over us,
15 And we, in turn, we will put to an end our transgressions,
And we will speak a pleasing word
[With regard to] the world and all that is in it.
Who is like you? None is like you!
O gracious and merciful one!"

77. Lit., "hard, harsh."
78. An epithet for the patriarchs.
79. I.e., tremble with pious fear, although protected by the aura of the ancestors.
80. Lit., "labors, efforts." I.e., God will be merciful to the pious of the present generation as a reward for the pious acts of the ancestors. The order of ll. 3–4 is here reversed, for the sake of clarity in English.
81. For this meaning of זוע, see *DSA*, 227, s.v. זוע. The poet here refers to the way Moses recounted God's covenant with Abraham, Isaac, and Jacob when he persuaded God to forgive his people after they worshipped the golden calf (Exod 32:13; see also Deut 9:5, 27).
82. Reading דכסיאתה as דכסי אתה with Ben-Hayyim (*RPH*, 60).

20 Mighty are the men
    Who turned aside the wrath of their master:
    Adam, the first [person],
        And Seth, his successor,[83]
    And Enosh, who proclaimed [Gen 4:26],
        And Enoch, who prayed [Gen 5:22, 24],
    And Noah, the righteous [Gen 6:9],
        And Abraham, the prince [Gen 23:6],
25 And Isaac, the devoted,[84]
        And Jacob, mighty in merit,
    And Joseph, who became a king [Gen 41:43],
        And Moses, the prophet,
    And Aaron, the priest,
        And Eleazar, the faithful,
    And Ithamar, the honored,
        And Phineas, the holy,
30 And Joshua, the leader,
        And Caleb, his heir [Num 14:24]:
    A multitude![85] And no other[86] like it exists!

    Happy are those who return,
    Who come at the word of their master.
    They come, and his mercies are with them,
35 And the master of all magnifies them.
    Happy is the world at the moment that they come:
    The Taheb[87] and the hosts[88] of the time of favor.[89]
    For he establishes peace,
    And mercies are extended,
40 And darkness is lifted up,
    And wickedness passes away,
    And creatures are at ease,
    And dew will be upon those who dwell in the time of favor,
    And the Creator of the world

83. Lit., "replacement."
84. Presumably a reference to his willing participation in his near-sacrifice in Gen 22.
85. See *DSA*, 584, s.v. סיעה.
86. Lit., "none."
87. The Taheb ("the one who returns," from the root תוב) is an eschatological prophetic figure identified with "the prophet like Moses" of Deut 18:18.
88. Lit., "ranks."
89. "Time of favor" translates רחותה, the beneficent end-time that will follow after the time of disfavor (lit., "turning Away" [*fanuta*, פנותא]).

45   Will be praised without perversion.

May God be praised!
There is no God but the one!

10 "The King Who Is over All" (*SL*, 42; *RPH*, 62–65)

This poem does not speak to God, nor does it directly address the people or speak self-consciously from within their midst. No one is addressed as "you," nor does anyone speak as "we." Instead, Amram Dare writes *about* God in this composition. He explores and expands upon aspects of God's nature and of human perception of God's actions in the world.

The poet here does not attempt to catalogue all aspects of the divine personality or presence. Instead, he focuses on the royal and martial elements of God's figure. The poet describes him as king, ruler, victor, and judge; the divine essence is power, used to create and to destroy, to judge and to vindicate, to condemn and to forgive. His unique potency defines him; "he does as he wishes / and no one can refuse," Amram Dare writes in the final lines.

As a secondary theme, this poem underscores the privilege that accrues to those who recognize God's unique power, trust in him, and revere him exclusively, as befits his potent majesty. And this understanding gestures toward the poem's twin purposes: praising the deity as his nature demands and deserves and, at the same time, conveying these truths to the community so that they may understand God's majesty and mercy and affirm their place among those who reverence God properly. This hymn serves as an affirmation of deep truths that both God and God's people must recognize in common. Recitation of the hymn offers God praise even as it reorients the people toward a deeply powerful truth.

Said at daybreak on Friday, on the Day of Atonement, and on the Day of Recitation.

The king who is over all
And whose authority encompasses those on high and those below,
And who can be found everywhere,
And all [mortal] kings exist within his authority:
5   A ruler who judges them
And may destroy them, should he so wish.
But there is no king as faithful and patient as he,
Whose kingdom is eternal life.
And happy is the congregation that trusts in him

10 And worships his name with devotion,[90]

For he protects from all harm.

Woe to those who reject him!

And seek to put their trust in abomination,[91] in anything aside from him,

For he has readied for them all kinds of traps.

15 For thus it is written in the great song:[92]

"He sentences them instantly,[93]

[With] judgments unlike any [other]."

Happy were the world and its creatures at that moment

When God proclaimed, "**I, I am He!**" [Exod 32:39].

20 In battle, God is singular,

And no other god is with him [see Deut 32:12].

And no imposter[94] shall seize his dwelling,[95]

And the heavens welcome no companion.[96]

As for those who belong to God, he will bring them;

25 They will come and wage[97] war,

And he knows[98] who bears the crown

Of the world, which he alone

Drew forth, by his hand, from within his power.

And one who has no portion in the world will become extinct,

30 And the imposter shall be expelled with hostility,

While the good will come and receive their reward.

For the world belongs to the one who made it,[99]

Doing as he wishes,

And no one can refuse.

---

90. This term (נצירו; see *DSA*, 545, s.v.) is cognate to the term that Amram applied to Isaac (נציר, "the devoted [one]") in Amram 9, l. 25.

91. See *DSA*, 830, s.v. רחקה. Ben-Hayyim translates as "put their trust in vanity," i.e., idols (*RPH*, 63).

92. I.e., Deut 32 (the Song of Moses, often referred to among Jews by its first word, *Ha'azinu*).

93. Lit., "he quickly designs judgments for them." The text here does not quote from SamT Deut 32, but it may be a kind of paraphrase of Deut 32:5. The targum to that verse states: וחש עתידות למו ("and fate rushes upon them").

94. I.e., an imposter deity, parallel to "other god"; lit., "sojourner, alien resident."

95. Lit., "dweller, sojourner," but here a reference to the "other god."

96. Lit., "the heavens do not receive a companion / one who sits (with God)." I.e., God is singular both above and below.

97. Taking יגחון from the root גוח, with Ben-Hayyim (*RPH*, 64); see *DSA*, 136, s.v. גוח.

98. Ben-Hayyim translates as "it will be known who bears/takes the crown" (*RPH*, 64).

99. Lit., "to him to whom he belongs."

May God be praised!
There is no God but the one!

11 "Exalted God, Hear Our Voice" (*SL*, 46; *RPH*, 65–67)

In this poem, Amram Dare juxtaposes God's magnificence and might with the people's worthlessness and weakness. Rhetorically, the poem constitutes a one-sided dialogue: the poet speaks exclusively to the deity ("you") as a member of the community ("we"). As a narrative, the entire poem is an extended plea for redemption, unearned but deeply desired.

The composition confines its attention to the present moment in the life of the congregation. The past is barely evoked: the poet offers fleeting references to God as a wonder-worker, alludes once to the figure of Moses, and acknowledges a history of Israelite sinfulness. The future is too uncertain to describe, as it may be a wonder wrought by divine mercy or a terror born, justifiably, of stubborn transgression. The present, however, consumes Amram. He writes from a perspective immersed in the moment. Amram Dare alternates between assuring God that he and his community are well aware of God's triumphant majesty and beneficence and rehearsing the people's unworthiness.

Perhaps Amram Dare's deftest act of rhetorical subtlety occurs when he writes, "We are not so brazen as to say before you: / 'Accept our [prayers] on account of your abundant forgiveness'" (ll. 25–26). In refusing to utter words he knows to be presumptuous, he presumes to utter the words. Thus, the poem attempts to do precisely what the poet himself cannot do: to compel God's mercy by asserting his forgiving nature and to cast Israel, unworthy but desperate, into his path. The poet, standing within his community, cannot throw himself on God's mercy, but he can make Israel's misery conspicuous and hope that God acts true to form.

> *Said on Friday in the morning, on festivals, and on the Sabbaths that*
> *fall during festivals.*

Exalted God, hear our voice!
O merciful one, spread your mercy upon us!
The whole earth is yours,
And who is like you?
5 Your hand firmly holds all.
The unseen victor,
Master of all miracles—

Your great power is limitless,
[As is] your strength and your might.
10 We are unable to stay upright before the multiplicity of your
        miracles;[100]
You see us wherever we turn.[101]
Watch out for us and rescue us!

O compassionate one, save us!
O merciful one, pity us in your mercifulness,
15 *Lest anger be our end.*
And indeed your goodness will be recounted forever,
For thus your mercy is upon the sinful.

O El Shaddai, O "**I am**"! Now is our moment,
And henceforth are we devoted unto you!
20 How we shall suffer and be scorned,
And be unable to stand before you.
No matter how often you purify[102] us,
Yet we did not learn, and we transgressed and we sinned.
Still you forgave us and did not cease your mercy upon us.
25 We are not so brazen[103] as to say before you:
"Accept our [prayers] out of the abundance of your forgiveness
And your goodness, [all that] you have done for us."
Overpowering were our sins and so excessive our transgressions,
But we were impudent and would not learn,
30 Despite all that happened to us.

O compassionate one, save us!
O merciful one, pity us in your mercifulness!
Lest anger be our end.
And indeed may your goodness be recounted forever,
35 *For thus your mercy is upon the sinful.*

100. This translation follows Ben-Hayyim (*RPH*, 65), which is also adopted by Tal (*DSA*, 137, s.v. גון).

101. Lit., "your seeing the direction of our faces." The translation incorporates Ben-Hayyim's suggestion (*RPH*, 65) that לן should be understood as לאן/להאן.

102. The word מזדכיך is difficult. The present translation takes it from the root זכי in the *ethpeʿel* stem (*DSA*, 230, s.v.); Ben-Hayyim (*RPH*, 66) translates it as צדקת, apparently taking the existing word as a corruption of the root צדק. Either way, the sense is that, while God keeps cleansing or excusing Israel, the people continue to besmirch themselves with sin.

103. Lit., "face," with a sense of bare-faced, immodest behavior.

May God be praised!
There is no God but the one!

12 "Lo, a Great Glory Is the Glory of the Sabbath Day" (*SL*, 44; *RPH*, 67–69)

Amram Dare here literally sings the praises of the Sabbath. The poet praises it because of its source (it is a gift from God, among the first of his creations), because of its intrinsic qualities (its holiness, uniqueness, and eternality), and because of its ritual power (the potency of observing sanctity in time and space and using the opportunity to praise the Creator). God's gift of the Sabbath to Israel (here, unusually, "the Hebrews") inspires the community to respond with gratitude.

The distinctive and emphasized quality of the Sabbath is its holiness, but this holiness is not merely an abstract quality. The root קדש has a basic meaning of "separation," and the poet alludes to this in his description of the Sabbath as a day "for resting" (apart from other days) and a day of limits, and he specifically describes it as a "separation" for the sake of God's name. In the opening stanza, the Sabbath is specifically juxtaposed with the other holy gift from God, the Torah. The two elements of holiness are entwined: both manifest themselves through rituals among the holy community (reading, resting), both elicit responses of thanksgiving and signify being chosen, and it was by means of the Torah that God conveyed the Sabbath to Israel. The Sabbath is thus embedded in the Torah, and the Torah—through the ritual of its reading—is embedded in the Sabbath. At the same time, the Torah is kept through action (reading, reciting), while the Sabbath is kept through restrictions on action. The emphasis on the Sabbath as something that the community keeps (a holy community is Sabbath-keeping, "keepers of the Sabbath" and its holiness) underscores that the Samaritan community ("the keepers") have been faithful not only to their distinctive Torah and their unique holy site but also to their singular understanding of the Sabbath. Keeping the Sabbath constitutes the congregation; failure to keep the holy day, the text implies, excludes one from the community. The "boundary of the Sabbath" delineates not only time and behavior, but social structure as well.

It is worth noting how the speaker's rhetorical stance changes throughout this poem, as brief as it is. Initially, the poet speaks somewhat abstractly in praise of the Torah, but his rhetoric becomes increasingly hortatory until he finally addresses the community explicitly: "Lo, keepers of the Sabbath!" (l. 19). But immediately following that vocative address, he turns back to a narrative voice, describing both God and community in the third person. At the very end of the poem (ll. 23–28), however, the poet speaks to God directly ("you") and places himself within the community ("let us ...") as he exhorts the community to full-throated praise of the God whose proximity is reflected in the directness of speech. Every aspect—literally, "every word"—of the Sabbath is holy, the poet has just explained, and what "word" could be holier than praise and thanksgiving to the deity, whose gift is this day of rest?

Said on the eve of the Sabbath and during the Sabbath day (except on the Sabbaths that fall during festivals).

Lo, a great glory[104]
Is the glory of the Sabbath day.
Happy are the Hebrews in the gift
That you gave to them: the holy
5   Torah and the holy day;
The Torah, for reading,[105]
And the holy day, for rest.

Great is the Sabbath!
May its Creator be praised and its maker worshipped!
10   The boundary of the Sabbath is an eternal pleasure,[106]
The premier[107] appointed time, which shall never be abolished,
And the holy [day] that shall never cease.
For it is greater than any other day
And it is holier than any other festival,
15   And the king sustains its separation for the sake of his name.
There is no festival like it,
And no holiness like it,
And no holy community like this one, which keeps it—
Lo, keepers of the Sabbath!
20   They were preserving[108] it on account of its holiness;

---

104. As Ben-Hayyim notes (*RPH*, 67), the word איקר used here and in the following line can also be translated as "gift" (a synonym of מתנתה in l. 3). The double meaning of the word underscores that the Sabbath is a glorious gift. See *DSA*, 358, s.v. איקר.

105. Torah and Sabbath are described as a single gift, which may allude to the inseparable relationship between the two: the Torah teaches about the Sabbath, and on the Sabbath, the Torah is revered.

106. The term עדן can mean "set time" (see *DSA*, 624, s.v. עדן I) or "delight, pleasure" (*DSA*, 625, s.v. עדן II). While the term poses a challenge to the translator, the association of the Sabbath with both pleasure and time is deeply evocative.

107. Lit., "the first appointed time"—first in terms of both existence and importance.

108. The root used here is שמר, the same root as in the name "Samaritan." In the previous two lines, the root (translated "keep") is נטר.

Its every aspect[109] is holy,
And the God who created it is merciful and gracious.

Let us hasten,[110] all of us, and open our mouths,
Let us recount your goodness, O merciful one,
25 O king, who sustains[111] us and grants us life and protects us,
Whose kingship it is our duty to praise.
O merciful one, to whom greatness belongs,
Praise [be] to your great and mighty name!

There is no God but the one!

13 "We Have Arisen from Our Slumber" (*SL*, 43–44; *RPH*, 70–72)

While the attribution of this poem to Amram Dare is dubious, its language is consistent with the time period of Amram Dare and Marqe and it has long been considered a genuine part of the *Durran*.[112] For this reason it is included in the present volume.

This poem is, like Amram Dare 7, a dawn song. But its presentation of daybreak and the significance of morning light differs from that of the other work. Amram Dare 7 offered a brief morning liturgy, as it were, while this poem describes morning rituals from a slight remove. The composition is rich with liturgical self-reference, particularly to the embodied elements of prayer: seeing, standing, bowing, and prostrating are all referenced multiple times. This work, then, offers a kinetic reinforcement of the experience and process of rising for morning prayer, which is physical, intellectual, and emotional. The sensory reality of perceiving the predawn lightening of the sky leads to the intellectual recognition that God, the source of the steady and reliable dawning light, needs to be praised and thanked and that these sentiments find expression through the actions of the body, which again assumes a horizontal position, but one of reverence rather than rest. The most commonplace of events—sunrise—becomes a pretext for deep theological reasoning that manifests itself in dramatic ritual practice. Just as the sun rises and sets, so does the human body. Both are creatures of God, and both, in hewing to their natural rhythms, offer God praise. The person who sleeps through dawn (and thus through daybreak prayers) is, by implication, as unnatural as a sun that fails to rise.

---

109. Lit., "word."
110. On this meaning of שוי, see *DSA*, 881, s.v. שוי II.
111. Or, more narrowly, "feeds."
112. On the authorship of this poem, see *RPH*, 70.

Elements within this poem evoke other textual traditions. The phrase "in the evening and in the morning" in line 24 refers back to the creation story of Gen 1, where "there was evening and there was morning, one day" (v. 5); this phrasing reflects the Samaritan custom of starting the day at sunset, which coincides with Jewish practice. More enigmatic are the poem's references to angels, for angels (and their religious practices) are not major figures in the Torah tradition of the Samaritans but do figure largely in later books of the Jewish Bible, as well as in Hellenistic and rabbinic Jewish writings. In particular, this poem evokes the tradition attested in various sources of angels uttering morning prayers, a tradition anchored in the biblical text of Gen 32:27, where the angelic being wishes to end its wrestling match with Jacob, saying, "Let me go, for dawn is breaking!" In the midrashim on this verse (e.g., GenR 78:1–2), the rabbis conjecture that the angels praise God in the morning just as Israel does, and according to SongR 3:9, Jacob's opponent pleads, "Let me go, for my turn has come to chant praises!" We need not look to rabbinic writings for angelic prayer and liturgy, however; the Dead Sea Scrolls preserve a rich repository of such materials, and the Samaritan writings can be understood as reflecting a very widespread set of understandings that would come to color Judaism, Christianity, and Samaritanism alike.[113] Among these is the belief that the angels pray in parallel with Israel, and that they are attentive to the prayers of Israel as well.

The visible, then, exists alongside the invisible; the dawning sun brings with it the attentions of the angels, who flock with delight to hear God being praised. Humans exist alongside angelic beings, and prayer is a moment when the two intersect: humans look to the sky and the rising sun, while angels descend and cluster around mortals at prayer. It is perhaps no wonder, then, that the moment when night changes to day feels so charged, for all its subtlety: it is a moment when Israel and the angels meet to offer thanksgiving to their Creator.

> *Said on the Sabbath day before the* qataf *of the book of Genesis ("Then he planted ... a garden in Eden, in the East"), on Sabbaths, and on festivals.*

We have arisen from our slumber,
And come unto you, O our master,
With devotion and with reverence.
We stand[114] before you,

---

113. See Chazon, "Human and Angelic Prayer."

114. The use of the root עמד here is unusual; while it is common in Hebrew and becomes common in the medieval, Hebrew-inflected Aramaic known as "Samaritan," it is highly unusual in classical Samaritan Aramaic.

5   And we prostrate ourselves before you
      At daybreak.[115]

      Happy is the one who arises from his slumber
      And comes to you in love,
      Rising and praising at daybreak
10   And magnifying your great power
      At the first light of dawn![116]
      Awed is the one who sees it.
      [Thus] it is fitting for every person,
      Anyone of the descendants of Adam,
15   Everyone who has been asleep,
      That he should wake from his slumber
      And gaze upon the light, just as
      It breaks and illumines the world.
      It is good that everyone who sees it
20   Should offer praise to the Creator and say:
      "May the Creator who created this be praised!"
      Woe to him who [still] slumbers
      When daybreak prayers occur.[117]
      In the evening and in the morning, the angels of YHWH[118]
25   Will be present everywhere,
      And wherever people pray,[119]
      The angels of YHWH will come and surround them,
      For the angels delight in hearing
      The praises of their master at all times.

30   Happy is the one who is able to stand in prayer,
      [For] he may stand, praising, and worship his master,
      And recite his prayer at its appointed time, every time.

      Happy is the one who arises then[120] and comes
        To you, O merciful one,
      Entreating and praying and praising,

---

115. Lit., "the portion of the morning," i.e., dawn.

116. Lit., "the opening of light."

117. Understanding אורעתה as "occurrence," from the root ארע.

118. The poet here uses the term מלאכי ה' (a term that does not occur in the Bible, although the phrase מלאכי אלהים is used in Gen 28:12 and 32:49, as well as in 2 Chr 36:16).

119. Lit., "wherever they are praying," with the humans being the subject.

120. Lit., "upon it (i.e., at daybreak)."

35 And bowing and worshipping and prostrating,
    And magnifying your name, as befits you.

Accept from us, O our[121] master,
Our prayers, in your great faithfulness![122]

May God be praised!
There is no God but the one!

14 "Great Is the God Who So Desires" (*SL*, 45–46; *RPH*, 72–73)

This brief composition is a hymn on the importance of resting on the Sabbath. The first half of the poem (ll. 1–9) connects the imperative for human rest to the divine model from the creation narrative, even as it makes clear that God did not rest because he was tired—an impossibility!—but because he did not want weary humans worshipping him on his holy day. The essential element of Sabbath observance here is its holiness; keeping the Sabbath results in blessings, while transgressing it leads to death.

The second half of the poem embeds a more subtle motif: the idea that the importance of rest constitutes a kind of divine mystery. While the story of the creation of Sabbath rest can be found in Gen 2:2–3, the poet here reminds his community that they are privy to this knowledge only because Moses received the Torah and taught it to their ancestors. The Sabbath and the laws and traditions for keeping it properly are not intrinsically knowable. Lines 5–9 describe the establishment of the Sabbath at the time of creation, but—for reasons that are not disclosed—this commandment is not revealed until it is shared with Moses.[123]

When these two portions are read together, this hymn presents the keeping of the Sabbath as the purpose for liberating the Israelites from Egyptian bondage. In the Torah, God tells Moses to tell Pharaoh, "Israel is my son, my firstborn.... Let my son go that he may serve me" (Exod 4:22–23); the service of God envisioned here is the keeping of the Sabbath. As Amram Dare writes, it was given "to the congregation that went forth from Egypt / in order that they might abstain

---

121. The base text has "my Master," which Ben-Hayyim corrects according to variants (*RPH*, 72).

122. The underlying term is חסד.

123. This problem is also treated in the book of Jubilees (2:17–20), a Jewish text from the second century BCE, but it is resolved through a tradition that the angels kept the Sabbath from creation until the time when it should be revealed to the chosen people as their inheritance alone (see Kugel, *Walk Through "Jubilees,"* 33).

(from work) on it" (ll. 13–14). The Sabbath, for our poet, constitutes a divine mystery that transforms the lived-in world. Sabbath rest can be seen as the engine underlying creation itself—rest can be defined only in the context of work—even as it is the essence of Torah revelation and the purpose of Israelite redemption.

> *Said on the Sabbath in the morning before the* qataf *of the book of Exodus, and on Sabbaths and festivals.*

Great is the God who so desires
Restfulness, lest any weariness[124] come before him,
So that those who abstain [from work] may rest.
For six days he worked to create the world and all its creatures,
5 And he ceased on the seventh day.
And he made it holy forever,
And said: "Whoever abstains [from work] on it is blessed!
And anyone who desecrates it shall be executed!"
Thus its boundaries[125] were fixed by the hand of God.

10 But Moses was appointed to reveal it,
And he imposed it on every kind of person.[126]
And he taught it before Mount Sinai
To the congregation that went forth from Egypt,
In order that they might abstain [from work] on it
15 And say, "Great is the great God, who bestowed such an honor!"

> *May God be praised!*
> *There is no God but the one!*

15 "O Faithful One, O Steadfast One" (*SL*, 46; *RPH*, 74–75)

This poem, like the previous one, offers lyrical reflections on the Sabbath, but here the poet speaks to God (at least initially) rather than narrating from a more philosophical remove. The poet uses his "conversation" with God to ponder the potential paradoxes of the Sabbath and its origins in the creation

124. In the form of weary people.
125. The word תחום is singular, but the plural reads better in English.
126. I.e., not just on Israelite men, but on all men, women, and children, Israelites and foreigners, and even the domestic animals belonging to Israelites.

story. God rests, though God is not weary; the act of creation does not diminish or weary God, nor does maintaining and sustaining creation ever weaken him. In this, God is entirely unlike people, who do find such work exhausting in terms of both energy and resources.

The poem presents the translator with a challenge, and the present version relies on Ben-Hayyim's understanding of its stichometry and structure. As he presents it, the work consists of three units: an initial address to God as Creator, an intermediate reflection on Israel's observance of commandments, and a final set of rhetorical questions that return to the uniqueness of God's creative works. While most of the poem speaks in relatively generic terms, the final lines employ a specific metaphor: architecture. Amram Dare notes that no mortal can "toil and constantly renew / an edifice" (ll. 15–16) without both expense and weariness; by extension, our poet compares God's work as Creator to a cosmic builder who, despite the vastness and scale of his project, is entirely undepleted.

The opening and closing lines of this hymn reflect this theme of divine effortlessness. God rests because he wishes to, not because he must. Essential to the implicit harmony depicted by this poem is the explicit role of Israel in keeping the unique gift of rest sacred. Indeed, while the festivals and holy days are connected to the observable cycles of the heavenly bodies and the natural world, and are thus in some sense naturally discernible, the Sabbath—like circumcision—exists independent of human discernment and became known only through God's commandment. Along similar lines, we can understand the Sabbath as woven into the fabric of creation, even if it was not revealed to Israel (and thus humanity) until Sinai, while the rite of circumcision and the other festivals were celebrated only after revelation (to Abraham in the first case, and to Moses for the latter). But the poet does not stress the revealed nature of circumcision and the Sabbath in this poem; instead, he highlights how the festivals are integral to creation, and creation is integral to the Sabbath. By closing his composition with rhetorical questions, Amram Dare transforms the liturgical cue affirming God's oneness into an answer: Only God could do this!

Said on the Sabbath in the morning before the qataf *of the book of Exodus, and on Sabbaths that fall during festivals.*

O faithful one, O steadfast one,
Happy are those who love you forever,
God, who does not exclude his creatures
From the fullness of this rest of his,[127]

---

127. The text as it is seems slightly corrupt, and Ben-Hayyim struggles with it, suggesting that the line be translated as, "The sum/fulfillment of His resting is this ..." (*RPH*, 74).

5   Which the God of all rested![128]

Only the congregation of Israel,
Which is called [both] son and slave of God,
Maintains circumcision and the Sabbath,
And the festivals, which are unceasing.
10   And he bound their observance[129] to the luminaries.[130]
In [their] passage, one perceives the festivals;[131]
And the festivals, just so, they come!

Who could interrupt the creation
Of the Creator, who endures forever?
15   Who could toil and constantly renew
An edifice[132] and be entirely unwearied?

May God be praised!
There is no God but the one!

16 "Lo, a Holy and Hallowed Day" (*SL*, 45; *RPH*, 75–78)

In this poem, Amram Dare offers his lengthiest and most complex meditation on
the importance of the Sabbath. No clear organizing theme governs the composition; instead, it offers a kaleidoscopic variety of interpretations of the sacred day.

The opening section of the hymn (ll. 1–6) emphasizes the transitive quality of
Sabbath holiness: it is holy, it acquired holiness from its Creator, and it imparts
holiness to those who keep it. Sabbath rest constitutes an echo of *imitatio dei*.

The next section (ll. 7–18) turns our attention back to the origins of the Sabbath, which Amram Dare casts as not simply a creation of God's but also as
a creature: God breathes life into it and names it, as if it were a living being
(although with six names rather than just one). Whereas the first unit emphasized the Sabbath's holiness, this second unit dwells on the idea of power.

The third unit (ll. 19–28) elaborates on the importance of, and the
rewards for, keeping the Sabbath. It begins with language reminiscent of an

---

128. Lines 3–5 are difficult, and the enjambment of the lines, while not unheard of, nonetheless
stands out.

129. Lit., "their names, pretexts."

130. I.e., the calendar, which is established by the cycles of the moon and sun and is thus eternal.

131. The poet here describes how observance of the heavenly bodies is connected to intercalation.

132. That is, Sabbath (as in Amram 18, l. 13: "a structure that cannot be shaken"), or perhaps the
entire heavenly "infrastructure" that governs the cycles of holy days.

incantation—"Whoever wishes ... / Let him ..."—which bestows an almost otherworldly orientation on the following lines. Proper observance of the Sabbath will result in a transcendent experience of proximity to the heavenly realm, as well as readiness to welcome the time of the redemption (the "time of favor") when it comes. The poet seems to imply that one who keeps the Sabbath "in purity" (see l. 20) will participate alongside the angels (who likewise observe Sabbath), thus experiencing "grace itself" (l. 24) and witnessing the acceptance of human prayers in the heavenly Temple.

To explain this bold imagery, the next lines (29–32) draw a comparison between prayer and a tree. Implicitly, the roots of the tree are in the earth—among the mortals—but its branches reach up to the heavenly realms, just as the prayers of the pure ascend. These prayers leaf out and provide protective shade to those down below. It is a virtuous cycle of beneficence, with Israel sheltering under the shade of its own piety.

The following passage (ll. 33–41), perhaps developing the generalized figurative language in the previous unit, drifts away from the specific topic of the Sabbath toward prayer and, more specifically, the potency of prayer to bring redemption. These lines anticipate the restoration to come under the Taheb, the returning one, who will be a new Moses. He will institute a time of peace, ensure the restoration of divine favor, and triumph over Israel's foes.

In the final unit (ll. 42–44), the poet weaves these various themes together through the deployment of theme words in catalogue form. He returns to the theme of the Sabbath ("this day") and describes it in terms of blessing, holiness, separation, and power, promising a tranquility and safety that will become the permanent way of being under the Taheb.

> *Said on the Sabbath in the morning before the* qataf *of the book of Leviticus ("And every grain offering you shall salt with salt ..." [Lev 2:13]), on Sabbaths that fall during festivals, and on the Day of Atonement.*

> Lo, a holy and hallowed day—
> Happy is he who hallows himself upon it.
> The Holy of Holies[133] hallowed it,
> And he entrusted it to the holy congregation:
> 5   The exalted God rested upon it,
> And he commanded that Israel should rest upon it.

---

133. The language here draws tight connections between God (the holy one), the Sabbath (the holy day), and the physical sanctuary (the holy space, i.e., "the holy of holies").

After he completed the [work of] creation,
His greatness breathed greatness into it[134]
And he titled it with good titles:
10 "Sabbath," and "holy," and "blessing,"
And "sign," and "refreshment," and "holy day."
As for the one who keeps it completely,[135]
[his] reward for resting greatly upon it
Is double that of any other day,
15 And this is a wonder, so very potent,
Deserving of powerful thanks.
May the God who distinguished it,[136]
Rested upon it, and hallowed it, be exalted!

Whoever wishes to see the time of favor,
20 Let him purify himself thoroughly on the Sabbath
And let there be prayer in his mouth.
Indeed, he will behold the ranks,[137]
And he will join with the good and perfect ones,
For he will have attained grace itself.
25 And the Gate of Repentance[138] will open,
And the altar of thanksgiving is there,
And it will receive the prayer of the happy ones,
And it will lift up [their] thanksgivings to the heavens.[139]

For praise is like a sapling:
30 Its branches ascend upward,
And its shadows offer shade
To those who speak [their words] with a pure heart.

---

134. The translation reflects the root נשם, which is usually translated as "refreshed, rested" but comes from the root meaning "breath" (as in the English idiom "to catch one's breath"). God imbued the Sabbath with the greatness of restoration. Alternatively, this line could be translated as "his greatness rested greatly upon it."

135. Or "peacefully."

136. The Sabbath.

137. The ranks of the angels (the good and perfect ones) who accompany the time of favor.

138. "Gate of . . ." is a relatively uncommon but hardly rare image in Samaritan literature; the specific image of the "Gate of Repentance" is unusual, however (see the preface to Amram 23). In rabbinic literature, the image of the "Gates of Repentance" appears in various sources that likely postdate Amram somewhat, including LamR 3:15 and PdRK Shuvah 2, where they are juxtaposed with the "Gates of Prayer." See DeutR 2:12 and MidPs 65:4.

139. The subject of the verbs here is the altar, which "receives" prayer and offerings on behalf of the people and conveys them to God. Amram Dare here uses the term *ma'on*, the level of heaven where God dwells.

Happy is the returning one,[140] and happy are
The students who resemble him.
35   And happy shall the world be when he comes,
For he will bring with him peace,
And he will manifest the time of favor and purify
Mount Gerizim, the house of God,
And remove [God's] anger from Israel.
40   And God will grant him a great triumph,
And through him shall he conquer[141] the whole world.

May God be magnified, he who gave to us this day
And blessed it, and hallowed it, and distinguished it,
And empowered it more than any other day!

May God be praised!
There is no God but the one!

17 "Among All the Days, None Is So Great as the Sabbath Day" (*SL*, 45; *RPH*, 78–79)

This hymn contains two stanzas that seem to address disparate themes: the first focuses on the Sabbath, while the second focuses on Moses. (The Sabbath appears here where we would usually expect to find the Torah mentioned; perhaps the Sabbath, so often linked with revelation in these poems, functions as a kind of synecdoche for scripture.) The two stanzas are linked by the poet's assertion that Moses ascended Mount Sinai "for its sake" (l. 13)—that is, for the sake of the Sabbath. Furthermore, subtle structural connections unify the two stanzas. Amram Dare articulates how the Sabbath is distinct from the other six days of the week, and in turn, he explores how Moses's experience differs from the experience of any other person. The hymn turns on implicit and explicit binaries that verge on paradox: a day of rest emerges from days of work, but the "wastrel" (l. 6) who rests on other days instead of working loses the sanctified day of rest, commandments reside with blessings, and fasting sates hunger. Both stanzas suggest that an encounter with the divine transforms: Moses's experience is immediate, as he

---

140. The Taheb, the prophet like Moses.
141. Lit., "battle, wage war." The sense of the line is that the Taheb will be the means for manifesting divine victory, although it might also be that the Taheb's victory comes only through God (i.e., "through God shall the Taheb conquer the whole world"). Ben-Hayyim suggests (*RPH*, 77) that בה could possibly refer to the Sabbath ("through it" rather than "through him").

temporarily joins the ranks of angels atop Sinai in the heavenly cloud. But the Sabbath also stems directly from the deity, as it comes from and is named by God.

The refrain constitutes a third element: the people. God has given the Sabbath to the people but the refrain tells them they must nonetheless summon it. The refrain's focus on the human perspective underscores the congregational perspective of the hymn as a whole. The first stanza focuses on the human experience of the Sabbath: a day of no labor, a day of prayer. The second stanza describes Moses's ascent but explains that he did so for the sake of "his generations"—the community. The congregation, however, cannot be passive and must do more than simply articulate gratitude. They must invite the Sabbath in, in order to acquire its gifts for themselves and their households.

While the Sabbath is one of the major themes of this hymn, the refrain refers to it as the "approaching jubilee." In Lev 25, "jubilee" refers to the forty-ninth or fiftieth year in a repeating cycle—Sabbath multiplied and magnified—but in Samaritan texts, it also refers to the day of the redemption that awaits the people in the future.[142] Here, however, it seems to refer to the weekly day of rest—a day that, in its respite from labor and through its implicit proximity to its divine origin, confers a foretaste of the ultimate redemption. But it is a rescue, a blessing, that will come only if called.

> *Said on the Sabbath in the morning before the* qataf *of the book of Numbers ("Then he ordained Eleazar and Ithamar as priests . . ."* [Num 3:4]*) and on the Sabbaths that fall during festivals.*

Among all the days, none
Is so great as the Sabbath day,
The source[143] named by the master in the world.
Within all other days, there is labor,
5   But the Sabbath? Its reward is no-labor;
The wastrel is driven out from its midst.
Blessings are ordained within it [see Lev 25:21],
From the mouth of the God of the beginning.

> *The entire house of Israel needs*
> 10   *To say: "Come!"*
> *[Come] in peace, O approaching jubilee,*
> *That comes and refreshes the mute and those who speak!*[144]

142. The Samaritans seem to have had a system that counted forty-nine years in each jubilee period, usually, but sometimes fifty years (Powels, "Samaritan Calendar," 713–14).

143. Lit., "root"—the idea is of something fundamental and essential.

144. "The mute" refers to animals, while "those who speak" refers to humans.

For its sake did Moses, the prophet,
Ascend Mount Sinai,
15 And he was concealed in cloud and in glory.
The fasting one was sated; he neither ate nor drank,[145]
For he stood among the standing ones[146]
And he brought life to the [future] generations.[147]

The entire house of Israel needs
20 *To say: "Come!"*
[Come] in peace, O approaching jubilee,
That comes and refreshes the mute and those who speak!

May God be praised!
There is no God but the one!

18 "God, Exalted and Honored" (*SL*, 45–46; *RPH*, 79–80)

This brief lyric is unusually rich with biblical quotations, which ground the commandment to keep the Sabbath in divine, prophetic, and scriptural authority. Deftly, Amram Dare creates an image of God, high in the realm of secrets, commanding his faithful prophet to impart the commandment to keep the Sabbath. The framing imbues the sacred day with both power and mystery.

Our poet's liturgical gem begins as a kind of storytelling: "Once upon a time, God commanded Moses . . ." The scriptural quotations function to ground the narrative in ultimate truth, however, and serve almost as talismans, underscoring the divine power within the commandments. The description of Moses as "the one entrusted with secrets" (l. 9) and his epithet "the great luminary" (that is, the sun; l. 8) translate the prophet into the realm of myth, while the treatment of the Sabbath as a "boundary" and a "building" lend this temporal structure a striking physicality. The final lines of the poem transform the story into an admonishment, however. The Sabbath, conceived of in spatial terms, is something that one could leave, but such an act would be a tragedy, for the Sabbath is no ordinary space. It is a garden that cares for the gardener, and within it are trees of life. Outside the garden of the Sabbath, the poet suggests, lies death.

---

145. See Exod 34:28, which describes how Moses neither ate nor drank while he was atop Sinai.

146. Angels (קעימיה). Like Amram 14, this poem seems to allude to a tradition in which the angels were already keeping the Sabbath before it was revealed to Israel by Moses (as referenced in the next line).

147. "Life" here refers to the Torah.

While the poet does not here connect the Sabbath to the divine rest of Gen 2:1–3, the final lines strongly echo the opening chapters of Genesis. The poet transforms the day of the Sabbath into a life-giving Garden of Eden where every tree is a tree of life. Paradise was, in fact, a foretaste of the Sabbath—this is the secret, shared by the prophet and reflecting the handiwork of the deity.

> *Said on the Sabbath in the morning before the* qataf *of the book of Deuteronomy ("Come and possess . . ." [Deut 1:8]), on festivals, and on the Sabbaths that fall during festivals.*

God, exalted and honored,
Commanded the holy prophet
For the sake of the holy congregation
Concerning the proclamation
5 That God proclaimed on Mount Sinai:
"Keep the Sabbath day, to sanctify it"[148]—
A festival that shall never be nullified.
And thus the great luminary[149] wrote,
Moses, the one entrusted with secrets:
10 "The children of Israel shall keep
The Sabbath day, enacting [its rites]" [see Exod 31:16].[150]
For its boundary was fixed by the hand of God,
For it is a structure that cannot be shaken.
Woe to the one who departs from it—
15 The garden[151] that tends its owners:
Every tree within it is life!

> *May God be praised!*
> *There is no God but the one!*

19 "To God, the Mighty and Triumphant" (*SL*, 46–47; *RPH*, 80–82)

This poem offers an unusually bleak vision compared to other works by Amram Dare. It spans from creation to the present and is associated with the *qataf*

---

148. The quotation here is in Aramaic; it aligns with the translation of Exod 20:7 (= Deut 5:11) found in the SamT.

149. I.e., Moses.

150. A paraphrase of Exod 31:16 as it appears in the SamT.

151. Lit., "the paradise that keeps its sustainers."

known as "the ring," which summarizes the entire Torah. Like the Torah itself, the hymn opens with great hope and ends in uncertainty at a precarious moment.

After an initial invocation directed to the deity (ll. 1–3), the poet offers a luminous description of the creation of the world symbolized by the kindling of the heavenly lights, which he connects to the creation of humanity, and specifically Israel, who mark their festivals by the calendar established by nature (ll. 4–16). The picture is one of beauty and beneficence: just as the sun, moon, and stars maintain their courses, so did the ancestors adhere to the ways God prescribed for them. They kept the festivals and the commandments, and in turn, God poured forth blessings upon them and kept the nations of the world at bay. It was a cycle of lovely reciprocity and mutuality, a time of favor—and it did not last.

The second main section of the poem turns to the disruption of early perfection (ll. 17–34). Favor has turned to disfavor, festivals pass by unobserved, sacrificial offerings have ceased, and Israel is no longer bathed in blessing but crushed under the feet of foes. God, the poet reminds his listeners, is not harmed by Israel's sin, but the people suffer acutely from their self-inflicted harm. They have spurned and neglected both divine blessings and protection.

Amram Dare offers few words of comfort, nor does he conclude the poem on an explicitly hopeful note. The only consolation lies in the sense of divine continuity that runs throughout the poem: good will be rewarded, and God is steadfast. Tangible offerings may no longer be sacrificed, but intangible offerings may still be made. The poet suggests, though he does not state it outright, that a return to piety and obedience will result in a restoration of the days of favor. People may be fickle, but God is steady, and his reliability applies to both punishment and forgiveness. At a moment when the sacrificial cult has been interrupted, the utterance of this prayer and the performance of the liturgy are offerings that in and of themselves constitute small steps toward restoration.

> *Said on the night of the Sabbath and the next day, when the new moon falls upon it, and thus on every new moon, evening and morning, and on Sabbath afternoons before the* qataf *of "the ring" (that is, the* qataf *that abridges the entire Torah).*

To God, the mighty and triumphant,
We offer thanksgiving, worship, and praise,[152]
For all greatness belongs to him!

He kindled illumining lights, inextinguishable,
5   And he distinguished holy festivals,

---

152. Lit., "we give thanks, we worship, and we magnify."

And he bound their name[s] to the lights,[153]
And he gave them to the children of his beloved ones,
So that they could rejoice upon them
And give thanks to his name and present offerings to him.

10 And he welcomed them,[154]
And he opened the treasury of the heavens to them
And poured forth blessings from there
And placated all the nations of the world.[155]
For they[156] are the children of those who fulfilled

15 All the commandments of their master
And sustained his festivals entirely.

We weep for you, O Israel![157]
Once you were in the days of favor,
But now, oh, you are in the days of disfavor [*fanuta*].

20 [Once] you were with your God,
Joining[158] him during all the festivals
And bringing him offerings,
The fullness of the work of your hands,
And he was accepting [them] from you,

25 Just like a father with his son.
And he subdued all the nations before you,
Acting as your shield,
And shielding you far from any harm.[159]
But from the day that you rebelled and abandoned him,

30 You became a stomping-ground for the nations.
New moons and festivals come and go;[160]

---

153. I.e., holy days are linked to the calendar, which is determined by celestial bodies.

154. Lit., "receives from them" (מקבל מנון). The translation "welcomes them" conveys the sense that God is greeting his people (cf. *kabbalat panim*) as well as accepting their prayers and offerings. The verbs here are active participles, but the translation renders them in the English past tense in order to sharpen the distinction between "then" and "now" about to be made in the poem.

155. The sense of this line is that the nations do not trouble Israel because they recognize that Israel's actions benefit them, and God placates (or sustains) the nations as a reward for Israel's service.

156. Reading אנון ("they") instead of אנן ("we").

157. The poet, speaking from within the congregation ("we") here, seems to address Israel's past self, lamenting what has become of the nation and what the present-day community, by extension, has lost.

158. Lit., "assembling with" or "rendezvousing with," in the sense of coming together at an appointed time.

159. Lit., "keeping every harm away from you."

160. Lit., "pass by just as they came."

No offering ascends upon them.
But God, whose greatness endures forever,
Is neither expanded nor diminished.[161]

May God be praised!
There is no God but the one!

20 "Blessed Is the House of Jacob" (*SL*, 47; *RPH*, 82–84)

In this poem, Amram Dare reflects on Israel's past, dilating on the time of favor when the virtuous patriarchs and ancestors of the nation lived. He touches briefly on Abraham, Isaac, and Jacob but focuses on two nonpatriarchs: Joseph, who led the people into Egypt; and Moses, who led them out. The poet recalls the miracle of Jacob's family entering Egypt as seventy individuals and emerging as sixty myriads and retells how they carried the bones of Joseph with them as they traveled toward Sinai.

Chronologically, the poem is quite fluid and delicately elliptical: it moves from Jacob to Abraham and, by allusion, Isaac, then leaps forward in time to the exodus before stepping back, via the bones of Joseph, to the beginnings of Israel's time in Egypt. The storytelling is not linear but impressionistic, and it avoids the negative dimensions of the story: there is no violence, no slavery, no fear. Instead, it is a story of triumph: Jacob's son becomes a king while Moses, the great prophet, becomes like a god to Pharaoh. These two figures constitute twin pillars of Israel's magnificent past bearing implicit promises for the future.

Said on the Sabbath of Assembly (fifty days before Passover) and every day from the new moon of Nisan until the conclusion of the holy day, and also on Passover Sheni.

Blessed is the house of Jacob!
A root that came forth from
Sixty myriads[162] were they,
Built up from seventy souls.[163]
5   Who is able to reckon their greatness

---

161. I.e., Israel's inability to make offerings may cause Israel pain but does not affect God.

162. Lit., "six hundreds of thousands."

163. A description of the expansion of the house of Jacob, which numbered seventy upon their entry to Egypt and six hundred thousand at the time of the exodus.

Or to exhaust their praise?

The fruit[164] of Abraham's field,

The harvest of "by myself I swear" [Gen 22:16],[165]

The children of the time of favor[166] went out

10   [To hear] the recitation at the base of Mount Sinai.

And they forgot nothing as they departed,

For their master had reminded them of it.

He reminded them to take the bones of Joseph,

For Joseph was great before he died,

15   And after his death, he was exalted:

His bones were taken by order of the great prophet,[167]

[Who] was proclaimed "God" by the power of the ruling authority.[168]

Two servants of the time of favor:

Joseph, the king, and Moses, the prophet.

20   As a reward for their good deed, save us, in your mercy!

May God be praised!

There is no God but the one!

21 "Great Is God, Who Thus Commanded" (*SL*, 47; *RPH*, 84–86)

In this brief and gem-like hymn, Amram Dare plays with numbers: seven, four, eight, and three. The seventh month is understood as analogous to the seventh day: a Sabbath among months. The first day of the month is not a singular holy day so much as the opening celebration of a month of festivities. Just as the weekly Sabbath contains a day of sanctity, the seventh month contains an abundance of holy days. These holy days themselves bear multiple names and serve multiple purposes, but all serve to nourish Israel in both body (through the harvest) and soul (through the purging of sin).

Just as the Sabbath is the crown of the week, the seventh month is the crown of the year, embellished with multiple holy gems: the Feast of the Seventh Month (celebrated on the first day of the month), the Day of Atonement, and the Festival of Booths. The holy days, likewise, are the Sabbaths of Sabbaths

---

164. Lit., "grain, crop," but a reference to Isaac.

165. Cited in Aramaic translation.

166. I.e., the children of Israel.

167. Lit., "by the hand of the great prophet," i.e., Moses.

168. I.e., Moses, who was "like God." See Exod 7:1, where God tells Moses, "See, I establish you as a god [*elohim*] to Pharaoh." Moses's "divinity" was recognized by God, the sovereign who bestowed the title, and by Pharaoh, the terrestrial ruling authority.

in their ritual observance, and the Festival of Booths in turn contains the additional holy day of the Eighth Day of Assembly (*shemini atzeret*). Holy days and festivals are layered within and among each other. Through the numbers and the emergent patterns, the month becomes a kind of ornate structure holding Israel and its piety within its bejeweled frame.

> *Said on the Sabbath of the Assembly of the Festival of Booths and on every day from the new moon of the seventh month*[169] *until the festival of the Eighth Day of Assembly.*

Great is God, who thus commanded
Concerning the beginning of the seventh month,
Premier among all the new moons,[170]
That it should be called, by the authority of God,
5   By four exalted titles—
Shabbaton,[171] remembrance, trumpet blast, and sacred convocation[172]—
In order that they should be a Sabbath-among-Months,
And a Sabbath of Sabbaths[173] among the festivals,
And the crown of the festivals of the time of favor.
10 Within it[174] are the Day of Repentance—
Holy, expelling sins—
And the pilgrimage of booths and the pilgrimage of the harvest,[175]
And the Eighth Day of Assembly,[176]
Seventh of the festivals and the holy of holies.
15 And all Israel is nourished [מהר] by them,[177]

---

169. The holy day is known among Jews as Rosh Hashanah, but whereas Rosh Hashanah is itself a festival in Judaism, among the Samaritans it inaugurates a penitential period that culminates in the Day of Atonement, which in turn prefaces the Festival of Booths and the Eighth Day of Assembly. See Powels, "Samaritan Calendar," 730–31.

170. The word ארשי literally means "foundation, origin"; see *DSA*, 67, s.v. ארש.

171. The seventh month is the "Sabbath" of months.

172. These four terms appear in Lev 23:24 in the SamP and in the MT. The Samaritan tradition of reading, as evidenced in the SamT of this verse, understands each of the four terms as a separate concept: מקרא קדש | תרועה | זכרון | שבתון. (The MT reads זכרון תרועה as a construct phrase, and understands the verse as listing three components.) These four terms provide the antecedents for the pronoun in the next line ("they").

173. For שב as "Sabbath," see *DSA*, 870, s.v. שב. The phrase "Sabbath of Sabbaths" (or "Sabbath of complete rest") echoes Exod 31:15 (where it refers to the weekly Sabbath) and Lev 16:31 (where it applies to the Day of Atonement).

174. I.e., within the seventh month.

175. Two names for the same festival.

176. I.e., *shemini atzeret*.

177. Israel is nourished—fed learning, as it were—by the holy day and its many names. The root of מהר is מור, lit., "to procure food," as befits the harvest festival.

And they are all appointed, one with another,
Three assemblies within it.[178]

May God be praised!
There is no God but the one!

22 "O Beneficent Rememberer Who Does Not Forget" (*SL*, 47–48; *RPH*, 86–88)

This final hymn of the *Durran* offers an extended meditation on God's nature. It includes a litany of divine attributes: God remembers and does not forget; he is merciful and gracious, but also terrifying and fearsome; he is good, and pure, and steadfast. These divine qualities stand in contrast to those of his people, who transgress, who sin, and who are inconstant. The poet does not articulate Israel's failings in order to lay blame or castigate his congregation, however, but rather to illustrate God's better nature and exalted magnanimity. It is precisely because God could do otherwise, perhaps even ought to do otherwise, that his care for his people is impressive and reliable. It is God's record of acting on behalf of Israel in the past that enables the congregation—those who recognize God's power but also his grace—to appeal to him to help them in the present.

As a closing to a collection of hymns, this work provides a hopeful, if not triumphant, conclusion. It praises God in ways that urge God to continue to act beneficently without presuming to paint Israel in a falsely positive light. What Israel excels at is praising God, in understanding God's nature and the importance of God's actions in their history. This poem frames all that came before in the *Durran* in that light, and read with Amram Dare I, it constitutes an *inclusio*: the collection begins and ends with praise that bears witness to God's saving power and graciousness in the face of Israel's weakness and sin.

Said on the Day of Atonement before the portion of Phineas.

    O beneficent rememberer who does not forget,
    Remember the covenant of your servants,
    And deal graciously with their children as their reward.[179]
    O, our God! O merciful one! Help!
5   We have no savior except for you.

---

178. This refers to the three holy days—the Day of Atonement, the Festival of Booths, and the Eighth Day of Assembly—that fall within the seventh month.
179. Lit., "on account of their labor/effort."

You are fearsome, oh, truly![180]
All the world trembles before you.[181]
Fear of you dwells in every heart,
And awe of you in every place,
10 And all know that there is none like you.
All beings, when terrified,
Seek refuge only with you.
Your potent splendor causes quailing,
While with your great mercy you put at ease.
15 Witnesses make known forever
That there is no divinity but yours;
Lo, gracious and merciful one,
You fulfill what you say.
O YHWH, a merciful and gracious God,
20 Praise is yours forever,
For you have not requited us
According to what our wickedness has earned.[182]
You, O YHWH, are pure, but we are sinful.
According to your goodness and your faithfulness,[183]
25 You have kept watch from your holy abode[184]
and saved us from the earthquake.[185]
We give thanks to you, O merciful one, for your faithful acts,[186]
For what you have done for us and continue to do.
O, swift helper,
30 No strength can sustain us except your strength, O my master,
And there are none whose deeds are like yours!

May God be praised!
There is no God but the one!

---

180. Lit., "the fear, it is yours, O true one!" The poet means to conjure how God casts fear upon others, even as the rather choppy syntax suggests the halting speech of the terrified.

181. Reading ממך in place of מן, with Ben-Hayyim (*RPH*, 86–87).

182. Lit., "according to the wickedness of our recompense"—i.e., the recompense merited by wicked doings. Ben-Hayyim translates as "the wickedness of our deeds" (*RPH*, 88).

183. The term חסד here is singular in form (חסדך).

184. *Ma'on*, the level of heaven where God dwells.

185. A more general translation of "terror" is also possible, but here I follow Tal (*DSA*, 227–28, s.v. זוע) and Ben-Hayyim (*RPH*, 88), who translate the term as "tremor," which suggests a specific geological event is being recalled. See, too, Marqe 1, l. 123: "Not from the earthquake [בזועה] did we learn."

186. The term חסד here is plural in form (חסדין).

23 "You Are the One Who Created the World" (*RPH*, 89–94; *D*, 226–28)

While the hymns of Amram Dare that are included in the *Durran* (1–22) are relatively brief and unstructured lyrics, the final six hymns of his *diwan* (23–28) have in common a significantly different form. All are lengthy—each contains twenty-two stanzas—and each is governed by an alphabetical acrostic; each stanza consists of four short phrases, often reflecting a single idea and employing a great deal of wordplay. This structure offers the poet a larger canvas, but he does not use the space to create narratives or systematic arguments. Rather, he crafts each stanza like a jewel, and a beautiful mosaic emerges from the composition.

One common device employed by Amram Dare that is particularly evident here is the rhetorical question. Sometimes he uses such questions not only to underscore the obvious nature of answers that need not be stated ("What other creator could create like God? None!" [cf. ll. 3–4]) but also to suggest that speculations about the divine nature cannot be fully answered. In other instances, these questions raise possibilities that he refuses to contemplate because the consequences of the answer exceed what he wishes to acknowledge: "If you do not rescue us, who will?" [cf. ll. 29–30]. This question implies the possibility that God will not, in fact, help Israel, and his refusal would leave Israel utterly unprotected. Rhetorical questions enable the poet to gesture toward what cannot be said without attempting to utter the ineffable.

While unanswered questions pepper many of Amram Dare's acrostic poems, two motifs appear in this poem with particular frequency. One is the motif of heavenly or divine gates, and the other is the image of the hand of God. This poem distinguishes multiple gates: the Gates of Divine Kindness, the Gates of Divine Goodness, and the Gates of Divine Favor. These complement other gates that appear in Amram Dare's works: the Gates of Mercy and the Gate of Repentance. The imagery of heavenly gates—distinctive paths of access to elements of the divine nature, or ways by which certain petitions may be pleaded on high—does not occur in the Torah but is a commonplace in Hellenistic and rabbinic Jewish writings.[187] The imagery reflects the intricate architectures of both royal space and royal power in antiquity. The idea of heavenly gates appears without fuss or fanfare in these poems precisely because they were a stock theological image. At the same time, it seems more than a coincidence that the great Samaritan reformer was known as Baba Rabbah—literally, "the great gate" (although these poems use the term תרח for gate, not בבא). Baba Rabbah, like a physical gate, provided some kind of access to the divine.

187. See Jacobus, *Zodiac Calendars*, 344–88.

The image of God's hand, by contrast, appears commonly in the Torah, where "hand" is often a figurative term for power (e.g., being in the hand of one's enemies). Certainly in these poems, "power" could function as a translation for "hand," whether describing the hand of God or the hand of Israel's enemies. But particularly with regard to God, I have retained the more literal rendering because Amram Dare so often seems to exploit the familiar and vivid nature of the image. For example, the radical nature of divine creation is expressed through images featuring hands. According to the opening stanza, God creates without using his hands—unlike human artisans, who rely on manual dexterity. The intangible force of God's creative power is juxtaposed in the next stanza with God's almost tactile protection of Israel, whom he guides out of Egypt by his hand. The image of the hand here resonates with its use in other works— by Amram Dare and even more so Marqe—that focus on the Torah as God's "handwriting" (a literal manuscript). Taken together, the examples of creation and exodus do not indicate that God lacks hands, but that God can achieve things without them that humans cannot. The resonances between the hand of God in Samaritan *piyyutim* and the depictions of the (disembodied) hand of God in the art of late antiquity—notably at Dura Europos—are particularly intriguing.

The nature of Amram Dare's longer compositions is such that the individual stanzas can be scrutinized on their own, like beads on a string; the structure of the hymns is determined not by thematic or narrative development but simply by the acrostic. Individual stanzas resonate with similar gems from other poems in this collection of this poet's more elaborate works.

> *Said on the fourth Sabbath of a month that includes within it five Sabbaths.*[188]

       א You are the one who created / the world without [use of a] hand
What other creator is able / to create creations like yours?

5–6   ב In the beginning, you revealed[189] / powerful creatures;[190]
By your power did they come forth / guided by your hand.

9–10   ג Praise belongs to you / whose fearsomeness is upon all;
Your creations reveal / that you are the master of all.

---

188. An unusual but far from rare occurrence, when a month begins on a Friday or Saturday (and depending on whether the month has twenty-nine or thirty days).

189. The language of "revealing" here describes creation.

190. Here, the phrase "powerful creatures" (בוראין חיולין) seems to describe a single class of angelic beings. In Marqe, we find two different categories of angels bearing similar names: "power-ful ones" (חילין) and "created ones" (בוראין).

ד For, you are the omnipresent one / who is present in all places;

15–16   For, you are he who endures[191] / from generation to
       generation.[192]

א "**I am that I am**" [Exod 3:14]: / [you are] the Almighty, who
       brings relief and favor;

19–20   Divinity is yours / in [days] past and [days] yet to come.

ו And you are the first, / he who preceded [all] creation,
   And you are he who will endure / after the world [ends].[193]

25–26 ז We cry unto you / with our bodies a-tremble;[194]
   O nourisher [זאון] of souls,[195] / if you see us, show us favor!

29–30 א If you do not rescue us—/ lo, who else is there, a reliable
       rescuer?[196]
   Who is there but you / who can rescue us from oppression?

ט Good one, who does good things, / who never ceases doing good,

35–36   Apportion us some of your goodness / that no other can give.

י O steadfast one, who endures / on account of his being timeless,

39–40   Rescue those whose lives / are borrowed against time.

כ All of us stand / before you, anxiously;
   If you look out, gaze upon us / with favorable regard.

45–46 ל Where can one who sins find refuge / from you, except at your
       hand?
   And whom can he entreat at the time / of distress, except you?

49–50 מ Who is present, when the heart / is distressed, as intimately as
       you are?
   And who may hope for favor, / if not out of your goodness?

---

191. Lit., "lengthens" (as in "lengthens days").
192. Lit., "upon generations of generations."
193. Or "after eternity."
194. The word ארתיתן here is from the root רתת, while the same word in the next line is taken
to be from the root רתי.
195. Or "living beings."
196. Lit., "one who is accustomed to rescue."

נ The relief of [receiving your] mercy—/ what wisdom could esti-
mate [its value]?

55–56   Deal favorably with the distressed, / who stand at the gate of
your kindness.

ס Your glory is our hope, / and our confidence is [in] your kindness;

59–60   Do not cast them away from us, / for the sake[197] of Moses your
servant.

ע We flee to be near your kind hand,[198] / for though our persecution grows ever worse,
Your goodness is greater / than our grave offenses.

65–66 פ Opener of the Gates of Your Goodness: / do not shut it in our
faces!
The Gates of Your Favor: / we place our hope in them.

69–70 צ Creator of bodies / and perfecter of limbs,
Gaze upon us with your kind eye, / for you are the source[199] of
our hope.

ק We stand / at the Gate of Your Kindnesses;

75–76   Accept our entreaties, for we / are the children of your servants.

ר O merciful one, abandon us not / to the mercy[200] of our foes;

79–80   Your abundant mercies exceed / the magnitude of our sins.

ש O goodly presence,[201] / we draw near to your goodness;
O hearer of prayers, / loosen our bonds!

85–86 ת Accept our repentance / out of your great compassion,
For you are merciful and compassionate, / as such is your
custom.

There is no God but the one!

197. Lit., "labor"—meaning "as a reward for his labor." The term suggests a parallel to the
rabbinic idea of *zekhut avot*, ancestral merit.
198. The image is one of intimacy and protection.
199. Lit., "locus, place."
200. Lit., "into the hands of."
201. Lit., "the dwelling that is good." Brown translates as "abode of goodness" (*D*, 228).

24 "Who Can Reckon Your Greatness?" (*SL*, 31–32; *RPH*, 94–100; *D*, 64–65)

This poem, like the others in this collection of Amram Dare's longer works, is composed out of small, jewel-like units. The stanzas do not construct a linear narrative but nonetheless create a mosaic of imagistic beauty. In this composition, Amram Dare turns his attention to the Torah and its revelation, weaving together images of scripture with reflections on the process of how the Torah was written and how it was conveyed to the children of Israel. A sense of the Torah's "dual authorship" (written by God, reinscribed and transmitted by Moses) emerges; this motif would become central to the works of Marqe.

In the early lines of this poem, the language of Genesis provides a constant counterpoint. This textual affinity underscores the narratives contained within the Torah, with special attention to the prominence of the Sabbath story. However, the use of Gen 1–2 as a touchstone also gestures toward the idea—developed in the writings of Marqe, as it is in Hellenistic and rabbinic sources—that the Torah preexisted material creation. (The association of this poem with the *qataf* of Genesis indicates an awareness of the intertextual references within the poem.) We know the story of the Sabbath and thus know to observe it, Amram Dare seems to suggest (as he revisits this favored theme of his, the institution of the Sabbath during creation versus its revelation on Sinai), precisely because the day of rest is contained within "the Teaching of great truth" (l. 5) that the congregation is charged to read and study. The Torah's narratives are intrinsically bound to the ritual practices of the Sabbath. Text and practice cannot be distinguished.

An even more provocative blurring of boundaries occurs in the poem in regard to the Torah's authorship. As the poet notes, "The tablets of the covenant / you entrusted to the son of your household" (ll. 45–46). These tablets are understood to be not simply the Decalogue but the Torah as a whole, which God revealed "by the hand of Moses" (l. 42). By the end of the poem, the poet no longer distinguishes between God and his prophet; for example, the following lines exploit the root קרא ("to proclaim, read aloud, call") in ways that permit the conflation of the author and his messenger:

> The proclaimer [קראה; lit. "the one calling out" or "the reader"] who
>   proclaimed: / "you shall have no (other) gods!"
> Proclaimed: "Keep / the Sabbath day, to sanctify it." (ll. 73–76)

God is certainly the origin of these words—earlier in the poem Amram Dare is clear that God speaks these words "from the fire" (l. 51)—but the divine words are conveyed to the people by Moses, who taught them to the Israelites and explained them. Without Moses, it seems, God's word might have been uttered but not received.

Lest this seem like overreading, we should note that the poet himself under-scores the deep intimacy and near-parity between God and prophet. He notes that God revealed the Torah "by the hand of Moses" (l. 42), crowning and cloth-ing him with prophecy (ll. 53–56). The phrase "by the hand of Moses" (ביד משה) is a common biblical refrain (it occurs eighteen times in the SamP and a total of thirty-three times in the Jewish Bible), but Amram Dare takes it seriously, even literally, with meaningful results. The sense of parallel exaltation is articulated when the poet asks:

> Where is there a god like / the God of our ancestors?
> Where is there a true prophet / like the faithful one of God? (ll. 61–64)

This does not equate God and Moses but exalts Moses so that he is the nearest to God that one can imagine a mortal being. And, as the poem draws to a close, the poet continues to juxtapose deity and prophet: God ("the God of the genera-tions"; l. 83) joins his name to that of Moses ("the prophet of all generations"; l. 84), and in the final lines of the poem God limits not only the speech of Moses but his own utterances:

> A limit to speech / the exalted one imposed:
> A limit to the words of Moses, / A limit to the words of his master!
>   (ll. 85–88)

No other prophet, except the Taheb (the "second coming" of Moses) will be a prophet so close to God, so intimate with revelation and with the revealer. It is not that Amram Dare deifies Moses, but rather that the words of scripture are so distinctive and potent in their own right that the relationship between author and scribe ceases to have meaning: Moses is so totally in synch with God as his conduit that the distinction between the two blurs.[202] Sinai constitutes the sum total of revelation: true words from the true God conveyed faithfully by a true prophet. Israel is distinguished not only by the possession of the Torah but by its claim on the one prophet worthy of hearing, recording, and teaching God's word. The Torah scroll in the midst of the congregation stands as vivid testimony to the covenant that was sealed and delivered by Moses's hand.

---

202. In this respect, we can consider Moses an analogue to conventional messengers who would read letters in the voice of another, speaking "I" and "me" but in the persona of a monarch or mili-tary attaché.

Said on the Sabbath before the qataf *of the book of Genesis and on Sabbaths that fall during festivals.*

ע O maker of the world, / who can reckon your greatness?
You made it, in [your] greatness, / in six days.

5–6 ב In the teaching of great truth[203] / we read and become wise.[204]
On each of the days it describes[205] / you raised up creatures.[206]

9–10 ג Raised in your wisdom,[207] / they make your greatness known,
Those who reveal your divinity, / only to display your
greatness.[208]

ד For you made, without wearying, / your works, which are
exalted.
15–16 For you fashioned them from nothing / in six days.

ע You made them perfect; / not one of them is flawed.[209]
19–20 You made their perfection known, / for you are the master of all
perfect things.

ו And you ceased [working], though not from weariness, / on the
seventh day,
And you made it a crown / for the six days [of the week].

25–26 ז You proclaimed it holy, / and you made it fundamental,[210]
The appointed time for every assembly / and pathway to everything holy.

29–30 ע You made it a covenant / between yourself and those who keep it.
You made known that you keep / him who keeps its keepers.

---

203. I.e., the Torah.
204. Ben-Hayyim translates as "and study" (*RPH*, 94).
205. I.e., each day of the creation narrative; lit., "on each of the days from them (its words)."
206. Lit., "raised [i.e., from infancy to maturity] creatures."
207. I.e., the Torah.
208. Lit., "revealers of your divinity / only for the sake of your greatness." There is a play on
"your greatness" (גלדך) and the "raising" (גדלת in l. 8; גדילין in l. 10) of creatures during creation.
209. The word pair of חסר and שלם here could also be translated as "complete . . . deficient."
210. Lit., "a foundation, base" (ארש), a term from architecture.

ט Happy are they who rest on it, / who are worthy of its blessing;

35–36   May its holy protection grant them ease / from all weariness and worry.

י With sublime glories, / our master glorified us;[211]

39–40   A day of rest he gave us, / that we may rest as he rested.

כ All of their greatness you lifted up; / by the hand of Moses did you reveal it.

Your holy writing / you entrusted to your faithful one.

45–46 ל The tablets of the covenant / you entrusted to the son of your household;[212]

Life is from their master,[213] / for all life comes from their living words.[214]

49–50 מ Giver of life, / from whom everything comes,

He spoke from the fire: / "You shall have no [other] gods!" [Exod 20:2].[215]

נ Prophecy has been his crown, / since the [first] days of creation.

55–56   Its light[216] was upon Moses; / as was fitting, he clothed him with it.

ס The structure[217] of our lives / is the tablets of the covenant,

59–60   A structure that will never cease, / forever and ever.

ה Where is there a god like / the God of our ancestors?

Where is there a true prophet / like the faithful one of God?[218]

---

211. Reading בון ("by them") in place of ביד, with Ben-Hayyim (*RPH*, 96). The pronominal suffix thus refers back to the first line.

212. The phrase "son [or member] of the household" suggests the intimacy between Moses and God. In rabbinic writings, it is typically angels who constitute God's household, and this phrasing suggests Moses's angel-like status. The term is also applied to Moses in *TM* 2 §51 (1012, p. 151).

213. Ben-Hayyim translates as "from that which sustains them," i.e., the tablets (*RPH*, 97).

214. Lit., "all lives are from their life."

215. An Aramaic translation of Exod 20:2 (but different from the translation of the SamT).

216. A reference to prophecy (and revelation) that crowned Moses in the form of beams of light.

217. Alternatively, "support, comfort." The concepts of structure, support, and comfort are all entwined, and the suggestion is that the laws and truths of the Torah will never cease.

218. I.e., Moses.

65–66   פ   Mouth to mouth he spoke [with him]—/ God with the son of his
house;[219]

            Wonders were revealed to him / such as were revealed to no
other.

69–70   צ   The Creator who created / the world and all within it

            Commanded Moses [to use it] to grant us / life to the living.[220]

         ק   The proclaimer who proclaimed, / "you shall have no [other]
gods,"

75–76   Proclaimed: "Keep / the Sabbath day, to sanctify it" [Exod 20:3;
Deut 5:12].[221]

         ר   Exalted is the great one, / to whom every great thing belongs!

79–80   He exalted the son of his house / more than any [other] son of
the house of Adam.

         ש   His Name to his name / he joined together in greatness:[222]

            YHWH, the God of the generations, / and Moses, the prophet of
all generations.

85–86   ת   A limit to speech / the exalted one imposed:

            A limit to the words of Moses, / a limit to the words of his
master!

            There is no God but the one!

25 "May You Be Worshipped and Praised" (*SL*, 27–28; *RPH*, 100–104; *D*, 73–74)

While this poem is no more linear or narrative than Amram Dare's other long
compositions, it nonetheless has a structure beyond the governing acrostic.
Broadly speaking, this poem can be divided into two halves: the first thirteen
stanzas attend exclusively to God (ll. 1–50), while the final nine (ll. 51–88)

219. Or, "member of his household," a term of intimacy; see n. 212 above).

220. I.e., the Torah; a text in one of the later portions of *TM* describes the Torah as "tablets
containing life for the generations"; see *TM* 4 §21 (1862, p. 249).

221. Cited in Aramaic translation.

222. The poet here refers to the way God allowed Moses to be called "god" by Pharaoh (Exod
4:16).

introduce the congregation into the work. The deity is consistently addressed directly throughout the poem as "you," while the human perspective embeds the poet within the community, where he speaks as "we" and "us." The first half dwells at length on the image of God as a Creator, using the verbs עבד ("to make, work") and ברי ("to create") with particular frequency, in both verbal and nominal forms, as an action, a product, and an epithet. Through his exploration of God-as-Creator, the poet articulates a clear philosophy: God can be understood only through his works. To understand God, study God's creation. Of course, subjects for study can be found near at hand, for everything is divine handiwork—including abstract elements such as time and, most significantly, wisdom, the intellectual capacity to pursue understanding. Indeed, wisdom determines the course of God's actions (ll. 25–28), and although Amram Dare's cosmogony does not posit a primordial Wisdom-Torah (such as we find in rabbinic interpretations of Prov 8, a biblical text not in the Samaritan canon), this reference to wisdom's creation is as close as this poem comes to a mention of scripture or revelation. Not even Moses is named; rather, the individual intellect, examining the world with reverent intensity, has access to the handiwork of God.

The poet does not lay out a philosophical treatise, however, and the structure of these stanzas veers away from analysis toward paradox. Particularly in these acrostic poems, where the individual stanzas are composed of very brief lines and are dense with repetition, Amram Dare conveys ideas through juxtaposition and wordplay. For example, in the fourth stanza he ponders, "For you are found in every place / but the like of you can be found nowhere" (ll. 13–14); God is omnipresent, a Creator manifest through all of his creations, and yet nothing compares to him. He is, as the poet writes in the previous stanza, "revealed among the concealed ones, / concealed among revelations // revealed to the enlightened / but concealed from the eyes" (ll. 9–10). Playing with the words כסי ("to hide") and גלי ("to reveal"), the poet attempts to convey how God makes himself known and yet, at the same time, remains utterly unknowable. And yet, this deity is not remote, for all his otherness; Amram Dare writes, "No one is able / to discern where you are; / Whatever way a person turns / his face, [there] he finds you" (ll. 45–48). God is both unknowable and inescapable, inside and outside, majestic and familiar. By putting these paradoxes, conflicts, and conundrums into poetry, the author does not resolve the tensions but revels in their beauty. Struggling to understand the conflicts within a stanza provides a way into the struggle to understand God.

For all the intellectual playfulness of these lines, the second half of the poem explores the human consequences of being a creature of God. In lines 53–56, where the poet pivots to speaking in the collective voice of the community, he acknowledges that the gift of wisdom has allowed people to perceive

God—and the human response is to worship God for this beneficence. The latter half of the poem turns to the present moment: God hears the congregation's appeals because he has given them the ability to discern their relationship to their Creator. This creation establishes a relationship of ongoing care. Throughout the final stanzas, the poet shifts his focus from the limited ability of humans to perceive a hidden God to expressions of wonder, gratitude, and need rooted in God's ability to see everything—and still forgive. If Amram Dare posits a theology in which God defies the senses, he offers an anthropology in which humans fully exist only when their Creator perceives them. The God who begins the poem as a primordial Creator and primary unity concludes the poem as one who hears, sees, and pardons. The poet's ability to share this message of hope with his community, and to submit his petition on their behalf, reflects perhaps the truest understanding of God's incomparable nature.

> *Said on the Sabbath in the morning before the* qataf *of the book of Exodus, on the Sabbaths that fall during festivals, and on festivals.*

ע   O maker of the World, / may you be worshipped and praised!
O maker who makes, / [but] not in the manner[223] of [a mortal] maker.

5–6   ב   New creatures / you made, from beyond the bounds of time[224]
In order to inform [them] that you / stand outside it, unbound by time,

9–10   ג   Revealed among the concealed ones, / concealed among revelations,
Revealed to the enlightened / but concealed from the eyes.

ד   For you are found in every place, / but the like of you can be found nowhere,
15–16   Concealer and perceiver of every secret / unlike any other who perceives.

א   You are the one who came before / any place and any time;
19–20   Every place and time / and every creature is of your making

223. Reading תשוית for תשבית.
224. Lit., "you created from time," meaning that the concept of time applies to them, as it does not apply to the deity, who stands outside the bounds of time.

ו   For you are apart from everything, / and you are unlike anything,

And you are the maker of absolutely everything / but unlike the appearance of anything.

25–26 ז   When your wisdom, which you created, / saw [something] fit [to do],

Your power made it so; / absolutely everything is according to your word.

29–30 א   You are the first, the fashioner, / the Creator, establisher of all;

You are the one to whom all belongs, / and [all] comes from you and relies on you.

ט   Happy is the heart in which nothing / dwells but you;

35–36   Happy is the one who thanks you, / for it is for your sake, all is on account of you.[225]

י   The unique priority[226] / of godhood is yours,

39–40   Unique in existence / and great of loyalty and truth.

כ   Nothing can encompass you, / but you can be found by all;

Every place—you are there / but no place can contain you.

45–46 ל   No one is able / to discern where you are;

Whatever way a person turns / his face, [there] he finds you.

49–50 מ   Who can understand you, / except through your handiwork?

Who is ordained to praise you, / except through righteousness granted by you?

נ   We are known to you from / our very creation;

55–56   We perceive your wisdom within ourselves, / and we bow before your greatness.

ס   Your handiworks bear witness / that you are singular in your greatness,

59–60   Witnesses of [your] truth, / unchanging.

---

225. The language here is elliptical (lit., "because of you, on your account"). I.e., all a person has comes from God and depends on God.

226. God is both first and unique. Nothing came before him or compares to him.

א Lo, you who are concealed[227] / from the gaze of all who see;
If you see fit, gaze upon us / gaze [upon us] in your mercy.

65–66 פ Rescuer of the oppressed, / [you] who are nearer to him than his
[own] heart,
Rescue us, for we have no / rescuer except for you.

69–70 צ Life-breath is a generous gift / that you have entrusted unto us.[228]
Deal generously with us, out of your generosity; / be generous,
in your mercy!

ק As we stand before you, / standing with [our] poor,[229]
75–76 Do not reject the clamor / of our petitions, if you see fit.

ר Merciful are you, and [you] suffice for us; / for your name is
"The Merciful."
79–80 Greater is your mercy / than the greatness of our transgression.

ש O hearer of cries, / hear the sound of our cries,
Our petition, which you know / before we speak.

85–86 ת Accept our repentance / and forgive our sins.
O my master! Do not lock / the Gates of Your Mercy[230] in our
faces!

There is no God but the one!

26 "You Are the One to Whom Divinity Belongs" (*SL*, 28; *RPH*, 105–10; *D*, 87–89)

In this poem, Amram Dare turns his attention to the deity directly. He speaks to
God (as "you") while recounting his various actions and attributes. Throughout

---

227. For פלא/פלי in the sense of "remote, hidden," see *DSA*, 685, s.v. פלי.

228. For צדקה as "gift, beneficence"—with the translation here extended to include "generosity"—see *DSA*, 724, s.v. צדקה. The second stich could be translated more literally as "which is in
our hands (and) comes from you."

229. Ben-Hayyim (*RPH*, 103) favors a variant reading in his translation: קיאמן קמיך קיאם דמסכינים
("Our stance before you is the stance of the poor").

230. This idiom evokes the rabbinic concept of the one hundred gates of heaven, including the
Gates of Atonement, the Gates of Prayer, and the Gates of Mercy. A gate of mercy is specifically
mentioned in MidPs 4:3 and b. Megillah 12b, as well as in the Apostolic Constitutions (7.23). See
Brown, *D*, 74.

the poem, the poet describes God's qualities: his power, his kindness, his great-ness, his mercy, and so forth. Two particular aspects of God's being stand out, however, and they are facets of the same quality. Amram Dare dwells on God's oneness—his radical singularity—as well as God's otherness. God is, in short, radically one, utterly unlike any other being. He has no analogue. (This poem can be seen as a corrective to Amram Dare 24, which makes bold statements about God's conferral of godlike status on Moses vis-à-vis Pharaoh that could be open to misinterpretation. Here the poet implies the prophet may exist on the highest plane proximate to the deity, but his status never rises to that of a divinity.)

The repeated assertions of God's oneness in this hymn accord with the liturgi-cal refrains that constitute the transitions between *piyyutim* and the other units of the Samaritan liturgy: "There is no God but the one." This radical unity, utterly unlike human individuality, reflects God's extreme otherness, and Amram Dare constructs here a theology that would resonate with later philosophers, includ-ing Maimonides: we cannot understand God as a personality per se, but only through what God has done in the world. The workmanship reveals the worker because it is an echo of his being.

And yet, for all of God's unknowability, he is not remote, nor is he utterly tran-scendent. Instead, he is a figure whose deeds indicate that he can be approached through prayer and petition. Our poet writes, "We are strangers / at the gate of your mercies" (ll. 61–62); the poet's plea does not come from a presumption that he has the right to call upon God. And yet prayer is effective, not because of the people who do it, but because God welcomes it: "We beseech you, for such is your nature, / not ours" (ll. 55–56). The poet depicts the people's utter depen-dence on God, who is known to them only through his acts of rescue and mercy.

The concluding lines, finally, offer a brief doxology, one that echoes in its language and repetitions the familiar Jewish prayer of the Kaddish. And yet, whereas the Kaddish consists only of praise, this poem ends with a rhetorical question: "May you be thanked, although who is able / to thank you (suffi-ciently) for your kindness?" (ll. 87–88). The poet cannot say that words fail, for all he has to offer is words. But where words fall short, will must close the gap. The poet offers up his words to God and trusts that God, as is God's nature, will find a way to catch them.

> *Said on the Sabbath in the morning before the* qataf *of the book of Leviticus and on festivals.*

א   You are the one / to whom divinity belongs;
     You alone are [the] Creator, / and all was created by your hand.

5–6   ב   Through the innovation[231] of your creations / it is known[232] that
you are the first;
By them you become known to all: / there is no god but you!

9–10   ג   Your power brought into being / everything, but not from anything prior;[233]
Your works reveal / that you are singular in your greatness.

ד   For you clothed your creatures: / [such are] the kindnesses of
your wisdom,
15–16   For you made it dazzling / and at the sight of it, praises [are
sung].[234]

ה   You spoke aloud,[235] voicelessly, / to the one who saw that you
are present,[236]
19–20   Just as perfect handwriting / is "heard"[237] by one who sees it.

ו   And this is your power, / [just] a portion of your greatness,
And greater than what you have made manifest / before the eyes
is what is still concealed.

25–26   ז   You proclaimed, without speaking[238] / words, and the world
came forth.
Your creatures hurried; / they bowed down at your words.

29–30   ח   You are the beginning / whose beginning no one can fathom;
You are the ending, / though you have no end or expiration.

---

231. On the term חדאות (related to חדד, "to renew, create"), see *DSA*, 249, s.v. חדת. Tal translates
"by the creation [חדאות] of your creatures [בוראיך]," but the present translation distinguishes between
the roots חדת/חדד and ברא.

232. The translation reflects Ben-Hayyim's understanding that ידע should be construed as אתידע
(*RPH*, 105).

233. Lit., "root."

234. Lit., "and its appearance is praises," presumably a reference to the magnificence of the
created world.

235. Lit., "made (yourself) heard."

236. I.e., to Moses, the one who perceived the divine presence.

237. The verb שמע here signifies understanding, but it is translated literally here to preserve
the tension between hearing and seeing developed in this stanza. The Torah makes God's voice
"audible."

238. Lit., "without a mouth."

ט   Burdened is the world / that bears[239] the dread of you,

35–36   And how can one not bear the fear / of the one who bears without hands?

י   Singular, you have no companion, / no second, and no partner:

39–40   Able, enduring, dreaded, / great, mighty, awesome.

כ   Any who might be compared [to you], / you do not resemble him;

Any who might resemble [you], / you are unlike him.

45–46 ל   You did not bring [the world] into being with a companion, / nor did you create [it] with a second.

By yourself you brought [all] into being, / and because of your greatness shall you be praised.

49–50 מ   Through [our] intellects, we understand / you through your deeds;

Through your scriptures, we understand / your workings, which are yours.

נ   We give thanks for your kindnesses, / for such is our ability;[240]

55–56   We beseech you, for such is your nature, / not ours.

ס   Your kindness is our hope, / and we await your mercy,

59–60   For where can we turn [our] faces? / Not away from you, but toward you!

ה   We are strangers[241] / at the Gate of Your Mercies;

Far be it from you to shut [it] / in the face of a needy sojourner.

65–66 פ   Outstretched of hands are we, / in need of beneficence;[242]

Extend your kind hands, / relief for our anxiety!

239. The root סבל denotes the physical act of carrying but includes the more existential connotation of "endurance, suffering."

240. Lit., "strength," in the sense of "strong suit." The only power humans possess is the power to recognize powerlessness.

241. Reading אכסנאי instead of הך סנאי or הך סנאין, which suggests enmity ("Lo, we are foes / at the Gate of Your Mercy").

242. Brown translates צדקה as "alms" (D, 89), but less material nuances are possible as well.

69–70 צ The soul's need is for relief / our need is for your mercies.
Deal fairly with us, / in fairness [that springs] from favor.

ק [When your] mercies are near, / [your] wrath keeps its
distance;[243]
75–76 If you see fit, bring us / into the respite of your mercy.

ר O most compassionate one,[244] / we have no rescuer except for
you;
79–80 Grant us that which cannot be given / by any giver except for
you.

ש Hearer of cries, / O one accustomed to being kind,
The petition of our humiliation / and our poverty—answer [it]!

85–86 ת May you be praised, may you be magnified, / may you be
exalted, O truth.
May you be thanked, although who is able / to thank you [suf-
ficiently] for your kindness?

There is no God but the one!

27 "You Who Were Our Creator" (*SL*, 30; *RPH*, 110–17; *D*, 93–95)

While Amram Dare 26 focused our attention on the nature of the divine, this
poem gives more attention to the human perspective. The poet's focus is not
God's radical uniqueness but rather the dynamics between God and nation,
and this covenantal relationship manifests itself rhetorically: almost every
stanza contains language addressed to God ("you") from the congregational
perspective ("we"). God and Israel are insistently juxtaposed, and the relationship between the two parties becomes essential to the definition of each. Israel
desperately needs God; God may not need people, but it is in God's nature to
be needed. One cannot be a Creator without a creation; one cannot be merciful without a people in need of mercy; one is not a parent until one has children. In short, while Israel would be impoverished without God, God would be
incomplete and unfulfilled without a people. In this poem, a relationship that

---

243. Lit., "near are mercies / far is wrath."
244. רתאה רתאיה.

could be entirely one-sided as a natural consequence of the impossible gulf separating the parties becomes a delicate but determined duet.

> *Said on the Sabbath in the morning before the* qataf *for the book of Numbers and on festivals.*

        א You who were our Creator, / you who were when all else was
            naught,
           Who created the world / and all within it, without a helper,

5–6   ב In you do we have faith; / there is no God aside from you.
           In your power do we trust, / for you have both ability and
            authority.

9–10 ג O mighty one whose might / subdues others' might,
           Subdue our enemies' might / with your great strength!

        ד Judge of the [other] gods, / you whose power is over all other
           powers,[245]
15–16   Put aside judgment of us / and subdue our foes!

        א If you do not rescue us, / and favor us in our humiliation,
19–20   O merciful king, / who will rescue us?

        ו And we are your servants, / and the children of your servants,
           And far be it from you to forget / the covenant of our ancestors.

25–26 ז We hasten to be near your mercies; / from within the midst of
           great oppressions,
           We cry out to you: "Relieve us / from all distress!"

29–30 ע In your kindness is our confidence, / and our requests [appeal to]
           your essence;[246]
           If you do not rescue us, / who would rescue us?

        ט Spread the shade of your mercy / over us, like a cloud!
35–36   Shelter us within [your] palm; / spare us before our enemies.

---

245. I.e., angelic beings.
246. For "essence," see *DSA*, 659, s.v. עקר; note the parallel phrasing in l. 49.

י The extinction[247] of [our] foes—/ those who singed our souls—

39–40 We[248] await [it] in the shade of your mercies, / for we are accustomed to patience.[249]

כ Conclude the judgments / that are becoming manifest in our time;
Bind the hand of our enemy, / which is stretched forth to destroy us.

45–46 ל The oppressions that with increasing intensity / have become manifest in our days—
Finish them, and bind / the wicked ones who oppose us!

49–50 מ Our requests are [made] of you, / O ruler of our spirits;
Without you, / our lives lack permanence.

נ We fear for our lives[250] / on account of our foes;

55–56 Grant us relief from oppressions / that arise from our sins!

ס Our foes are pitiless, / and we are subdued by them;

59–60 Forgive and rescue [us], for we / are like the living dead.[251]

א O, you before whom / all kings bow down
And before whom all heroes / tremble and quake,

65–66 פ Rescue us from [our] foes, / for their hearts lack pity;
Relieve the frightened, / for they are fearful on their own.

69–70 צ Those who need relief / live[252] in despair,

247. Lit., "consuming by fire, burning."

248. The unemended text, influenced by the acrostic, reads, "they await."

249. This stanza is difficult. The term יקדני סניה (lit., "the burning of the enemies") is ambiguous but is here taken as referring to the punishment of the foes. The root כמר can mean "to have compassion" or, secondarily, "to hide, protect" (*DSA*, 393–94, s.v. כמר I; כמר II). Ben-Hayyim translates "They are taught to conceal" (*RPH*, 114), but Tal favors the meaning "to have compassion" (*DSA*, 393). *CAL* (s.v. *kmr*) lists "to hide, to keep safe" as the primary Samaritan definition (from the root sense "to cover, to keep warm") but notes that, in late Jewish literary Aramaic, in proximity to the root רחם, the root כמר can have the meaning "to bestow mercifulness." The translation here attempts to capture the dual nuances of safe concealment and trust in God's mercy.

250. Lit., "our souls are fearful."

251. Lit., "standing like dead ones."

252. Lit., "stand, exist."

Despairing before [their] foes / who come against them in rage.

ק   Sustain our lives, / for they are yours, in justice, for [the sake of] justice,

75–76   And enact judgments, / as you are accustomed to instructing.[253]

ר   O merciful one, appoint for us / a portion of your redeeming mercies,

79–80   Running swiftly / and redeeming us.

ש   [We are] stripped[254] of your mercies, / but for the sake of our ancestors,
Command our redemption / and the destruction of our enemies.

85–86   ת   O [you who are] strong in pity, / relieve our misery!
Your harsh judgments / subdue, on account of our lowliness!

There is no God but the one!

28 "O Merciful God, Rescue Us" (*SL*, 29–30; *RPH*, 117–22; *D*, 105–7)

This poem shares the defining structural features of Amram Dare's other long poems (23–27)—it has short stanzas, is dense with wordplay, and is built on an acrostic scaffold—but the focus of the poem is distinct from those of the other exemplars. This poem may be classified as primarily petitionary and penitential, as it places its primary emphasis on the human condition and the human need for redemption. The poet's hope for rescue emerges from his understanding of God's essential nature: God is attentive and defined by his mercifulness. The opening stanza states, "If the merciful one does not rescue us / what rescuer have we?" (ll. 3–4). Without a people to redeem, a redeemer lacks fulfillment.

From the first stanza onward, the poet's focus is his community. Of this poem's twenty-two stanzas, fifteen include some form of the communal plural ("we, our"), and in all but three of those stanzas, first-person plural forms occur more than once. The poet here speaks emphatically for and from within

---

253. Alternatively, אלוף אלוף could be understood not as two forms of the root אלף but as two forms from different roots: אלוף חלוף (homonyms in Samaritan pronunciation), meaning "accustomed to change." I.e., God is well accustomed to changing (just) punishment to (compassionate) mercy.

254. For this meaning of שלח, see *DSA*, 897–98, s.v. שלח II.

the community. (Only once does he address God individually, as "my master," in l. 57.) Yet the poem is just as emphatically a plea to the deity. Every stanza addresses God as "you," describes an attribute as "yours," appeals to God using a vocative, or indicates his need to act through an imperative. The poem constitutes a very self-conscious oration, one that subtly instructs the congregation how to regard God (with trust and expectation) and reminds God how to respond to his people (that is, by living up to their expectations). While the word "covenant" occurs only once, the relationship implied by that term governs this poem as a whole.

Only seven stanzas lack the interiority and explicit identification of the poet with his community indicated here by the use of first-person plural forms; nonetheless they too articulate a strong relationship between God and humanity. Each of these stanzas addresses God directly (as "you") and speaks to the deity in terms of his relationship with humans—specifically, with individuals. For example, couplets stating, "Every soul trusts / in the abundance of your compassion" (ll. 41–42) and "In whom [else] could he trust, / he who [relies on] you and only you?" (ll. 61–62), describe the same qualities that place God in relationship to the congregation, but as categorical aspects of the bond between people and God. It is a relationship that is both unequal—humans are entirely dependent—and yet reciprocal. Without God, the people have no hope; without people, God has no one to praise him. Note how the poet articulates how utterly dependent the community is upon God, how utterly unified the two parties are:

> Our souls are yours; / our lives depend on your justice.
> Our confidence counts on your loyalty; / our hope relies on your mercy.
>   (ll. 53–56)

A literal translation of these lines would be even starker:

> Our souls are yours; / our lives, your favor;
> Our confidence, your loyalty; / Our hope, your mercy.

The pairings make the dependence radically clear: nothing human, not breath and not hope, exists outside of God. A relationship in which all that one party has derives from the other creates a situation of complete reliance, which could engender significant anxiety—a reality the poet has already acknowledged a few stanzas earlier by juxtaposing the assertion "every soul trusts" with the fact that "every body trembles" (ll. 41, 43). The poet intermixes fear and faith—fear of what one's actions may merit but faith that God will forgive. To some extent, praise of God is contingent upon that relationship, as the poem suggests in its concluding stanza:

May you be praised; may you be extolled! / May you be exalted forever!
May you be honored, may you be blessed! / May you be worshipped
    forever! (ll. 85–88)

The implicit conclusion of each stich is "... by us!" The poet expresses confidence that God will redeem the people; in return, God can be confident in the people's praise.

The poet articulates hope in God's mercy, but he also makes clear that the people need mercy: they are far from flawless and do not merit redemption intrinsically. God's nature, not their own, assures a happy ending. Divine nature consists of mercy, loyalty, and compassion; although God is far, he is also near, and he is also all-powerful. Humans, by contrast, are dependent and wanting: people, being weak, need forgiveness and support. And people need hope. The poet acknowledges that some will fail to trust in God—"Woe to the one who keeps far from you" (l. 35)—but sin alone will not cause a rupture with God because God is merciful: "Our transgressions would endure / were it not for your forgiveness" (ll. 37–38). The relationship is not one of equality by any means— "What is [our] weak dust / confronted with its Creator?" (ll. 51–52)—but, more consequentially, it can be one of intimacy. When Amram Dare calls God "closest of the close" (l. 73), he offers his congregation a reason to pray, because he reminds them that God will surely listen.

> *Said daily, on the Sabbath before the* Qataf *of the book of Deuteronomy, and on festivals.*

א   O merciful God, / rescue us in your mercy!
    If the merciful one does not rescue us, / what rescuer have we?

5–6   ב   Through your merciful eyes / and your loyalty, behold us!
    With your faithful hand outstretched / relieve our trembling!

9–10   ג   O mighty and awesome one, / you shall be praised forever!
    God of gods! / you shall be worshipped forever!

    ד   We fear you / and trust in you;
15–16   We fear your anger, / and we seek your mercy.

    ה   "**I am that I am**" [Exod 3:14]:[255] / our Creator and our rescuer—

---

255. A divine name based on God's self-description in Exod 3:14.

19–20   Banish us not, / for you are our place[256] of refuge!

ו   Do not reject us, / for you are our hope!
Do not punish us, / for you are our security!

25–26 ז Our cry unto you / is the cry of the poor;
None can find for themselves / relief, if not from you.

29–30 א We set our hopes / at the Gate of Your Mercies;[257]
Far be it from you to reject / those who put their hope in you.[258]

ט   Happy is the one who draws near to you, / O distant one who is near;
35–36   Woe to the one who keeps far from you, / O near one who stands aloof!

י   Our transgressions would endure / were it not for your forgiveness,
39–40   And our sins would be great / were it not for your mercy.

כ   Every soul trusts / in the abundance of your compassion;[259]
Every body trembles / at your dreadful power.

45–46 ל Do not deny your mercy / to those who spread their hands [to you],
Nor [your] pity to those who do not have / the courage to come seeking favor.[260]

49–50 מ What would we be, in the grasp of your anger / were it not for your mercy?
And what is [our] weak dust / confronted with its Creator?

נ   Our souls are yours; / our lives depend on your justice.
55–56   Our confidence counts on your loyalty; / our hope relies on your mercy.

---

256. Reading "house" (בית) in place of ביד with Ben Hayyim (*RPH*, 118).

257. See *D*, xxii.

258. Lit., "those whose hope you are."

259. רתותך.

260. I.e., the poise or arrogance to seek God's forgiving gaze; see *DSA*, 50, s.v. אפים, meaning 6. Ben-Hayyim compares the phrase with the Hebrew idiom in 2 Sam 2:2 and Job 11:15 (*RPH*, 120).

ס Forgive us, O my master, for we / are alive [but] like the dead,

59–60   And remember to our merit the covenant / with the dead as [you do] with the living.

ע In whom [else] could he trust, / he who [relies on] you and only you?

And whom can he petition,[261] he / whose needs are for you and only you?

65–66   פ O apportioner of life / and extender of mercy,

Open your kind hand / in favor to the poor!

69–70   צ We need your mercies / in our old age:[262]

Thus we need you / during our prime,[263] now more than ever![264]

ק O closest of the close, / yet unseen,

75–76   Accept our petitions / and respond to our pleas!

ר Favor [us in] our fearfulness / [on] the day when we stand before you,

79–80   And do not withhold from us / your favor and your mercy!

ש At this hour of our renewal / after we withered,[265]

If you do not watch over[266] us / in your faithfulness, how can we be healed?

85–86   ת May you be praised, may you be extolled! / May you be exalted forever!

May you be honored, may you be blessed! / May you be worshipped forever!

There is no God but the one!

---

261. Understanding ישול to be from the root שאל (see *DSA*, 859–60, s.v. שאל/שול I).

262. Lit., "after we are withered." See n. 265 below.

263. Reading בחיינן instead of וחיינן, with Ben-Hayyim (*RPH*, 121).

264. The implication is that, if the elderly need God, those in the prime of life need God even more. Alternatively, if כדמות is understood as כ+ד+מות, the translation would be: "Just as one who is dead needs you—/ while we are alive, even more so!"

265. "Withered" (בליותן) here refers to aging; see SamT Gen 18:12 and *DSA*, 99–100, s.v. בלי.

266. Lit., "gazing upon."

Marqe ben Amram

MARQE BEN AMRAM WAS, according to Samaritan tradition, the son of the priest Amram ben Sered—Amram Dare, the first great Samaritan poet and a participant in the Samaritan reformation under Baba Rabbah—and the father of the last major classical Samaritan poet, Ninna ben Marqe. Whereas Amram Dare and Ninna are both known exclusively as poets, Marqe wrote not only poetry but also prose, in his magisterial exegetical composition known as *Tibat Marqe* (also sometimes referred to as *Memar Marqe*).[1] Indeed, later Samaritan tradition refers to Marqe as "the source [or "Creator"] of wisdom" (Aramaic, *bedawah de-hakhamatah*) and "the fountain of wisdom" (Arabic, *yanbū 'al-hikma*).[2] While Marqe's poetic works have remained a central part of Samaritan worship down to the present day, *Tibat Marqe* has received more attention from modern scholars. Samaritan liturgical poetry has, like Jewish hymnography of the same period, been neglected in favor of more "scholarly" midrashic works. As the present study illustrates, however, Marqe's poetry should also be reckoned a crowning achievement of Samaritan exegetical as well as literary creativity.

Marqe's name most likely derives from the Latin "Marcus." It reflects the lingering influence of Rome in classical Samaritan culture and resonates with the names of his father, Tuta (Titus), and his son Ninna (Nonus). Later Samaritan tradition records a hagiographic legend concerning his name: an angel appeared

---

1. *Tibat Marqe*, in its final form, is divided into six books. The first book and sections of the second book are written in the Aramaic of Marqe's time, while other sections of the second book and the remaining four books use the literary Hebrew of later Samaritan writings and probably postdate Marqe by several centuries. Reinhard Pummer notes, "It is conceivable, however, that they [the Hebrew sections] too—or at least some parts of them—are from [Marqe's] time but were edited in a style characteristic of the last centuries of the Aramaic literature" (*Samaritans*, 224).

2. The title "founder of wisdom" occurs in the Samaritan chronicle known as the *Tulida* ("genealogy"), the earliest sections of which date to the twelfth century CE, where it is written, "This is Amram—he is Tuta—the father of Marqe the source of wisdom" (§129). See Florentin, *Tulida*, 90. The description of Marqe as "the fountain of wisdom" occurs in the *Annals* (*Kitāb at-Ta'rīḫ*) of Abu l-Fatḥ of Damascus, written in Nablus ca. 1355 CE; for a translation of this passage, see Stenhouse, *Kitāb al-tarīkh*, 184.

in a dream to Amram Dare shortly before Marqe's birth and informed him he was to name his son Moses. However, because Samaritan interpretation of Deut 34:10 prohibits giving such a name, Amram Dare named the child Marqe, which has an equivalent numerical value (345) according to gematria.[3] While this account is of questionable historicity, it nonetheless reflects Marqe's great stature among the Samaritans and underscores his particular affinity for Moses as a teacher, interlocutor with the deity, and scribe.

Marqe lived in the late third or fourth century CE; unlike his father he is not included among the ranks of Baba Rabbah's reformers, which suggests that he was young or at least not yet prominent at the time of the reformation. Marqe's influence on Samaritanism, however, is evidenced by his enduring literary significance. In addition to *Tibat Marqe*, he composed twenty-five liturgical poems, and the Samaritans consider him to be the greatest of their hymnographers. While some of his poems are performed in abbreviated form in contemporary Samaritan liturgy (Ben-Hayyim published only the abbreviated versions), the complete texts were preserved in earlier manuscript traditions (and thus are available in Cowley's edition).

Marqe's poetry differs noticeably from that of his father, although there are similarities as well, particularly with Amram Dare's longer compositions outside the *Durran* (Amram Dare 23–28). Like Amram Dare, Marqe writes in a distinctive Palestinian dialect of Aramaic, akin to the Jewish Palestinian Aramaic (JPA) of their Jewish neighbors, and like his father, Marqe composed without end rhyme.[4] Marqe makes frequent use of alphabetical acrostics as a structural device, as Amram Dare does in his longer poems; in the works of both poets, these compositions typically have twenty-two stanzas, but whereas Amram Dare's acrostic poems consist of four short lines per stanza, Marqe's almost always have either four or seven lines, and his lines tend to be lengthier. Finally, Marqe's poems are less psalm-like than his father's *Durran* poetry—longer and more regular—and also intertextually richer and more theologically developed. Their resonant language and turns of phrase were influential in Samaritan literature and liturgy.

There are, of course, exceptions to these generalizations. Thus, while Marqe 1–17 are fairly consistent in formal structures (alphabetic acrostic poems of twenty-two stanzas, with each stanza containing four to seven cola), Marqe 18–25 display significant diversity. Marqe 18 lacks any obvious stichometry, although its use of repetition makes clear that it is not simply a prose text. Marqe

3. See Tal, "Mârqe," 152.

4. It should be noted that Ben-Hayyim includes transliterations indicating the contemporary Samaritan pronunciation of the poems he edited. Presumably the pronunciation from the late third century CE to the early fourth differed.

19 and 20, while structured as alphabetical acrostics, have noticeably shorter stanzas than Marqe 1–17, and both include a refrain. Poems 22 and 23 are the shortest of Marqe's works—only seven and eighteen lines, respectively—and they lack any obvious structural devices. Finally, Marqe 25 includes a name acrostic—the initial stanzas spell out M-R-Q-H—as the opening to a poem that lacks a conventional alphabetical acrostic. Three other poems (15, 16, and 21), although written in Marqe's conventional acrostic form, were in practice read only in part, not in their entirety (Ben-Hayyim included only the initial portions of these poems, those still in use among the Samaritans, while Cowley provides the full texts[5]). Within the individual poems, however, Marqe tends to concentrate on specific themes and to revisit specific motifs and turns of phrase; thus, while the individual poems in the latter portion of this anthology may differ from each other, they reflect consistent and developed theologies and anthropologies.

Several poems provide clear evidence of refrains, while others employ repetition with conspicuous density. Marqe 16, 19, and 20 include short refrains at the conclusion of every stanza. Other hymns, such as Marqe 1 and 24, have refrain-like repeated phrases that do not recur in a regular fashion. The lack of refrains or "fixed-word" (מילת קבע) rhetorical structures, as attested in Hebrew, JPA, and Syriac poetry from this period (as well as in certain biblical psalms, such as Ps 118) nonetheless marks these Samaritan poems as different—not just in form but perhaps in terms of performance as well.

While Amram Dare's poetry creates an initial impression of formal diversity in which common themes can nonetheless be discerned, Marqe's poetry initially appears more uniform in structure, but when examined closely, it displays a range of subtle and significant themes and concerns. Marqe adopts a variety of perspectives within the poems: he speaks to God directly (as "you") but also indirectly ("he"); he speaks from within the community ("we") or at some remove ("you") or even from afar ("they"). Only rarely does he write from God's perspective, and even then only through brief quotations, and never in a sustained fashion; he does not write extensively in God's voice, as Jewish and Christian poets do. At other times, Marqe speaks not to God but to the Torah (Marqe 14 and 20), which he addresses directly as "you." Indeed, the Torah, often dramatically personified, constitutes one of the most important and distinctive elements of Marqan poetry. The only figure as prominent as God, Israel, and the Torah in Marqe's poems is Moses, who (like the poet himself) links

5. Ben-Hayyim notes his use of Cowley but explains that he included only units in common use; for example, in his introduction to Marqe 15 he writes, "Presented here are stanzas 1–7 because with regard to this piyyut it was the custom to say those alone, and the rest were not in use (from when?)" (*RPH*, 224).

the other figures together. Moses mediates between God and people through his conveyance of the Torah. The Torah—in particular the Ten Utterances—is divine in origin but must be taught to the people by God's chosen prophet. Each figure is singular: a singular God, a singular nation, a singular writing, and a singular prophet. The radical uniqueness of each "character" constitutes a key element of their commonality.

Marqe's poetry reflects a distinctive spatial orientation, as well: the revelation at Sinai (and, by implication, the remembrance of that moment during the prayer service) constitutes a moment when heaven and earth meet. God descends with his angelic hosts, while Moses ascends, on behalf of the people. Torah constitutes the point of contact. Within this spatial construct, Marqe also creates a specifically visual understanding of revelation: it is the moment when the concealed is revealed, when the invisible becomes visible, the intangible is manifest. Marqe's focus on the Sinai theophany resonates powerfully with the liturgical moment in which the hymns themselves are sung: the people assembled and ready; the deity and the angels hovering above, invisible yet present; the Torah visible and tangibly manifest in their midst; and the poet-performer, an heir to Moses, mediating among the parties and orchestrating the dynamics that bring the parties into relationship and affirming the covenant that links Israel and God through time, from Sinai to the present. Marqe uses the potency of poetic rhetoric to collapse the distinction between past and present, between foundational moment and ongoing significance. In some fundamental way, Marqe's poetry brings his community to stand again at Sinai, with the affirmation of Torah as a renewal of the revelation (in a fashion akin to the Eucharist in Christianity[6]).

While humans—specifically the Israelites—are the recipients of God's gift of Torah, when God descends to bequeath it, he is accompanied by the angelic hosts. The imagery that Marqe develops resembles the meeting of emissaries or wedding parties: Moses and God lead their entourages toward a chosen point of contact. Their journeys take place along the vertical axis: Moses and his host ascend; God and his host descend. And other changes occur as well: Moses undergoes a kind of apotheosis, transformed into something slightly more than human, if not exactly angelic or divine; and the angels are transformed, fleetingly, from invisible to visible creatures. As Marqe writes in poem 15:

To the rank of divinity did Moses, the prophet, ascend,
And he was honored atop Mount Sinai.

---

6. The term for this reexperience of crucial sacred moments is "anamnesis." For examinations of this phenomenon in the context of the Jewish liturgical setting and rituals, see Langer, "From Study of Scripture"; Lieber, "Rhetoric of Participation."

God descended, and all his creatures saw his descent;
All his troops from his abode went forth,
Above the entire house of Israel. (ll. 73*–77*)

It is unclear whether "creatures" in this stanza refers to angels, humans, or both—indeed, from the perspective of the singular God, it may well be a distinction without a difference. Furthermore, the Torah is not the only "revelation" at Sinai: "Standing ones, concealed / Went forth, revealed" (Marqe 9, ll. 73–74). Elsewhere Marqe refers to the angelic hosts as "the concealed congregation" (Marqe 14, l. 56) who become "the revealed ones" (l. 65) when they descend, and in another hymn he writes: "The powers and the mighty ones were seen / On the day when the Torah descended" (Marqe 24, ll. 33–34). When God gave the Torah to Israel, he gave them insight into the aspects of the very heavens.

Marqe's angelology is not substantially developed here. He often employs terms that are ambiguous, such as "standing ones" and "creatures," and he seems to intentionally blur the boundary between angels and humans (living mortals may also be described as "standing ones," and both angels and people are creations of God). Specific categories of angels do seem to exist: standing ones, powers (or "powerful ones"), mighty ones, and primordial beings (or "foundations"). The angelology is not influenced in any obvious way by late biblical writings such as Ezekiel or Zechariah, or by the emerging rabbinic traditions of Hekhalot and Merkavah mysticism. Instead, what emerges is a picture of God traveling in the company of a divine court that is splendid yet invisible—and for a moment, splendid and visible—yet one that in no way impinges on the radical singularity of God. Only Moses approaches that boundary.

The abiding topic of Marqe's poetry is the Torah as the source and embodiment of the covenant between God and Israel, as witnessed by the angels, transmitted by Moses, and kept by the people—faithfully or not—through the generations. Recurrent themes permeate Marqe's hymns, often in the form of binary pairs: God's forgiving nature and faithfulness to the covenant is balanced against Israel's sinful ingratitude; the merit of Israel's ancestors and the steadfastness of Moses as prophet act as counterweights against Israel's fickleness and waywardness; God's eternality is juxtaposed with human transience. At times, specific commandments (studying Torah, praying, keeping the Sabbath, circumcision) and ideas (God's uniqueness, the Torah's potency, the wonder of creation) are singled out, but in many cases the language is more general and elliptical. Unlike Amram Dare, Marqe does not focus on the larger arc of history; only one mention each is given to the time of disfavor (Marqe 1, l. 113) and the time of favor (Marqe 5, l. 87), and the second Moses—the Taheb—is never mentioned (aside from a possible allusion in Marqe 21, l. 97*). In this respect, Marqe is quite unlike his father, who repeatedly cited these historical epochs and looked forward to the advent of the Taheb. Broadly speaking, Marqe seems to prefer to focus on the more quotidian (routine transgression, routine forgiveness) rather than epic drama. These poems are very much "in the moment," standing at a Sinai that resonates with the present. "Now" itself becomes cosmic, as Israel— a singular people—stand in the presence of their singular God.

1 "Gaze upon Us, O Our Master" (*SL*, 12–14; *RPH*, 133–46; *SAP* 433–39)

In this lengthy acrostic poem, Marqe strikes an unusually melancholic tone. The language of despair, darkness, exposure, and shame colors the depiction of humanity in this work; anything positive and redemptive derives exclusively from God. Marqe dwells on human failure as a foil for divine mercy and expresses a sense of almost morose wonder that such miserable creatures as humans could merit not only God's attention but his compassion. The poet voices a fear of abandonment—anxiety that God will turn his face and not come to his people's rescue—for, indeed, such has happened before: "Just as they left him, he left them / And gave them over to all kinds of punishments" (ll. 67–68). So unworthy are the people that Marqe personifies death as the priest who administers the ritual of bitter waters to the people, who stand accused of infidelity. The poet repeatedly stresses the community's stubborn resistance to repentance and the guilt of all, rejecting any claim that they merit anything other than suffering. The poet's appeals to the community, such as that in the closing stanza, encourage them to praise God despite their transgressions ("But we freely incite his jealousy" [l. 152]) because God possesses power over both life and death and he may be persuaded to incline to the side of compassion and life, for his own mysterious reasons.

For all its pessimism—tempered only by a tremendous confidence in the deity—this poem provides a powerful example of the interplay among form, content, and performance. The poem's stark forcefulness derives largely from the relentless binaries that structure the piece: "Your merit is that you are merciful / And our weakness is that we are wicked" (ll. 15–16). God is good, the people are sinful; God is a redeemer, but the people unworthy of redemption. The bareness of the rhetoric and the way the poet revisits, deepens, and develops themes echoes the biblical psalms, with which this hymn shares a preference for intensive parallelism. The short lines of the work, structured along binaries and parallels and featuring multiple refrains, in turn strongly suggest the antiphonal mode of performance that would become typical of these poems (although we do not know how they were performed in Marqe's time). Each line invites the completion of the following one, and the simple bleakness and faint hope of the poem both accrue inexorable forcefulness. Human worthlessness becomes oppressive, and doom all but inescapable, and yet God's compassionate mercy feels almost—*almost*—assured.

> *Portions are said on all the Sabbaths in a month and on all festivals.*

א Gaze upon us, O our master!
We have nowhere else to turn our faces.

We know that we have sinned,

5 And we repent [תהי] of our transgressions;
Act charitably[7] toward us, O our master
And do not decree against us according to our deeds!

ב With a mighty hand and an outstretched arm
You rescued our ancestors from their foes.

10 They crossed the sea and the Jordan [River],
And you rescued them from every dire strait,
And you relieved them from every affliction.
So now, help us, O our master,
And do not decree against us according to our deeds!

15 ג Your merit[8] is that you are merciful,
And our weakness[9] is that we are wicked;
But your goodness does not suffer when [you] forgive us,
For we are a bad bet[10] and our inclination is toward evil.
But you are God, good and merciful;

20 *Acting charitably toward the guilty*
Lest they be destroyed by punishments!

ד A great fear is in the world;
O people, look and be afraid!
Woe to us that we were unready to learn

---

7. Normally, the root צדק is translated as a form of the word "justice," but here the later meaning (familiar from the translation of צדקה as "charity") seems appropriate, as the petitioners seek not justice—which would be bad for them, albeit fair—but mercy.

8. Lit., "praise," in the sense of "a reason that we praise you."

9. Lit., "shame."

10. The root זוף has meanings of "to lend, to be in debt," and is more commonly translated as "sinner" in nominal form.

25   The rewards and the punishments,
These and those, this with that;
Quails are heaped up high,[11]
While those who grumble are handed over for judgment.[12]

ה Just as we committed sins,
30   So we are stricken with afflictions.
We have no right to grumble against your goodness;
All [our] grumblings are against ourselves.
For we have destroyed ourselves on our own:
A person who strikes himself with his own hand—
35   Who is able to come and judge[13] him?

ו *And if the merciful one does not help and remember those who love him,*
Let us all weep for ourselves;
We have no right[14] to cry out "Help!"
A sinner, if he cries out "Help!"
40   And there is no helper who will help him,
What is the value of his cry?
He cries out "Help!" but compassion [רתי] is denied him.

ז Merit is yours, O my master;
Glory befits your divinity.
45   In all generations that span from Adam until now,
And from here and henceforth until the day of judgment,
Your glory shall be undiminished.
Toward the innocent and toward the guilty,
Toward these and toward those, you are compassionate.

50 א A day on which he is not praised—
Darkness engulfs anyone who walks in it;
He may have a lamp in his hand, but he cannot see.
A night in which he is not magnified—
He who sleeps does so in mighty distress;

11. Lit., "quail are gathered into heaps."
12. The final two lines of this stanza refer to the events of Num 11:31–34.
13. The root פשר has connotations of "to judge, explain, interpret"—all of which imbue the idea of self-harm with a sense of bafflement.
14. Lit., "face," with a connotation of partiality or expectation. Later in the poem (l. 70), Rodrigues Pereira translates the same Aramaic word as "cheek" (*SAP*, 470).

55 He who is led but leaves his leader,
He suffers unceasing blows.

ט We have strayed since the day we left you;
Our straying is easy to mend,
But we incline not toward repentance.

60 Moses, the master of the prophets,
Sent [word] and said to us in his writing:
"Return unto YHWH!" [Deut 30:2].[15]
Happy is the one who returns and finds his master!

י Days filled with suffering:
65 Such are the days of sinners!
For they each forgot the one who helped them,
And just as they left him, he left them
And gave them over to all kinds of punishments.
And every punishment that comes, it is he who beats them,
70 But they have no right to cry out, "Help!"

כ Indeed, fear lurks in the clearing,
Indeed, desolation within the towns.
For the good one has turned his face from us,
And if the merciful one will not help,
75 *And will not remember those who love him,*
Lo, fathers and sons
Will perish in [his] anger, for it is fierce.

ל The punishments do not frighten the sinner,
Nor do afflictions fill him with fear—
80 He pays no mind at all;
A rebel regards himself as rejected
And knows that all he has will be consigned to fire.
He turns to his money[16]
But knows that he will have no pleasure from it.

85 מ Death resembles the priest

---

15. Cited in Aramaic translation (but not that of the SamT). The text here reads ותחזור לסעד ה';
the SamT reads ותעזור ליד ה'. On the preposition סעד, see *DSA*, 601, and also the discussion in *RPH*,
138–39.

16. Taking אפריו as a form of חור ("money, silver"), but with a wickedly sharp pun on "ashes."

Giving a person bitter waters to drink.[17]
Woe to one whose sins are discovered;
Woe to all sinners.
For they will be in terrible distress;
90   The recompense with which they will be afflicted
Is a reward for all their transgressions.

ב   The soul stands, terrified,
And the living suffer terribly.
For the Good has turned his face from us,
95   *And if the merciful does not help*
And does not remember those who love him,
Let the sinners weep for themselves,
For they are in terrible distress.

ס   Signs—they inform [us]
100   That there is not in [this] generation, the one we are in,
A person untouched by sin.[18]
Fathers and sons,
Mothers and daughters,
Just as they joined together, all of them, in rebellion,[19]
105   So are they afflicted by punishment.

ה   Lo, because of our sins,
We, ourselves, are killers:
Killing those who are mute and those who speak,
Even innocent beasts,
110   Even children, free of transgression,
Even youths, children of the good.
They suffer for sins they did not commit.

פ   The time of disfavor [*fanuta*] is the source[20]
Of all that great affliction—
115   May it be cursed in every place!
The fruits of the womb are blocked
And the fruits of the land destroyed.

17. An allusion to Num 5, the trial of the suspected adulteress, who is compelled to drink bitter waters.
18. Lit., "who is not friends with sinners."
19. Lit., "and rebelled."
20. Lit., "it caused."

The mouth of punishment opens against us
To swallow up young and old.

120 צ Great despair that is in the world—
   O people, look and be afraid!
   Woe to us that we were unready to learn;
   Not from the earthquake[21] did we learn,
   Nor from the plague of locusts did we gain knowledge![22]
125 Let us at least fear the punishment of death
   Before the fountains of plenty cease flowing!

   ק Darkness engulfs us from above and below;
   Darkness suits those [far] reaches,[23]
   For his anger extends to every place.
130 The appearance of the luminaries changes,
   And the abyss withholds its waters;
   Wickedness can find no place to flee to,
   And so it turns upon itself.

   ר O merciful, O good,
135 Act charitably, as is your custom.
   We are unable to withstand your judgment;
   A tree's leaf makes a sinner tremble.
   So how can we withstand the judgment of the one who causes the
      world to tremble?
   Act charitably toward the guilty,
140 *Lest they be destroyed by punishments!*

   ש Your name is "merciful and gracious";
   Strip not your glory from us.
   For the living are naked,
   And were you not to cover them in your goodness,
145 Then they would perish in a blink,
   For they are like fragile grass
   And the storm of guilt is mighty.

   ת Let us utter praises and hymns.

21. See Amram Dare 22, l. 26.
22. Lit., "recite a teaching," parallel with "to learn" in the previous line.
23. Lit., "darkness suits them."

Before turning away from here
150   Toward the one who lasts[24] forever.
His power, freely given, grants us life,
But we freely incite his jealousy.
Whether he grants us life or death,
Both lie within his realm of greatness!

2 "God Who Shall Be Worshipped" (*SL*, 16–17; *RPH*, 146–53; *SAP* 439–40; *D*, 198–99)

In this acrostic, Marqe meditates on God's role as Creator and develops the inherent mystery of that divine power and prerogative. The poet, as is his custom, employs binaries to convey the sweep of creation (heaven and earth), as well as the enigma of the act (stressing the divine power to both reveal and conceal). All creation and all creatures bear witness to God's power and constitute an embodied act of praise, and no portion of the world—visible or invisible—exists beyond his care and presence. Everything is *of* him, but he exists beyond it all.

This sense of paradox undergirds much of the poem, and lends the composition a sense that it strives to articulate the ineffable, and that by not quite doing so it underscores God's majesty and otherness. Marqe juxtaposes God's intimate presence (he carries the world, touches his creatures with his mercy, feeds all mouths, and even suffers when people sin) with assertions of his radical transcendence. From silence is brought forth noise; from darkness, light; from muteness, speech. Throughout the poem flows a sense of slightly startled, wondrous love and adoration of the miracle of being created, of being able to grasp any of this mystery. Marqe returns repeatedly to the goodness of God and of creation, and while he acknowledges humanity's flaws—the final word is "repentance," which signals imperfection—he focuses on the potent synthesis of God's power and mercy. The ability to recognize the majesty of God's actions inspires the poet's praise.

One key concept here, developed more explicitly in later poems in this collection, is the idea of Torah as a kind of preexistent Logos. In the second stanza, Marqe depicts God as dwelling in "in the beginning" (l. 5)—that is, in Torah—and from within that space he spoke the world into being. And four stanzas from the end, the poet returns to that image, describing God's "dwelling place" (Torah; l. 73) as preexistent. The Torah, as Marqe develops in more detail in

---

24. The language here suggests ארך אפיים, i.e., "length of nose," with the meaning of "patient, forbearing."

other poems, provides the means by which the poet and his community understand God, his power, his compassion, and his demands.

> *Said on Sunday, on the first Sabbath of the month, and on festivals.*

ע   Maker of the world,
   God who shall be worshipped,
   God of the righteous,
   Master of the penitent,

5   ב   "In the beginning"[25] is the province
   Within which your goodness dwelled.
   In the silence you sowed
   Words, and life[26] arose.

ג   Your powers, lo, they are
10   The produce of your knowledge;
   Its foundation is revealed,[27]
   But its choicest part is concealed.

ד   The choicest part of the foundation was
   Selected by your hand for yourself;
15   The choicest parts among the hidden things
   Belong to YHWH our God.

א   The four quarters of the world
   Were established by your hand;
   Your great power carries
20   All of them, yet is not near them.

ו   And you, at the summit of the world,
   Higher than all the heights,
   Surveying all that lies below
   While staying steadfast[28] on high.

25   ז   Your proclamation yields creation,

25. Creation, but also the Torah.
26. Lit., "creatures."
27. I.e., the basic elements of creation can be discerned through the senses, but other aspects of true reality must be revealed to humanity.
28. The root of the participle ממן is אמן.

And your utterances, worlds.
The touch[29] of your mercy
Is the happiness of your servants.[30]

ה O mighty one, you whose divinity
30   Fills above and below,
Your riches in things concealed
Exceed in might what is revealed.

ט Happy are the souls
Of those who prostrate themselves;
35   Happy are the bodies
That bear the dread of you.

י O giver of life,
Let all greatness be ascribed unto you
Day and night;
40   [All] living beings give thanks to your name.

כ All mouths, [both] mute
and speaking, you feed;
Every mouth that possesses speech
Proclaims your praise.

45 ל From on high, on Mount Sinai,
You proclaimed that you are merciful [רחם]
Unto all generations,
That you are merciful and compassionate.

מ No one knows the dwelling place
50   Of your great divinity;
From the silence you brought forth
The world and all within it.

נ O unsleeping guardian,[31]
You are God forever,

29. The word here has connotations of physical proximity and trembling, with implications of
fearfulness and awe.
30. Or "those who worship you."
31. The image here echoes Ps 121:4: "Lo, the guardian of Israel neither slumbers nor sleeps."

55 Guardian of the covenant,
And trusted by those who love him.

ס The one who sustains, the one who lifts up,
The one who suffers[32] but is unharmed,
Forgive our sins,
60 Pardon us in your mercy!

א Remember the first ones
And forget not the last ones;
Those who serve you and those who love you,
You swore to them by yourself.

65 פ You who protected Isaac
From his father, Abraham,
Protect us, O our master,
From the hands of our foes!

צ O fashioner of children,
70 Gaze upon us in your mercy;
Deal justly with us,
For you are our master and our Creator.[33]

ק Creator of the dwelling place,
Preexistent is your divinity,
75 Your truth fills the world
And your goodness exceeds even that.

ר "The Merciful" is your name—
Upon us, have mercy!
May your mercy protect
80 The children of those who love you

ש Peace do you apportion;
The perfect do you seek.
[To you who are] completely perfect,[34]

---

32. Lit., "who bears with, tolerates."
33. Or "sustainer."
34. Brown translates as "giver of peace to the peaceful" (*D*, 199). The present translation follows Ben-Hayyim, *RPH*, 153, and *CAL*, s.v. *šlm*.

Let them give thanks and praise to you.

85 ת May you be praised forever,
    O God of the righteous;
    May you be exalted forever,
    Master of the repentant.

There is no God but the one!

3 "You Are Our God (1)" (*SL*, 17–18; *RPH*, 154–59; *D*, 199–201)

Marqe here meditates on God as Creator, and on the consequences of this for God's human creatures. For Marqe, the simple existence of the world constitutes a reason to praise God: creation exists to testify to God's glory. Prayer, for Marqe, is the most natural response to the miracle of being alive, whether one is a mere mortal or an angelic being. Even the most wondrous beings are God's creations, and God's magnificence outshines anything of his own making.

And yet, God did not create the world merely in order to receive the thanksgiving prayers of his creations; he loves life, he loves the living, and he loves the world. God is, the poet assures his listeners, near to those who call out to him, though they cannot see him. When the world suffers, God opens his treasury and dispenses relief. And in a stanza that seems to poetically retell the Genesis account of the creation of the heavens—"Your breath filled the expanse / Over the world you established"—the poet adds an evocative detail: "You sent dreams / To console those who love you" (ll. 29–32). It is not clear whether the poet has a specific episode in mind (the stories of Joseph, for example) or something more general and existential. God's visions become reality—he speaks and they exist—but the human gift of dreaming is a kind of echo of this power.

Indeed, while this poem is addressed exclusively to the deity, its words clearly respond to the hopes and concerns of the human congregation. While occasionally acknowledging the existence of powers beyond the human realm—angels rush about on missions, and God's power binds the invisible and imperceptible as well as the visible and tangible—the poet's focus is on the relationship between God and the community of the faithful. The poem's words overtly remind God of humanity's dependence on his beneficence and implicitly reassure the congregation of divine providence and care. God deserves praise and rewards it, and that is precisely what this poem supplies: an expression of awareness of gifts received and blessings granted. If such words are what God desires, Marqe here ensures that his community offers them up.

Said on Monday, on the first Sabbath of the month, and on festivals.

א   You are our God
    And the God of our fathers,
    The God of Abraham
    And of Isaac and of Jacob.

5 ב   Above and below,
    Your power is great and commanding;
    Among the invisible and the visible,
    You are a merciful God.

 ג   The magnitude of your might—
10   Who can understand or know [it]?
    The Almighty and the awesome one,
    Over all the generations of the world—

 ד   [You] who preceded the world,
    And [who] established it magnificently,
15   So that it might testify of you, of your greatness.
    For you are God forever.

 ה   Where is there a reliable one as good
    And as close as you?
    Or where are there creations
20   Aside from what you created?[35]

 ו   And you, in your greatness,
    Are an unchanging God,
    And whocvcr prays to aught but you
    Seeks but does not find.

25 ז   Righteousness is yours;
    The righteous are your lovers.
    At no time or moment
    Do we lack your goodness.

35. The poet here puns on the dual meaning of the root קנׂי, "to create" but also "to possess." God possesses all because God created all.

ע Your breath filled[36] the expanse
30   Over the world you established;
    You sent dreams
    To console those who love you.

ט Happy is the world
    That you are its master and leader;
35   Your commandments are good,
    And happy are their keepers!

י Singular one, you preceded
    The world you sustain;
    O giver of gifts,
40   [Our] thanks to you, on account of your greatness!

כ You see all,
    And nothing is unseen by you;
    All your works are good,
    O my master, and you are better than they!

45 ל Eternal is your mercy,
    Eternal is your compassion.
    We worship your magnificence,
    For you exalt those who worship you.

מ Trusting are we,
50   For you are our God, and we are happy;
    We owe you our praise,
    For all our gifts come from you.[37]

נ Leader of the world,
    The path follows you;
55   Guardian of life,
    Unto your goodness does one draw near.

ס Abundant is your goodness;
    Your lovers abound;
    Abundant are

---

36. Lit., "inflated," from the root נפש. The image here is of God creating the heavenly expanse by exhaling, as if filling a balloon.

37. Lit., "from us to you is praise / and from you to us is a gift."

60   Your wonders: you shall be praised!

ע   Your many works
        Are subservient to you;
        Your servants reign,
        In service to you, [over] all magnificence.

65 פ   You opened your treasury,
        And the world felt relief;
        Mouths praise you
        Unendingly.

 צ   We need you,
70   [both] standing ones and mortals;[38]
        Prayers, in faithfulness,
        To your name shall be said.

ק   In the presence of your holiness
        We cry out: "O God Most High!"
75   You are close to your worshippers,
        Though unseen by them.

ר   Beginning without end
        Are your praises;
        O lover of all,
80   Life is what you love.

ש   Your name is fearsome,
        For you are glorious and awesome;
        Your messengers rush about,
        Your order[s] in hand.

85 ת   May you be praised forever,
        For all praise belongs to you;
        May you be blessed forever,
        For you are the one who blesses the world.

There is no God but the one!

---

38. The underlying text (קעימין ומאתין) is a merism. It seems to describe angels and humans but could also be translated "the living and the dead," as Ben-Hayyim does (*RPH*, 158); Brown renders it, "We need Thee in life and in death" (*D*, 201).

4 "You Are Our God (2)" (*SL*, 18–19; *RPH*, 159–65; *D*, 201–3)

This poem highlights a key dynamic in the relationship between God and his people: the people depend entirely on God—the phrase "If it pleases you" is repeated several times—and in return they attest to God's oneness. God is not said to need people in the way that people need him, but nonetheless, the rhetorical questions at the midpoint of the poem—"Who can praise you / As befits your works? / Who can exalt you / As befits your wonders?" (ll. 49–52)—suggest both a negative answer (it is impossible, no one can) and a positive response (the present community can certainly try). Similarly, the rhetorical question "Who can recount what you are?" (l. 54) elicits implicit answers that simultaneously assent to the impossibility of such an achievement and acknowledge that the current composition is nothing if not an attempt to do so.

Marqe here delights in God's awesomeness and otherness. There is an optimism and confidence in the poem, a sense of delight and wonder that, for all of God's uniqueness and power, he has chosen to attend to this community. Almost every line speaks to God directly as "you," and while the poet articulates a sense of complete dependency on God—"our lives are yours" (l. 8)—there is no anxiety or fearfulness in this poem. This is a poem of full-throated praise of God that assumes with a deep and secure confidence that the human voice is not only heard but listened for. God works wonders, but without the congregation, there would be no one to bear witness.

> *Said on Monday and on the first Sabbath of the month and on festivals.*

א   You are our God
     And the God of our fathers,
     Our exalted God,
     Mighty and awesome!

5   ב   Through your goodness the world came into being,
         And by your might is it ordered.
         We are at your mercy;
         Our lives are yours.

     ג   May your great power
10   Have mercy on us;
         What is revealed and what is concealed
         Are great things [coming] from your goodness.

ד   The awesome one, the praised one,
    Working wonders,
15 For you are, throughout the day,
    Praised by your creations.

ה   If it pleases you—
    You are beneficent and merciful;
    And if it pleases you—
20 Triumph belongs to you.

ו   And however it pleases you,
    You honor those who love you,
    And when it pleases you,
    You triumph over your foes.

25 ז The touch of your praise[39]
    Is the healing of our lives;
    The rush of your compassion
    uplifts our bodies.

ח   Your strength exceeds any other's strengths,
30 And all strength comes from your strength;
    Our strength would be weak and puny,
    Except that you are merciful.

ט   The whole world is happy
    That you proclaimed that you are merciful;
35 The generations are happy
    That you are merciful and compassionate.

י   Your right hand bears
    All that is above and below;
    Your oath [which you swore] to our fathers
40 You will not nullify for their sons.

כ   All proclaim unto you
    That your mercy is without end;

---

39. Tal translates as "The motion of your glory" (*DSA*, 228, s.v. זוזע), while Brown has "The elation (evoked) in praising Thee" (*D*, 202).

All tremble before you,
Though no eye sees you.

45 ל Above, you have no companion,
And moreover, below, how much the more so are you [alone];
Forever you stand
In the dignity[40] of your kingdom.

 מ Who can praise you
50 As befits your works?
Who can exalt you
As befits your wonders?

נ O awesome one, O wondrous one,
Who can recount what you are?
55 You remember, and do not forget,
The covenants of those who love you.

ס Your forgiveness extends,
In the end, to all sinners,
Forgiving and doing no harm,
60 So that penitents may come back.

ע You who seek out[41] our faces,
Gaze down upon us and free us!
You see us and show [us]
That you are merciful and compassionate.

65 פ You are present and can be found
By anyone who seeks you in truth;
Free all who worship you,
Who seek you in devotion.

צ We need you,
70 And all the world with us:
The need of the generations
Is for your eternal sovereignty.

---

40. Lit., "rank, level."
41. Lit., "see for."

ק You proclaimed that you are merciful,
    And this [mercy] shall be a cure for the generations;
75 O proclaimer of mercy,
    Forget not your proclamation!

ר "The Merciful" is your name
    Before "Let there be . . ."[42] and for how long?
    Those who love you[43] bear witness
80 That you do not oppress your creatures.

ש Your name is "The Merciful,"
    And all things testify that you are so.
    [Ours is] the greatest witness:
    There is no God but the one!

85 ת May we recount your praises,
    May we be steadfast in great honor,
    May we return to you,
    And then nothing may harm us.

There is no God but the one!

5 "It Is Incumbent upon Us" (*SL*, 19–20; *RPH*, 166–71; *D*, 204–5)

In this poem, Marqe revisits two of his favored themes: God's majesty and power, as revealed through his work as Creator, and the ungrateful, baffling sinfulness of humanity, despite knowledge of God's beneficence. Two elements of this conventional Marqan theology stand out in this poem, however: his evocative use of the image of "the Deeps"—the primordial waters of the creation narrative that opens Genesis, echoing creation-by-combat narratives of Mesopotamian lore (תהום, "Deep," is cognate with the sea god Tiamat)—and his brief, allusive historical sketch as the poem ends.

At the center of the poem (stanza 13, constituting the letter מ in the acrostic), the poet expands on God's actions in Gen 1:6–11, the separation of primordial waters into those above the firmament of heaven (understood to be a vault that keeps the upper waters at bay) and those beneath (including groundwater, upon which the dry land was thought to float, as well as the sea):

42. I.e., since the creation story of Gen 1.
43. Or "your mercies."

The waters of the Deep he crushed,
While the waters of the Firmament he lifted;
He breathed an expanse between them,
A pathway for those who love him. (ll. 49–52)

The language here recalls the familiar ancient Near Eastern narratives of theo-
machy in which creation is staged as a battle between gods. God conquers "the
Deep" (תהום) and splits it into the waters that are above and below the dry land.
Indeed, the language here echoes a source from the Jewish Bible: "Are you not
he who dried Sea [ים], the waters of the great Deep [מי תהום רבה]; who made
the depths of Sea [ים] a way for the rescued to pass through?" (Isa 51:10). Just
as God controlled the primordial waters at the time of creation, he parted them
when Israel passed through the Sea of Reeds. The creation narrative, as Marqe
tells it here, anticipates the redemption of Israel: dry land constitutes the pathway between the waters upon which God's beloved tread. Exodus 15 becomes
an implicit intertext for Marqe's reading of Gen 1. The rebellion of humanity
against God's powerful beneficence (ll. 16 and 32) anticipates the rebellions of
Israel in the wilderness, as well as the failures of Marqe's own community in
his day.

The idea that the past anticipates the present finds somewhat more explicit
articulation in the final stanzas of the poem. Here Marqe refers to the prayer of
Adam, who appealed to God and was forgiven; to Jacob, who bested an angel;
and to Balaam, whose curse became a blessing. In each instance, a transgression—real or potential—was averted and transformed. Adam's sin led to the
invention of forgiveness, Jacob's struggle yielded not only victory but blessing,
and Balaam's slander turned to prophetic praise. The trajectory—from the first
human being, to a patriarch, to the wilderness generation—suggests that the
final two stanzas (ll. 81–88), whose time frames are not specified, speak directly
to the present community. The images of triumph and penitence that color these
final stanzas evoke the ancestral stories even as they describe the present and
future (the time of favor). The imagery of the *Urzeit* resonates with the imagined
experience of the *Endzeit*.

*Said on Monday, on the second Sabbath of the month, and on
festivals.*

ה It is incumbent upon us to ascribe praise
To the master of the world;[44]

---

44. The Aramaic of these opening two lines (הב לן משבחה / למרה דעלמה) is an approximate
equivalent of the Hebrew opening of the prayer known as the *Aleinu* (עלינו לשבח לאדון הכל); see the
introduction to Marqe 6, below.

We are greatly obligated
To speak praises unto him

5 ב By the mouth with which he created,
With the words that he established;
According to a man's labors
Does he grant him his reward.

 ג He revealed a lovely world
10 From out of nothingness,
And he lit within it luminaries
That shall never be extinguished.

 ד Fearsome one, praised one,
Worker of wonders,
15 Before whom all things tremble,
Yet dust[45] rebels against him.

 ה He was and he shall be,
And his name is eternal,
He who was shall be,
20 And who can stand against him?

 ו Ascribe greatness to our God!
For this [purpose] have we come into being,
And it is incumbent upon us to say of him
That the [earth's] fullness is his on account, of his greatness.

25 ז He who feeds every mouth
Shall be praised by every mouth.
He feeds us and sustains our lives;
Let us ascribe his praises!

 א Dread of him and fear of him
30 Alarms the world,
And this is the great shame:
That dust rebels against him.

 ט We have strayed and we have sinned;
It is time for us to return!

45. I.e., humans.

35   There is no shame in a child
      Returning to[46] his teacher.

 ׳   He has given us writings
      Containing life;[47]
      If we use the writings [well],
40   He has given us life.

 כ   How long will he testify against us?
      Until punishment comes?
      He who loves us abundantly
      Dismisses evidence against us.

45 ל Hearts and mouths
      The great good one seeks;
      [When] the two of them are joined in fear,
      The tabernacle is revealed.

 מ   The waters of the Deep he crushed,
50   While the waters of the firmament he lifted;
      He breathed an expanse between them,[48]
      A pathway for those who love him.

 נ   Moses, the great prophet,
      Taught us in his writing,
55   That he accepts sinners
      If they abandon their sinful ways.

 ס   Endure [your] fear of him
      And recall his greatness!
      To anyone who recalls him with honor
60   He grants his reward.

 ע   He sees and knows
      What is concealed within every heart;
      He seeks out goodness revealed,
      He who understands the unseen.

46. Lit., "turning back" (הפך), akin to the idea of *teshuvah* (repentance).
47. Lit., "life is within them."
48. This idiom recalls that in Marqe 3, l. 29.

65 ‏פ‎ He opened the mouth of the Deep
And brought forth for us the waters of life;
He shut the mouth of the serpent,[49]
For it destroys life.

‏צ‎ Cry out in fear
70   And recall his greatness;
Adam cried out in this way,
And he was forgiven by his master.

‏ק‎ He stood with Jacob
At the Jabbok's ford,
75   And he granted him victory over the messenger
And gave him his blessing.

‏ר‎ Regarding the chief of all slanderers,
Balaam, son of Beor,
He changed his utterance[50] to blessings,
80   And he blessed Israel.

‏י‎ YHWH[51] the great, the singular one,
He who triumphs in every battle,
His lovers praise him;
Within every battle, they triumph.

85 ‏ת‎ They are the penitents,
Those whom he grants triumph in battle;
They reveal the time of favor
And serve their God.

There is no God but the one!

49. The underlying term is ‏נחש‎; this may refer to the serpent of Gen 3, but given this specific context, it may also be conflated with the ‏תנינים‎, the great sea serpents of ancient Near Eastern lore (see Gen 1:21).

50. Lit., "mouth." See Num 22–24.

51. The written text has the Tetragram, but presumably "the Name" (‏שמא‎) was pronounced here instead. Indeed, the letter shin (‏ש‎) is expected here in the acrostic, but I have labeled the stanza with a *yod* (‏י‎), as in *RPH*, 170. This usage of the Tetragram where one would expect "the Name" occurs in Marqe 16, l. 152, as well.

6 "Render Praise unto Him" (*SL*, 20–21; *RPH*, 171–76; *D*, 206–7)

This poem resonates to a striking degree with the familiar Hebrew prayer of rabbinic Judaism known as the *Aleinu* (usually dated to around the fourth century
CE, or perhaps a bit earlier—the same period as Marqe). It twice uses phrases
reminiscent of the Jewish prayer—indeed, Ben-Hayyim's Hebrew translation
makes the resonance explicit: first in the opening lines ("Render praise unto
him, / To the one who is accustomed to praise") and again at the beginning of
the sixth stanza ("Let us render greatness to our God / With a word that befits
him"; ll. 21–22). These are not, to be sure, direct "translations" or borrowings
of Jewish and Hebrew liturgical language, but the affinity in sentiment and
phrasing is unmistakable. Praise of God is not only an instinctive response to
the wonder of God's actions in history or an impulsive reply to recognition of
the majesty of his creation; it is a duty. And it is a duty that is fulfilled even as
the imperative itself is articulated.

It is not simply the repetition of the obligation to pray, however, that links
this poem to the *Aleinu*; it is the issuing of that command in the context of God's
status as both "master of all" (in Hebrew, אדון הכל) and Creator (in Hebrew,
יוצר בראשית). The early stanzas of the poem recapitulate the events of Gen 1
(a favored theme of Marqe), treating God's creative agency as a manifestation
of his lordship. Much of this hymn's imagery—including the association of God
with luminescence—draws on that formative scriptural chapter.

Furthermore, while the *Aleinu* focuses on Israel's chosenness and draws a
sharp contrast between the proper worship of Jews and the improper worship of
the gentile nations, Marqe focuses primarily on the obligation of his community
to praise God. And yet, Marqe does note that "Superior to [other] nations / Have
you appointed us" (ll. 63–64). He does not dwell on the improper worship of the
nations but rather on the loftiness of the people chosen by the lofty one.

Finally, just as the *Aleinu* repeatedly stresses God's oneness and ends with
the proclamation of God's unity—"on that day, YHWH will be one and his name
will be one" (Zech 14:9 in the Jewish Bible)—this poem likewise stresses God's
singularity and, in particular, his varied names. All the diversity of human perceptions of God, and all the variety of God's manifestations in the heavens and
upon the earth, cannot obscure his radical, mysterious oneness. It is this name
that, as Marqe writes, "bears / All that is above and below" (ll. 83–84).

The *Aleinu* prayer contained within it seeds of a kind of early, latent mysticism, one rooted in speculation on God as Creator and cosmic power, manifested through divine names.[52] This poem, while distinctive from the Jewish

---

52. See Swartz, "*Alay le-shabbeaḥ*."

liturgical work in both language and themes, nonetheless offers striking echoes
of it, evidence of a shared fascination and perhaps even an attenuated kinship.

> *Said on Tuesday, on the second Sabbath of the month, and on
> festivals.*

ה Render praise unto him,
To the one who is accustomed to praise;
Those whom he fashioned—
Who [but they] could praise him?

5 ב He created the heavens and earth,
Before aught else he brought forth.
In his great wisdom
He established the heights and the depths.

ג He revealed the dry land
10 From the muck[53] of "**wilderness and waste**" [Gen 1:2];
Laud his might,
He who is master of his works!

ד For these are [his] creations,
Exceedingly honored;
15 The choicest of his "words":[54]
Light that goes forth to illumine.

ה Wherever he kindles light,
May he be praised by every mouth;
Wherever he spreads out darkness
20 Let hearts offer him thanks.

ו And let us render greatness to our God
With a word that befits him—
But who is able to speak of him
As befits his might?

25 ז An appointed time is propitious
For praising him, for he is a great God;

53. Lit., "waters."
54. I.e., the first thing "called" into existence on the first day of creation.

O feeder of the living,
To you all the living offer thanks.

ח   Eternal life is yours,
30   And you need nothing.
      You lower yourself to be praised
      By ephemeral mouths.

ט   Good is he who is proper,
      Who praises him, for God is great;
35   Happy is he who awakens and rises early
      According to the will of his master.

י   O singular one, you endure;
      To you are thanks owed, in keeping with your greatness,
      O giver and provider
40   Of the needs of ephemeral mortals.

כ   You see all,
      O God, in [your] heavenly abode;
      Every body and soul
      Your might freely sustains.

45 ל   Your might cannot refuse
      The prayer of a pure heart,
      And there is no rejecting the worship
      Of the person who is devoted to you.

מ   O revealer of all hidden things,
50   And knower of all concealed things,
      Who is able to conceal
      Anything from your dominion?

נ   O enlightener, whose light
      Fills all the world;
55   O enlightener, from whose goodness
      All light derives!

ס   Many are those who transgress against you,
      But by the barest minimum are you appeased;
      No harm can come

60   To one who worships you devotedly.

א   "God Most High" is your name,
     "Almighty God," "**I am**."
     Superior to [other] nations
     Have you appointed us.

65 פ Many wonders
     You set in motion for us;
     Pharaoh and his troops[55]
     You sank into the Sea of Reeds.

צ   It is necessary for us to do
70   Repentance and to pray unto you:
     Moses prayed to you,
     And the six hundred thousand [with him].

ק   O eternal one, whose covenants
     Endure forever,
75   Your covenants with our ancestors
     Are a covenant that cannot be nullified.

ר   "The one who is far from wrath, completely,"[56]
     Wrote Moses for the generations;
     Have mercy on us,
80   For your name is "The Merciful One."

ש   Your name is a great truth,
     And trustworthy, O our master;
     Your name, O God, bears
     All that is above and below

85 ת May your greatness be repeated
     At all times;
     May you be praised by every mouth,
     By all the generations of the world.

     There is no God but the one!

---

55. From the Greek ὄχλος; see *DSA*, 29, s.v. אכלס.
56. An allusion to SamT's rendering of Exod 34:6.

7 "You Are the Merciful One" (*SL*, 21–22; *RPH*, 176–82; *D*, 208–9)

Most of this poem constitutes praise directed at the deity. With only a few
exceptions, God is consistently addressed directly as "you" rather than indirectly as "he." When the poet speaks of his human community, he generally
does so indirectly, referring to them rather impersonally in terms of their
actions: they bear witness, they worship, they sin. To be sure, in some cases
Marqe speaks of God rather than to him, and at times he stands with his people
("we") rather than at a remove (when he speaks to them as "you"). Primarily,
however, the poet's audience is God, and the congregation eavesdrops on his
monologue.

In the latter part of the hymn, however, the poet breaks through the fourth
wall of his conceit. He speaks directly to his congregation:

> Open your mouths
> And utter praises unto him;
> He opens his treasury
> And replenishes all the world,
> Gazing down from the abode.
> All we need comes from him;
> His gaze is one of mercy,
> Giving life to the world. (ll. 65–72)

First Marqe speaks to his community using imperatives, compelling them to
join him in praising God. The presence of the community, implicit earlier in
the hymn, is here foregrounded. In the next stanza, the poet makes clear that
he aligns himself with his community—they are "we" rather than "you." If the
majority of the poem has been oriented toward God, with the poet turning his
eyes upward, here he leads his congregation's gaze upward as well, so that they
may imagine themselves sharing a divine perspective, as if they were looking
at the human world with God. The poet envisions the community envisioning
God envisioning the community.

In the lines before his congregational address, the poet pleads with God to
pity his people for the sake of their ancestors and by virtue of their suffering;
four imperatives structure the stanza. He directs God's gaze downward:

> Remember the ancestors
> And rescue their children!
> See how they are oppressed,
> And do not harass them! (ll. 61–64)

God is obviously Marqe's audience here. Each line implores the deity to act, while the people are adduced indirectly, as "they" and "them." In the stanzas after his congregational aside, however, the poet's perspective changes. In the next stanzas of the poem the poet resumes his direct address of God, but now the people are directly present as well. Marqe asks God to "Stand now with us … / And redeem us" (ll. 75–76), and while he acknowledges that "the heights and the depths are yours" (l. 79), he also reminds God that it is "we" who "are within your dominion" (l. 80). Only in the final two stanzas (ll. 81–88) do the people fade away again, as the poet's focus returns, under an irresistible impulse, entirely toward God.

> *Said on Tuesday, on the second Sabbath of the month, and on festivals.*

א   You are the merciful one
    Whose mercy is endless;
    Look upon us and rescue us,
    For such is your way![57]

5   ב   "In the beginning" is in your right hand,
    And "the day of judgment" you possess.[58]
    Your creations bear witness:
    There is no God but you!

ג   The revealed and concealed
10   Grow great out of your goodness;
    The [human] body trembles
    At the mention of your dominion.

ד   True is the judge,
    He who shows no favor;
15   He judges kings,
    And no one offers objections.[59]

ה   Where in the world
    Is there [another] God like you?

57. Lit., "faithfulness," but in the sense of "habit, custom, predictable way of behaving."
58. These lines employ time—*Urzeit* and *Endzeit*—as bookends.
59. Lit., "and no one afterward objects."

Or where can there be found
20   Worship like yours?

ו   And can any [mortal] king
Stand against you?
For you stand firm and endure,
While we are ephemeral dust.

25 ז   Righteousness is yours,
While we are sinners;
You rescue the righteous
And have compassion on sinners.

ח   You are exceedingly mighty,[60]
30   Such that no knowledge can express it;
O singular God,
Rescue us in your mercy!

ט   Happy are we, forever,
That you are our God!
35   Happy is the mouth that offers
Praise to your name!

י   May he be praised forever,
The king who[se reign] never ceases!
May praises be uttered unto you,
40   For you are worthy of even more than this![61]

כ   The whole world rejoices
At the sound of your praise;
All four corners of the world
Tremble at your might.

45 ל   High above the world
With all beneath your hand,
Above and below
Your dominion is over all.

---

60. Lit., "your might is exceedingly mighty."
61. Lit., "for you are filled by more than this." Brown translates it, "Thou art the fullness and more so" (*D*, 208).

מ From you the world comes,
50   And to your hand does it return,
Rescued by your splendor
At a word from you.

נ You are greatly expansive,[62]
Meeting the needs of all;[63]
55   Your radiance shines
At a word from you.

ס O forgiving one, O forbearing one,
Forgive our sins!
Our transgressions are many,
60   But you are merciful.

ה Remember the ancestors
And rescue their children!
See how they are oppressed,
And do not harass them!

65 פ *Open your mouths*
And utter praises unto him;
He opens his treasury
And replenishes all the world,

צ *Gazing down from the abode.*
70   *All we need comes from him;*
His gaze is one of mercy,
Giving life to the world.

ק The first, who stood
Over the wellspring of silence,
75   Stand now with us, O our master,
And redeem us from your wrath.

ר "The merciful one" is your name,

---

62. Lit., "your expanses [or: respites] are great." The root נפש connotes breath and breathing room, the promise of restoration and revivification. By extension, the idea of "expansiveness" can connote forgiveness and redemption.

63. Brown translates these two lines, "Thy redemptions are many / necessary for all who are in need (of them)" (*D*, 209).

And greatness befits you.
The heights and the depths are yours,
80   And we are within your dominion.

ש   Your name is honored and awesome,
Such that no knowledge can express it;
Send redemption to your servants,
And forget not your covenant.

85   ת   Return and have mercy,
For you are merciful and compassionate;
The repentant come,
Desiring your great divinity.

There is no God but the one!

8 "Happy Are We" (*SL*, 22–23; *RPH*, 182–87; *D*, 210–12)

Thematically and theologically, this hymn is conventional for Marqe: it stresses
God's nature as Creator and redeemer, and it underscores the imperative for
humans to revere God and the consequences of their failure to do so. What
is particularly evident in this poem is a rich, if subtle, intertextuality. In other
poems, we see how Marqe weaves together two creation narratives: Gen 1 (the
creation of the world) and Exod 19 (the creation of Israel). The themes of creation and revelation from those chapters permeate much of Marqe's writing and
can be discerned in this hymn. But here we also find potent, recurring allusions
to two other passages from the Torah: Exod 15 (the Song at the Sea) and Deut
6:4–5 ("Hear, O Israel," the passage known in Jewish liturgy as the Shema).
The poem's references to the earth trembling and the parting of the sea and the
quotation of "Who is like you?" all resonate with Exod 15 (and also with the
psalms known to the rabbis as the Egyptian Hallel, Pss 113–18, which are not
included in the Samaritan canon). The references to the imperative to hearken
to and love God—joining together "strength, soul, and flesh"—in turn echo
the command "Hear, O Israel! you shall love YHWH, your God, with all your
heart [i.e., mind], with all your soul, and with all your substance" (Deut 6:4–5).

These allusions are subtle, far less overt than the kinds of intertextuality one
encounters in the *piyyutim* of Marqe's Jewish contemporaries, such as Yose
ben Yose.[64] Writing in Hebrew, Yose quotes scripture directly and deploys full

---

64. See Mirsky, *Yosse ben Yosse*.

phrases, either intact or in modified but recognizable form. Marqe's engagement with scripture is less transparent (particularly given the language gap between the Hebrew Torah and his Aramaic poetry, with the SamT as a possible mediator), and his canon more narrowly defined. The Samaritan Bible consists only of the Pentateuch, which limits the quantity of sacred text at his disposal. At the same time, ideas and phrases known from sources not canonical within Samaritan tradition (e.g., the Prophets and Writings of the Hebrew Bible, the Christian New Testament, and even rabbinic writings) were nonetheless known to him. In this hymn, Marqe draws his intertexts from the Torah, but the prominence of Exod 15 and the Shema in Jewish liturgy suggests a point of cultural sympathy between the two communities—a shared reverence for two particular passages in a foundational text.

> *Said on Wednesday, on the third Sabbath of the month, and on festivals.*

א   You are the Creator
Of the world, and happy are we;
You bring forth whatever you wish
From your creative imagination.[65]

5 ב   In you we trust,
For in every place you triumph;
In you the righteous of the world
Place their trust.

ג   The righteous offer praise to you,
10   And they become [your] praise;
You reveal your goodness to them
In every place.

ד   Indeed, this is the prayer
For sustaining life,
15   For it arises, hidden,
Before the discerner of hidden things.

ה   Where is there a god who rescues
His worshippers, except for you?
Who is able to redeem

---

65. Lit., "from the vision of your knowledge."

20   The world, aside from you?

ו   Woe to him who sees your works
        And fails to praise you;
        Woe to your foes
        Who come, provoking your anger.

25 ז   A trembling: [they] hear you
        But none can describe you;
        You rattled[66] your dominion
        For the sake of those who love you.

ח   Strength, soul, and flesh
30   Join together in their love of you [cf. Deut 6:4–5];
        You nourish the living
        With your word.

ט   Good are your commandments,
        Good the world that you created;
35   Your goodness is sustained
        By those who fulfill your commandments.

י   You parted the sea for your servants
        That they could pass through its midst;
        Israel praises you
40   From the midst of all the nations.

כ   Let every mouth possessing speech
        Proclaim praises unto you;
        Any greatness and dominion
        Is exceeded by your great glory.

45 ל   Unto you do we offer praise,
        Saying: "Who is like you?" [Exod 15:11].[67]
        To you is it fitting it offer praise,
        Night and day.

מ   From the depths to the heights,

66. I.e., God makes creation tremble on account of his redemption of Israel.
67. Cited in Aramaic translation.

50　　Our praises rise unto you;
　　　From the heights to the depths,
　　　All honor is yours.

ב　We offer thanks unto you forever,
　　For you are our God;
55　　We trust in your might,
　　　For no other is as trustworthy as you.

ס　Those who worship you are honored,
　　For all honor comes from you.
　　Those who bear witness to you endure,
60　　With all the generations to come.

ע　The wellsprings of the deep
　　You made flow before the assembly;
　　You made the cloud
　　To shade them.

פ　You lifted to the summit of the mountain,
65　　The mouth of the deep;[68]
　　　Mouths and hearts
　　　Will praise your kingship.

צ　The cry of the oppressed
70　　You heard, and you rescued them;
　　　Receive our appeal,
　　　For thus is your way.

ק　The voice of the shofar
　　You made heard, for the sake of your servants;
75　　Standing ones and mortals[69]
　　　You made tremble on their account.

ר　The chief of all gods are you,
　　And thus you bear witness[70] to your greatness;

---

68. The order of the first two lines of this stanza has been reversed for the sake of clarity.

69. The underlying text here is קעימין ומאתין, which as indicated above (n. 38) could also be translated as "the living and the dead."

70. The translation follows Ben-Hayyim (*RPH*, 187); alternatively, it could be translated, "and thus they (the other deities) bear witness to you."

O merciful one, O good one,
80   Gaze upon us and rescue us!

ש Your name is fearsome,[71]
And happy is he whom you protect;
Your dominion gives life
To those above and below.[72]

85 ת You seek the penitent
So that you may give them the world;
Turn back to us
And forgive our sins!

There is no God but the one!

9 "God Is the First" (*SL*, 23–24; *RPH*, 188–93; *D*, 212–13)

In this poem, Marqe positions his congregation not as immediate participants in a theological drama but as intimate witnesses to their own history. The past—specifically the Sinai event—is presented with terse and vivid immediacy.

The hymn sharply juxtaposes two key events from scriptural history: God's creation of the world and his revelation of Torah. The two events become facets of the same divine act. In each case, a transcendent God, high in his heavenly dwelling, transforms a radical silence into something tangible—the world and the Torah. Both creation and revelation are depicted as the transformation of something invisible and immaterial into something visible and concrete. The creation of the world in essence anticipates or foreshadows the revelation of Torah. Scripture contains Eden within it.

Structuring the poem is a series of pairs: concealed–revealed, unseen–seen, above–below, angelic–mortal, and possibly even living–dead. The events of creation saw the fashioning of both humans and angels, and at Sinai the heavenly host itself was transformed from invisible to visible. In short, Sinai is a moment when various binaries collapsed: the unseen was seen, the still moved (mountains, "standing ones," the dead), the hidden became manifest, and mortals and angels shared a singular moment. Presiding over this transformative

71. Or "Fearsome" may be understood as one of God's names, as in "Fear of Isaac" (פחד יצחק) in Gen 31:42.
72. I.e., angels and mortals.

event, however, is a singular God—a being untouched and untroubled by binaries. In the final stanza, Marqe deftly summarizes his vision:

> They trembled there,
> Standing ones and mortals,
> As constantly he proclaimed
> The words that were (written) upon them:
> *There is no God but the one!*

In the collapse of multiple binaries—as the worlds above and below come together, as God reveals the concealed words—God manifests his radical singularity. The liturgical proclamation of God's oneness can be heard as a synopsis of the Torah, the lesson of both creation and revelation.

> *Said on Wednesday, on the third Sabbath of the month, and on festivals.*

א   God is the first;
    He preceded the world;
    It is God who began the world
    And concluded [creation] with "Very good!" [Gen 1:31].

5   ב   In the supernal abode
    He is God forever,
    In the holy abode,
    The place he set aside for himself.

ג   His[73] power is more concealed
10   Than all the [other] powers;
    Power went forth
    On the day that he proclaimed his name.[74]

ד   For he is the mighty one who stands
    Over the wellspring of the silence,
15   He who is destined to say
    "I, I am He!" [Deut 32:39].

---

73. The text says "your might," which would be the only instance where God is directly addressed in this hymn; the translation emends the original for consistency.

74. A reference to Exod 3:14 or Exod 20:2 (and similar phrases, e.g., Deut 5:6).

א His divinity is great;
  None other possesses a portion of it.
  His divinity is great;
20   It fills the world.

ו Woe to the one who does not believe
  In his great power;
  Woe to the one who does not bear witness:
  There is no God but the one!

25 ז When he proclaimed his name,
  The world trembled,
  When he proclaimed and said:
  "You shall have no other gods!" [Exod 20:3].

ח Strength-angels and creature-angels[75]
30   Were assembled there
  When the incomparable God
  Descended to reveal his name.

ט He crowned Mount Sinai
  With cloud and with glory;
35   The mountain trembled mightily
  Out of great fear of him.

י That great voice,
  Never to be repeated—
  How fitting to hear it
40   Coming forth from the flame.

כ All the powers[76] that had been concealed
  Went forth revealed,[77]
  When God proclaimed:

---

75. The underlying Aramaic is חילין ובוראין. Brown translates as "Angels and mortals" (D, 212).
See Ninna I, l. 79, where the same pairing occurs. Depending on how the phrase is understood, the
scope of the phrase is either horizontal or vertical: the poet either evokes and amplifies the scope of
the heavenly hosts, as God's retinue accompanies God to participate in the theophany (horizontal),
or alternatively he stresses the parity between heaven and earth (heavenly hosts and terrestrial
crowd) at that same moment (vertical).
76. Angelic hypostases.
77. Lit., "went forth as revealed things"—i.e., the invisible became visible. Marqe here connects
the content of revelation to the angelic realm.

"I am YHWH, your God" [Exod 20:2].

45 ל   Within two tablets
        He wrote the Ten Words;
        He gave them to Moses:
        Life for generations

      מ   A great vision
50   Were they, the two tablets,
          Pillars engraved
          By the finger of consuming fire.[78]

      נ   Radiant were they,[79]
          Like lightning flashing forth;
55   The awesome one[80] wrote them
          With his own finger.

      ס   Long were they hidden away
          Within the heart of the fire;
          Long did Moses pray
60   Before he received them.

      ע   [It is] an Eden, extending life
          To those who drink from it—
          An Eden that is rooted
          In eternal life.

65 פ   The wellspring of concealed things
          Are the tablets,
          The wellspring that brings
          Wisdom to all the generations.

      צ   The will of God
70   Are these tablets,
          The will that he made [tangible]
          During the six days [of creation].

---

78. God is described as a "consuming fire" in Deut 4:24 and 9:3.
79. The words of the writing.
80. A pun on "awesome" and its homograph "flame, lamp."

ק   Standing ones, concealed,[81]
    Went forth revealed;[82]
75 Thunder and lightning
    Assembled there.

ר   The merciful one wrote them
    With his own finger;
    The merciful one descended[83]
80 In order to give them.

שׁ His divine name
    Is on both their sides:[84]
    YHWH, to whom none can be compared,
    Not among the concealed or the revealed.[85]

85 ת   They trembled there,
    Standing ones and mortals,[86]
    As constantly he proclaimed
    The words that were [written] upon them.

There is no God but the one!

10 "O God, O Enduring One" (*SL*, 24–25; *RPH*, 193–98; *D*, 214–15)

Marqe's poetry is rich with descriptive appellations for the deity. He is equally
expansive in his descriptions of God's primary manifestation among his people:
the Torah. This poem in particular offers a catalogue of the Torah's attributes.
In many ways, the writing resembles its divine author: as God is good, so is the
Torah; God gives life, and he does so in part through his Torah; God is merciful, and the Torah is an instrument of his mercy. The Torah is the symbol and
evidence of God's covenant with Israel and the ultimate sign of the trust between
both parties. At the same time, the Torah is very much God's possession—his
treasure, his wealth—and God's decision to share it with Israel represents a
tremendous act of generosity and intimacy.

---

81. I.e., invisible angels became manifest as thunder and lightning.
82. See ll. 41–42 above.
83. Or "caused trembling (when He gave them)."
84. Both sides of the tablets (Exod 32:15).
85. I.e., neither in the angelic (invisible) world nor in the mortal (visible) world.
86. The underlying text, קעימין ומאתין, could also be translated as "the living and the dead."

A commonplace in Marqe's writing and in his theology more generally is that Torah provides a point of access to the divine. God's writing enables people, however partially and incompletely, to understand the author. As Marqe writes here, Torah is "a spark from [God's] garment" (l. 14). The Torah acquires divine attributes precisely because it is through the Torah that people come to know God. At the same time, the Torah possesses a unique potency; it is a creation unlike other creations, because it retains some fundamental connection to God's wellsprings of power. The Torah does not merely convey sacred history and divine commands to the people; it acts as God's agent in the world.

Here, as in other poems, Marqe connects the revelation of Torah at Sinai to the creation narrative of Gen 1. Sinai constitutes a creative act with consequences for the natural world and the heavenly realms that are on par with the original cosmogony. In particular, Gen 1 and Exod 19 both narrate moments when God gives life to his creatures: in Genesis, that life is literal, in the form of life-breath and animation; in Exodus, this life may be metaphorical—Torah provides insights that permit people to renew and extend their lives—but also literal, if we understand Marqe's description of the Torah as "the breath of life" as referring to a kind of spiritual reanimation of Israel.

Throughout the poem, Marqe gives voice to an exuberant sense of wonder at God's power and kindness, at his deeds and his acts. He rejoices in the implicit paradox that the Torah, a creation, testifies to the majesty of a God who preexisted all creation, and he asserts that serving God is incumbent not just upon Israel but upon all who trace their line back to Adam. God gave life to humanity, and God gave the Torah to Israel to keep his people alive.

> *Said on Thursday, on the third Sabbath of the month, and on*
> *festivals.*

א O God, O enduring one
   Who endures forever,
   O God, superior to all the mighty ones,
   And trustworthy, indeed, forever,

5 ב In your great might we trust,
   For you are our master.
   In your divinity, which brought forth
   The world from the beginning,

   ג Your power is concealed,
10 But your goodness and mercy are revealed;
   [All that is] concealed and revealed

Is in the dominion of your divinity.

ד   The choicest of creations
     A spark from your garment;
15   The choicest of all the nations
     You chose for yourself [as] your worshippers.

א   Where is there a trust
     As holy as that of those who belong to you?
     Trust in you is life-giving
20   To the one who is equal to [its] keeping.

ו   And that which is life-giving
     Needs keeping—one must keep them;[87]
     And from within the writings of the Torah,
     We learn [them] and teach [them].

25 ז   You summoned a great sign
     For the breath of life;
     A great trembling occurred
     Before it[88] was revealed.

ע   The wealth of your divinity
30   Was set upon Mount Sinai;
     The wealth of your kingship—
     Who can reckon it?

ט   Your goodness yields
     Israel's exaltation;
35   Happy is the House of Jacob,
     For what it heard from its master.

י   The sea and its waves[89]
     Are conquered by a glance[90] from you;
     Your right hand shelters
40   All your works.

87. I.e., the commandments.
88. I.e., the Torah.
89. God's control over the sea and its waves is mentioned in Pss 65:8 and 89:10. For more on Marqe's use of this motif, see the introduction to Marqe 5, above.
90. Or "by your will."

ב   All things hearken to you
    And come at your word;
    Absolutely everything bears witness:
    There is no God but the one!

45 ל   There is no divinity but yours,
        On high and down low;
        Only in your Torah
        Do we put our trust.

    מ   The abode that is on high
50   Is the place of your dominion,
        The waters of [the] deep and the waters of [the] sea
        And the very waters of the heavens.

    נ   Your radiance spread out
        The world; at a glance[91] from you,
55   O most radiant one,
        Praises are uttered unto you.

    ס   The signs of your divinity
        Display your dominion;
        O forgiving one, O beneficent one,
60   Forgive us in your mercy!

    ע   You created the world
        Without any helper;
        You drew forth from within it
        Creatures, from nothing!

65 פ   You split the dust
        And brought forth from it what we need;
        You apportioned[92] with your right hand
        Creatures, from where had been nothing!

    צ   He was fashioned from the dust,
70   And all was created for his sake;

---

91. Or "by your will."
92. Lit., "divided"—creation is depicted as done by separation.

All who descend[93] from Adam must
Serve you.

ק Before your divinity
    We cry out, all of us:
75 O first of the world,
    Who preexisted all!

ר Beginning of all are you,
    And its conclusion;[94]
    O merciful one, O beneficent one,
80 Gaze upon us and rescue us!

ש Your name fills all good things
    For him who merits receiving them;
    We praise your dominion;
    There is no God aside from you.

85 ת You seek the repentant,
    So you may give them the world;[95]
    Turn back unto us
    In your mercy, for you are able [to do so]!

There is no God but the one!

11 "O God, O Singular One" (*SL*, 25–26; *RPH*, 198–203; *D*, 216–18)

Here Marqe speaks both of and to God, and in the course of doing so he catalogues a variety of divine names and attributes. As the poet notes, "Though it is easy to mention your name, / you defy description" (ll. 15–16). He does not include here actual divine names from the Torah (e.g., YHWH, "I AM"), although he does so in other poems. Instead, he includes a litany of divine attributes and activities: God is singular, just, eternal, enduring, expected, radiant, awesome, holy, lofty, true, and exalted; he is Creator, judge, owner, hope, and victor. God transcends space and yet is described in terms that wed his actions

93. Lit., "all who are from Adam."
94. Lit., "and the end of all." This line suggests Rev 22:13 ("I am the alpha and the omega, the first and the last"); see also Rev 1:8.
95. Or "eternity."

with the physical world, such as the "dwelling place of goodness" and "source of peace" (ll. 81–82). These epithets address the poet's paradox: Marqe regards God as indescribable and yet devotes this poem (and others) to describing him. The heaping up of adjectives and activities gestures toward God's immensity and greatness: the poet offers all this, yet none of it is even close to sufficient! The task of description is impossible, and yet the need to try is urgent.

> *Said on Thursday, on the last Sabbath of the month, and on festivals.*

    א O God, O singular one,
        For whom there is no companion,
        We appeal to you,
        In [your] righteousness accept us!

5   ב O Creator who created
        The world in his singularity,
        With [our] feeble mouths
        May hymns be uttered unto you.

    ג Most powerful of the gods,
10   Joined to no second [power],
        Your praises shall they utter—
        [All] who pass through the world.

    ד O true judge,
        Who shows no favor,
15   Though it is easy to mention your name,
        You defy description.[96]

    ה Indeed, O God, you bind
        Everything to your great divinity.
        He answers the one who appeals to him
20   Without any perversity of heart.

    ו And everything, whether concealed or revealed,
        Holds fast to his divinity;
        And every king and ruler
        Extends to him his crown.

---

96. Lit., "no one can describe you."

25 ז They implore his authority
    Without any perversity of heart,
    [And] he implores all day long:
    "And now, O Israel!" [Deut 4:1].

    ח Eternal life is his,
30   And all life he makes pass away;
    Eternal life is his lot,
    Which distinguishes his divinity.

    ט Keep his commandments,
    For they give you life;
35   Whoever worships
    Another god strays.

    י The singular one, who dwells
    In the holy of holies,
    His right hand carries
40   The upper and lower [realms].

    כ All that is above and below
    Is attentive to his glory;
    All of them are within his dominion,
    And eternal life is his.

45 ל Eternal life is [his] garment,
    And he clothes no other with it;
    Sapphire-stones
    [Line] his honored pathway.

    מ Enduring one, expected one,
50   Owner of all,
    By your deeds do we know
    What you are capable of.

    נ O radiant one, O awesome one,
    Triumphant in battle,
55   We trust in your might,
    For there is none so trustworthy as you.

נ O hope of his lovers,
Forget not your promises;[97]
Your worshippers are fearful—
60 Rescue them in keeping with what you teach!

ע He sees what is concealed and revealed,
But he is concealed and unseen;
Upon the cloud of his divinity
Is the one who relies on no second [being].

65 פ Offer praise unto him
From heart and from soul;
Whoever voices his greatness
Is accustomed to rescue.[98]

צ He hears appeals,
70 He accepts prayers,
He supplies our needs,
[We] who sustain his words.[99]

ק O holy one, O true one,
Preeminent in your divinity,
75 Receive the wretched,
Those seeking justice from you.

ר O lofty one, O exalted one,
Wellspring of compassion,
Have mercy on us,
80 You whose name is "Merciful One"!

ש O dwelling place of goodness,
O source of peace,
Dwell with us,
O our God, in your goodness!

97. Lit., "proclamation." Brown and Ben-Hayyim both translate as "covenants" (*D,* 217; *RPH,* 202).
98. The order of the last two lines of this stanza is reversed for clarity.
99. I.e., who keep God's commandments.

12 "O God, 'El Elyon'" (*SL*, 25–26; *RPH*, 203–8; *D*, 218–20)

This lyrical address to the deity, which speaks to God directly and indirectly, constitutes a catalogue of divine attributes. Each stanza singles out an aspect of the divine, one manifest through actions or simply as an intrinsic quality, an element of godhood. The poem begins with the enigmatic divine names "El Shaddai" and "I am," but from there it moves toward explaining in more concrete detail why the community ("we") praises God.

Some attributes are cited only once, such as God's wealth, steadfastness, splendor, role as Creator, and goodness. Others recur multiple times: God's justice, mercy, power, and uniqueness. As the poem progresses, however, Marqe weaves the attributes together in ways that hint at the unique complexity of the deity. God's power as Creator invests him with attributes of both justice and mercy. Without one, the other two no longer cohere. Similarly, Marqe illustrates God's uniqueness as it manifests itself in both his providence (his unique concern for his particular creations) and his generosity.

The essential recurrently underscored, essential divine attribute is God's singularity. In some ways, the liturgical affirmation that concludes this hymn (and so many others)—"There is no God but the one!"—determines this thematic feature. But on a deeper level, Marqe's composition highlights the paradox of uniqueness: as the source of all, God in some sense embodies all. Every attribute worthy of worship, worthy of God, occurs within God, and these manifest in a ripple throughout creation. They are facets of the deity, elements of a divine and singular whole.

Said on Friday, on the last Sabbath of the month, and on festivals.

א   O God, "El Elyon,"[100]
   We render praise unto you;
   "El Shaddai" [and] "I am,"[101]
   We exalt you.

5   ב   On account of your divinity we offer praise:
   "There is no God except for you!" [cf. 2 Sam 7:22]
   In your great power we trust:
   You protect[102] those who worship you.

---

100. A name of God ("God Most High") used by Melchizedek and Abraham in Gen 14:18, 19, 20, 22.

101. Two names by which God identifies the divine self. "I am El Shaddai" appears in Gen 17:1 and 35:11, and "I am" in Exod 3:14.

102. The idiom קום עם (lit., "to stand with") has the sense of "protect" (akin to the English phrase "stand up for"); see *CAL*, s.v. *qwm*, 4.d.1.

ג Great one, mighty one,
10   Greatness belongs to your divinity;
     [You are] great in strength
     And wondrous in mighty deeds.

ד He who dwells in the abode
     Never neglects a petition.
15   The judge of all the earth is
     True and trustworthy!

ה **He is God**;
     No second adjoins him.
     He is abundant with wonders,
20   *True and trustworthy!*

ו **And ascribe greatness to our God,**[103]
     O portion that he set aside for himself![104]
     He numbers himself alone,[105]
     And beyond that, he has no companion.

25 ז The just one, whose justice
     Fills all the world,
     The just ones of the world,
     Keep his commandments.

ע The rich one, whose riches
30   Consist of all property[106]—
     The rich and the destitute
     He provisions from the storehouse of good.

ט The good one, whose goodness
     Endures forever,
35   Let his good works be recounted
     By every mouth.

י Unique, you endure

103. This stich is a near quotation of Deut 32:3.
104. This line resonates with Deut 32:9.
105. Lit., "he counted himself as his essential nature / as an individual"; cf. Deut 32:12. Brown, reading מנה as a prepositional phrase instead of the verb "to count," renders the line, "From Himself is He Himself" (*D*, 218). The sense of the line affirms God's individuality and uniqueness.
106. Lit., "require all property" (צריך כל מדלה)—i.e., God's "belongings" consist of everything.

In the dignity[107] of your kingship;
Day and night
40   Shall hymns be uttered unto you.

ב O herald to the creatures,
All of whom hearken unto you:[108]
Establish us in your mercy,
For you are the God of our fathers.

45 ל There is no divinity except yours,
Above and below;
Forever and ever,
May you be worshipped and praised!

מ You are the owner of all,
50   And your rule encompasses all;
What in the heavens or upon the earth
Is not under your power?[109]

נ O radiant one, O awesome one,
May you be worshipped and praised!
55   We bear witness to you all day long:
There is no God but the one!

ס O pardoner, O forgiver,
Knower-of-all,
Pardon us in your goodness,
60   And help us, out of your mercy!

ע Our maker and our sustainer,
Our master, sustain us!
Answer us and help us,
For such is your faithfulness.

65 פ O rescuer who rescues
The beleaguered and beset,
Release us from judgment
And redeem us from wrath!

107. Lit., "level, rank."
108. Lit., "him."
109. Lit., "hand."

צ Creator of Adam,
70   And God of all his sons,
Deal generously with[110] us
In your goodness, for you are merciful.

ק O preeminent one, who preceded
All in [your] uniqueness,
75   Pay heed to the impoverished
Who seek justice[111] from you!

ר O "rider upon the heavens" [Deut 33:26],
O "ruler of the earth" [cf. Deut 33:27],[112]
Have mercy on us,
80   For your name is "Merciful"!

ש Hearer of appeals,
Who does not deny our requests,
Hear our voices, O our master,
And have mercy on us!

85 ת Mighty in awesomeness,
Accustomed to authority,
Forgive our transgressions,
And absolve our sins!

There is no God but the one!

13 "Lo, the Merciful King" (*SL*, 26–27; *RPH*, 208–14; *D*, 220–21)

This poem explores God's singularity—the divine oneness that is, at the same time, a divine aloneness—and couches it in terms of the story of the creation of humanity and God's ongoing relationship with humankind. The picture that emerges is of a God who desires (even if he does not need) the companionship that people offer. The fact that God created the world with no companion testifies to his power, but also his solitude. Indeed, the poet gives God a line to speak in this poem, the only reported speech in the hymn: "Come, for I would receive [you]!" (l. 28)—a divine command that is also a plea, one that God calls out

110. Or "Act charitably (justly, righteously) toward us."
111. Or "charity."
112. Lit., "and the world is under your arm."

every day. God created his creatures to bear witness, but also to attend to him. He forgives their transgressions for the sake of their companionship. Humans are utterly unlike God—transient rather than immortal, unknowing rather than all-knowing, ruled rather than regnant—and yet mortal company pleases God. God and people seek each other, but to outsiders, each might seem to be on a fool's quest. What does God need of people? How can people hope to find God? And yet, this is the wonder Marqe describes: "He who rises early to seek him, / Indeed, he finds him nearby" (ll. 81–82).

Said on Friday, on the last Sabbath of the month, and on festivals.

ה   Lo, the merciful king
    Praised by every mouth:
    It is he who made
    The world, he alone.

5   ב   He created creatures
    Steady and strong;
    Your creatures bear witness:
    There is no God but you!

   ג   The powerful one, the awesome one,
10   Able to act as he wishes,[113]
    We are ephemeral beings
    But he permitted us[114] to praise him.

   ד   For he is unique in his divinity,
    And he has no peer;
15   For he knows all
    And needs no informing.

   ה   Where is one who can comprehend him?
    How can there be one who knows him?
    [Yet] wherever he is sought,
20   He is found nearby.

   ו   And he is above and below,
    And everything is within his dominion,

---

113. Or, more figuratively, simply "omnipotent."

114. Reading with Ben-Hayyim (*RPH*, 209), who emends וארשתין (and we are beginning [to praise Him]) to וארשתן, from the root רשׁי. Ben-Hayyim translates, "he commanded us."

And he is God,
And no second is adjoined to him.

25 ז He implores his creatures,
And they come, listening to him.
He implores, every day:
"Come, for I would receive [you]!"

ח Eternal life is his,
30 But all [mortal] lives he makes pass away;
Our lives and our souls
Are given into his dominion.

ט Goodness and mercy,
They are his handiwork;
35 He does good for the wicked,
Until at last they repent.

י May he be praised forever,
For he is the master of life;
May he be exalted forever,
40 For he sustains [all] living beings.[115]

כ All the creatures of the world
Hearken unto his word;
He gathered the waters of **nothingness** [Gen 1:2],[116]
As suits his dominion.

45 ל He called out to his creatures
And swiftly they answered him;
But he was by himself
When he made his works.

מ He spoke and brought it to pass;
50 All of it was pleasing to him.
At his utterance there came into being
His craftsmen and his workers.

---

115. Lit., "souls."

116. Marqe uses the Hebrew phrase תהו ובהו, lit., "wilderness and waste," familiar from the King James Version as "formless and void."

נ   The lights that he kindled
    Shall never be snuffed;
55   Their radiance fills
    The heavens and the dry land.

ס   The signs[117] show
    The greatness of their craftsman,
    The signs of the appointed times
60   [Marking] days and years.

ע   Great are [the] works,
    [But] greater is he who made them,
    The Creator of all:
    May he be praised and magnified!

65   פ   The rescuer is near
    To whoever seeks him,
    Redeemer of our ancestors
    From the hands of their foes.

צ   They appealed to him,
70   And he answered them and redeemed them;
    He is the fashioner of their bodies,
    And the nourisher [זאון] of their souls.

ק   He endures forever,
    Lengthening his own existence;
75   The standing ones and mortals[118]
    Are under his dominion.

ר   "The Merciful" is his name,
    And thus it bears witness to his greatness,
    The heights are in his dominion,
80   And the depths under his power.

ש   He who rises early to seek him,
    Indeed, he finds him nearby;
    He grants forgiveness

---

117. Perhaps a reference to constellations and heavenly bodies.
118. I.e., angels and humans (קעימין ומאתין), or "the living and the dead."

To the one who abandons his sins.

85 ת He who regrets his transgressions—
        Indeed, he acts with compassion for him;
        Praises and hymns
        We utter to him at every time and season

There is no God but the one!

14 "Lo, Our Souls Are Sated" (*SL*, 60–62; *RPH*, 214–23; *SAP* 440–44; *D*, 290–94)

This hymn is one of several Marqan poems that focus on both the Torah's revelation and its existential significance for humanity and creation more generally. Marqe describes the revelation in highly kinetic, even frenetic, terms: Moses moves upward, the Torah descends, God sits, the angels stand. He creates a sense of tremendous, overwhelming motion atop Sinai. The nonlinear, recursive structure of the poem recreates for the congregation the dynamic, confusing experience of revelation. There is always something to "see" and "hear," a new direction to "turn," in one's mind's eye. The poet offers the congregation a literary, liturgical echo of what their ancestors experienced, as the Torah is once again received by the community.

Here Marqe speaks of God, not to him. Instead, he speaks to the Torah—"O writing!" (l. 43)—and to the congregation, telling them to look upon scripture, simultaneously inviting them to imagine the Sinai theophany and to gaze upon the Torah scrolls in their midst. But while the Torah is the focus of the poet's and his congregation's direct attention, God is a dynamic presence. The poem evokes the burning bush from which God first addressed Moses (Exod 3:2) and consistently compares the divine presence to a fire into which Moses steps (unharmed) to acquire the Torah written by God's fiery finger. This God, a consuming flame, brought forth the world and his Torah through fire.[119]

Marqe's preference for fiery imagery in this poem results in paradoxical images: Moses, acquiring scripture, is said to have "gleaned fruits from the flames" (l. 107). Indeed, the central paradox of the poem is the insistent juxtaposition of fire with food. While Marqe consistently likens God to a dangerous fire that miraculously permits Moses to survive the acquisition of Torah, Torah itself is routinely and consistently compared to food.[120] It nourishes, sustains,

---

119. See MacDonald, "Samaritan Doctrine of Moses."

120. A metaphor rooted in scripture, as in Deut 8:3 ("a person does not live by bread alone, but by every word that comes forth from the mouth of the Lord").

and gives life. Fire, which might seem antithetical to life, instead provides the writing that, while not food, nonetheless sustains life. In some sense, scripture transforms Moses—and by extension Israel—into something other than human, something akin to the divine fire that can thrive without consuming fuel, a community nourishing itself through study and praise.

> *Said in its entirety on the three festivals and in abbreviated form on the other holy days.*

א Lo, our souls are sated[121]
    By a meal of the writing;
    It is not a meal of food,
    Such as mortals prepare;
5   It is a meal of the eternal,
    And anyone who is sated[122] by it lives.

ב Its Creator is a consuming fire.
    From within the fire, it was given;
    The great prophet received it.
10   Into the fire he stepped:
    The priest who would serve him[123]
    Ate from what remained from the fire.

ג Praiseworthy became the prophet
    When he received the writing on the mount;
15   A pillar of cloud concealed him [it[124]],
    And a pillar of fire illuminated him [it],
    And the great king who wrote it
    Extended it to the prophet with his right hand.

ד A great fear did he fear—
20   The holy prophet atop the mountain—
    The powers gave him strength,
    And the primordial beings [יסדיה] supported him.
    And the voice of the shofar rang out before him,
    And the voice of the prophet grew strong.

---

121. Or "nourished" (סביעין).
122. Or "nourish themselves" (סבע).
123. Alternatively, "serve it" (the Torah, whose words are fire).
124. The prophet and the mountain here become interchangeable.

25   ה   These were the Ten Utterances,
         And from their substance was creation completed;
         Written on tablets of stone [were they]
         And set within the ark.
         And Mount Sinai was trembling
30   For fear of them, when they descended.

     ו   And because of them, the eternal[125] descended
         From the heavens to the earth
         And said: "Make for me a tabernacle,
         A dwelling for my sovereignty" [cf. Exod 25:8].
35   And all the days that he was in their midst
         There was peace in the world.

     ז   A sacred seed that Moses brought down
         He sowed upon the two tablets;
         Ten specks were they,
40   But upon them were laid all the foundations.
         And he hewed[126] from them five books,
         And all Israel is fed by them.

     ח   Come in peace, O writing,
         O lamp that illumines all Israel.
45   For it is the writing of the eternal king
         Written by the finger of the eternal,
         And there is no writing like it
         Wherein life itself is written.

     ט   Happy is the world, and that which is within it;
50   Happy are the living, with what [i.e., Torah] is in their midst
         Lives from [words] of eternal life,
         From the source of life.
         And as for the heart in which they dwell—
         No mishap can come upon it.

55   י   The day when its[127] words were said
         Within the concealed[128] congregation,

125. The term here has connotations of "existence, standing, sustaining."
126. Or "expounded."
127. Alternatively, "his" (i.e., God's).
128. I.e., heavenly.

Trembling overcame the standing ones:[129]
The powers and the mighty ones and the primordial beings,
They besought the peace of their master
60   Before he descended to the revealed world.

כ   The great honor roused itself;
All the powers arrayed themselves.
The concealed ones[130] let themselves descend
To hear the voice of the master proclaiming,
65   And the revealed ones[131] were amazed and understood
Who it was who received it from the abode.

ל   Let us only go unto the writing
With songs and praises.
Let there be songs before it,
70   And [let] praises follow after—
From within the great praises[132]
The prophet received it on the mount.

מ   From the concealed world of the abode
Did the Ten Utterances go forth,
75   From the right hand of his divinity
Into the right hand of the prophet;
And divine nourishment [מירה],
Descending, gave life to the generations, forever.

נ   The lights on high declared its greatness;
80   He extended it, the torch of light,
To the prophet, bedecked with a beam of light
As he descended, bearing the tablets
Written by the finger of God,
By the right hand of God, a consuming fire.

129. "Standing ones" (קעימין) refers to angels, as do the terms "the powers and the mighty ones and the primordial beings" (חילין וגבוראן ויסדין) in the next line.

130. "Concealed ones" (כסיאתה) is another term for angelic beings. It also suggests their role in "concealing" the Torah.

131. "Revealed ones" refers to humans, made of material substance, who also receive the revelation. Here it seems to refer to the idea that the nations were aware that Israel had been chosen by God to receive the Torah (see Exod 15:14–16).

132. Angelic song.

85 ס Many creatures descended,
       Declaring the greatness of the holy writing.
       The king who is in the heavenly heavens
       Said that it should descend, but he did not move;
       [Rather] he moved the mountains and the valleys,
90   And the world was calm in his mercy.

    ע See[133] the writing that Moses brought
       And worship the master alone!
       Much did the prophet pray
       And fast, before he received it;
95   Let us multiply our praises of the great God,
       For the good one saw fit to grant us his handwriting.[134]

    פ The divine mouth speaks
       The Ten Words on Mount Sinai;
       Let every mouth possessing power of speech recite
100   The recitation that grants life to the reciter,
       And let his soul be sated by that which is not food—
       Just as happened to Moses the prophet.

    צ From within his terror, Moses prayed,
       And he fasted until he received it;
105   For one hundred and sixty set times[135] he fasted.
       Sated [סביע] by the saying of praises,
       He gleaned fruits from the flames,
       And his soul was sated, but not by food.

    ק Read, in God's proclamation,
110   How he called to the light and it shone forth shining!
       The mute heard his words,

133. This translation follows Ben-Hayyim, whose understanding reflects living liturgical traditions of pronunciation (*RPH*, 221). Brown renders in the past tense: "They saw ... they prostrated ..." (*D*, 293).

134. *CAL*, s.v. *kyr, kyrʾ*, translates כיר אדה as "autograph."

135. What Marqe intends here is unclear, as this number quadruples Moses's forty days upon the mountain; it may result from adding together various references to "forty days" in Exod 24:18, 34:28, and Deut 9:9, 11, 18. In antiquity, a tradition appears according to which Moses fasted for one hundred twenty days: forty days for each set of tablets and another forty in atonement for the golden calf. An eighteenth-century Samaritan author (Ibrahim ibn Yaʿqub ibn Murǧan) offers a version of this account, which is paralleled in ExodR 47:7 (see also Midrash Tanhuma, *Ki Tissa* 31). See Bowman, *Samaritan Documents*, 232, and see also the discussion in Zsengellér, "Day of Atonement."

And the speaking obeyed them;[136]
The world diligently obeys the good person
Who obeys all the words of his master.

115   ר   "Mercy!" proclaimed God,
         For all the generations are in need of it;
         The prophet received mercy
         From the one whose name is "Merciful."
         It was gleaned from the wellspring of the "very good" [Gen 1:31]
120   By the right hand of the fearsome one, a consuming fire.

       שׁ   A shining sun, never extinguished,
         Are these Ten Utterances;
         The sun [of Torah] was kindled among the concealed ones
         By those who dwell within the concealed [realm],
125   And the prophet, bedecked with a beam of light,
         Composed five books from them.

       ת   Chaos and wasteland: God sufficient unto himself,
         No other companion was there.
         But there his power and his goodness said:
130   "Let the gate open and let Moses enter
         And let him take the Ten Utterances
         And let him know how the world came into being!"

15 "God, upon Mount Sinai" (*SL*, 50–51, 877–78; *RPH*, 224–27 [ll. 1–49]; *D*, 271–75)

Marqe's focus in this poem is the theophany and revelation of Torah on Mount Sinai. He does not offer a linear retelling of the events or a straightforward embellishment of Exod 19; instead, Marqe elaborates on selected aspects of the events episodically and elliptically. He introduces multiple metaphors in his attempt to articulate the nature of the Torah: it is a treasure from God's storehouse, seeds that sprout and sustain the people, and water that quenches a deep thirst. He provides different descriptions of the revelation: the Torah descends from the heavens but also emanates from the "great deep" (l. 58*).

---

136. The poet here offers an interpretation of נעשה ונשמע in Exod 24:7; it is worth noting that the SamT reverses the order of these two words from what is found in the MT and the SamP. Cf. Ninna 1, ll 105–6: "All that YHWH spoke to Moses / Let us hear and let us do!"

Throughout the poem (only the first seven stanzas of which remained in common usage among the Samaritans[137]), Marqe underscores that the audience of revelation was not only human but angelic; indeed, Sinai represents a moment when the boundary between mortals and angels blurs:

A gathering of standing ones occurred atop Mount Sinai.
On its [the Torah's] account were they gathered
In order to hear it, and mortals were gathered
In order to hear [it], word by word. (ll. 109*–12*)

Angels and mortals alike witness the revelation, but they remain segregated by status and location. Moses, however, is practically deified atop Sinai:

To the rank of divinity did Moses the prophet ascend,
And he was honored atop Mount Sinai.
God descended, and all his creatures saw his descent. (ll. 73*–75*)

Moses experiences in heightened, intensified form what the people experience more generally through their proximity to God and God's word. The drama of these lines develops what Marqe wrote in the opening stanza: "God lowered himself and descended; / The prophet rose and ascended" (ll. 3–4). The constellation of images that texture this poem brings together the heavens, the earth, and the deeps, together with mortals, angels, and God. It is a moment of transcendent and transformative unity, yet transient. The cue that prefaces this work—"with humility"—indicates that the performance of the work should not stress pride, but rather humbling awe at the receipt of this gift.

The radical uniqueness of God is stressed throughout, and three times the first of the Ten Utterances is reiterated: "You shall have no [other] gods!" (ll. 103*, 116*, 137*). This divine imperative is anticipated in the fifth stanza (ll. 28–36), which offers a fleeting synopsis of the speech-acts that occurred at Sinai: God, or perhaps Moses, proclaims, "There is none but God!" (l. 33). And the people respond, "The prophet, who is steadfast forever, / Taught us all that was written within it!" (ll. 35–36). The moment of revelation, like God, his prophet, and his Torah, was singular, but the imperative to study and to teach scripture extends the moment into the present. The dynamism of the poem, with its repetitions and elliptical reiterations, recreates some of the cacophony that marks the unmooring experience of Exod 19, even as the essential content of scripture—the Ten Utterances, and most of all the radical oneness of God—is underscored.

---

137. *RPH* contains only the first seven stanzas of the poem (ll. 1–49); *SL* draws on a second manuscript to supplement the abbreviated version of the poem in its main manuscript. Here asterisked line numbers indicate the sections taken from *SL*.

Said on festivals.

Cue: "With humility"

א God, upon Mount Sinai, made tremble
The powers and the mighty ones and the primordial ones.[138]
God lowered himself and descended;
The prophet rose and ascended.
5   Mount Sinai quailed and quaked
Out of fear of its Creator
When he came to receive
Life for all generations [to come], forever.

10 ב By a finger of consuming fire was it written,
In divine knowledge;
With fasting and praying was it received
By the hand of Moses, within the flaming fire,
From the lofty arm
15   Upon which the world depends.

ג The powers descended with him
From the abode, above the mount's summit;
All the mighty ones of Israel trembled
When he spoke the Ten Utterances,
20   Going forth from the mouth of the divinity,
Life for all generations [to come], forever.

ד For this is the choicest of his utterances
Which the God of Gods uttered;
And Moses, steadfast forever,
25   Received the choicest of them from the right hand of his master,
So that all the generations would trust
In God and in Moses.

א The storehouse[139] that feeds those needing feeding,
Light and wisdom for those who inquire of it,
30   A treasure that enriches
All who seek within it—the enduring one

138. I.e., various kinds of angels (חילין וגבוראל ויסדין).
139. I.e., the Torah; this metaphor, like "schoolhouse" (see Marqe 16, l. 87, and Ninna 1,
ll. 68–69), comes from the world of building and infrastructure.

Uttered, with the blasts of the shofar,
Proclaiming: "There is none but God!"
On high and down below, they joined together, saying:

35   "The prophet, who is steadfast forever,
Taught us[140] all that was written within it."

ו   Woe to the one who keeps far from knowledge
Woe to the one who does not keep the commandments.
For it is the scroll of the Torah,

40   Expounded by Moses the prophet at the command of his master,
Which he set within the ark,
So that the repentant could read within it.

ז   The seed sown within the fire,
The Ten Utterances, rose and sprouted

45   Ten Utterances,
Ten treasures.
Moses the prophet is trustworthy,
Steadfast in the house of God,
The giver of Israel's harvest.[141]

50*   ח   Life from him who lives eternally
Is the great writing that is among us;
The living testify that there is none else like it
That it is from above the world
And brought down from the heart of the heavens

55*   And explained by the mind[142] of Moses.

ט   Happy are we that he bestowed among us
The wellspring of life, unchanging,[143]
That was from the great deep of the Name,
Divinity inscribed by the hand of the prophet;

60*   And all the generations yet to come
Forever will drink from its waters and thrive.[144]

---

140. Lit., "made us wise."
141. *RPH* ends with this stanza; for the following stanza (ll. 50*–55*) and the last stanza (ll. 132*–37*), see *SL*, 50–51, and for the remainder (ll. 56*–131*), see *SL*, 877–78.
142. Lit., "heart."
143. The phrase דלא שני may also suggest (via Hebrew) "there is no second"—i.e., an affirmation of monotheism.
144. From מתח, "to prolong, extend, propagate."

י   The day that it[145] descended upon Mount Sinai
God descended, and all his creatures saw;
Because of the greatness of his prophet, who received it,
65*   No one shall transgress its precincts, stepping
Behind the curtain [פרכתה] before the writing,[146]
Except for God and Moses.

כ   All the world is bound to his [or: its] words;
Every heart will be bound to it, for it is his [or: its] knowledge
that reveals
70*   The secrets of his divinity, and they tremble greatly.
For the great prophet received it from the domain
Of the great king, life-giving to the generations forever.

ל   To the rank of divinity did Moses the prophet ascend,[147]
And he was honored atop Mount Sinai.
75*   God descended, and all his creatures saw his descent;[148]
All his troops[149] from his abode went forth,
Above the entire house of Israel.

מ   From his abode on high was it given,
And on Mount Sinai was heard some of his knowledge
80*   That Moses, his prophet, expounded
From the five books, its pericopes;
From the summit of Mount Gerizim were the decrees
And the instructions taught to Israel.

נ   A light, never to be extinguished, was kindled
85*   Since the days of the covenant,
By the mouth of the one who spoke and kindled another [light]—
Light, mighty and abundant, that is from the mouth
Of the one who spoke—he who is YHWH, a consuming flame.

145. I.e., the writing, as indicated by the following reference to God's descent to bequeath it in the following line, and Moses's subsequent receipt of it.

146. Lit., "none of the generations shall step near [or: violate], for there is no being near it [i.e., it is prohibited to be near it] / behind the curtain of the writing."

147. In *TM* I §35 (86א, p.137), Marqe makes a similar suggestion concerning Moses's proximity to and imbuement with divinity: "Divinity and prophethood were combined to honor him" (אלהותה ונביותה אזדמנו לוקרתיה). In drawing near to divine space, Moses acquired something akin to divinity himself.

148. Reading נחתו for יהות, as Cowley suggests (*SL*, 877n9).

149. From the Greek ὄχλος.

ס They testified that they are the writings of truth:
90* The heavens and the earth testify
To Moses the prophet that all his writings are truth.
Truth testifies to Moses the prophet:
In [the revelation of] Mount Sinai
And also in you[150]
95* Shall they trust forever.

ע His creatures[151] saw; summoned, they descended with him.
His mighty ones[152] and Moses were upon Mount Sinai,
And Mount Sinai feared and trembled out of fear of its maker;
But Moses was steady upon the earth.
100* And his head reached into the clouds.

פ Great and powerful wonders were seen
There upon Mount Sinai. The mouth of God
Proclaimed: "You shall have no [other] gods!" [Exod 20:3]
The mouth of Moses spoke with his master
105* Mouth to mouth;
Mouths become pure,
Coming to mention his name—
By which he drew forth the world.[153]

צ A gathering of standing ones[154] occurred atop Mount Sinai;
110* On its[155] account were they gathered
In order to hear it, and mortals were gathered
In order to hear [it], word by word,
[Words] filling the world with mercy
From the name of God, our God.

115* ק Thunder and lightning there was when his voice spoke,
Proclaiming, "You shall have no [other] gods!" [Exod 20:3]
The voice of Moses was heard with the voice of
The shofar; the congregation of Israel paid heed

150. The structure of the line (בטור סיני ואף בך) implies a parallel between Sinai and God.
151. A kind of angel (בוראיה).
152. A kind of angel (חיליה).
153. The verb חלץ ("to draw forth") is used in Samaritan Aramaic to describe the process of creation (*DSA*, 275, s.v. חלץ).
154. Angels (קעימין).
155. I.e., the Torah's.

To his words and came, trembling,
120*   From that great dispersion.[156]

ד   His mercies descended with him upon Mount Sinai;
The merciful one proclaimed that he is a God of mercy;
The greatest of the prophets trod within the fire,
The most exalted of all men, who kept
125*   His decrees and served his Torah.

ש   Six hundred thousand, on the slopes of
Mount Sinai, were hearing his voice;
There went forth from the fire arrows[157] of lightning
And a flashing fire, darkness, a cloud, a thick cloud,
130*   And God came, a consuming fire,
Proclaiming the Ten Utterances.

ת   The congregation of Israel beheld something delightful, twice![158]
God commanded them [that] they should remember
The three days until they were readied for Mount Gerizim.[159]
135*   Three witnesses went out to summon them: darkness, cloud, and
        thick fog.
And God, a consuming fire, came and proclaimed the Ten
        Utterances,
Beginning: "You shall have no [other] gods before me [Exod
        20:3]; I am the enduring one!"

16 "This Is His Great Writing" (*SL*, 53–55; *RPH*, 228–38 [ll. 1–75, 76–141, 142–71])

This magnificent composition, one of Marqe's longest hymns, celebrates the Torah at length.[160] From the opening line, the congregation is invited to hear

---

156. The flight from Egypt.
157. Taking חז from זוז (*DSA*, 225, s.v. זוז).
158. Perhaps a reference to the two separate events that follow: "God commanded ..." (Omer day 46) and "God came ..." (Omer day 49); see Crown, *Samaritans*, 685, 729–30.
159. This line draws a strong connection between Sinai and the Samaritan temple, suggesting that revelation was a prerequisite for temple-based worship. It may also suggest an association between the temple and ongoing divine speech, in a fashion akin to what is written in Isa 2:3 // Mic 4:2, "Torah goes forth from Zion."
160. An earlier version of this translation was originally published in Lieber, "Forever Let it Be Said." Ben-Hayyim included only the stanzas in common liturgical usage when he assembled his

the poem in the presence of the physical Torah scroll(s) in their midst. "This is his great writing!" Marqe exclaims (l. 13). And in doing so, he makes explicit the connection between the revelation at Sinai, when God bequeathed the text to Moses, and the faithful extension of that text into the present moment. It is a poem that is akin in spirit to the line recited by the congregation in Jewish liturgy as the Torah is held aloft and its text presented to the public after it has been read in the synagogue: "This is the Torah that Moses set before the children of Israel, according to the utterance of YHWH by the hand of Moses." The Jewish text, in turn, is a composite of two biblical phrases, Deut 4:44 and Num 9:23. The Jewish and Samaritan claims reflect the desire of rival parties to identify their own Torah with the Torah given at Sinai. In neither case is the language explicitly polemical, but it is bold in its unambiguous truth claims. These are the words and this is the scroll, asserts Marqe—anything else (implicitly, the Jewish Torah or Christian copies of scripture) must be considered fraudulent and misleading.

Marqe is not content here to collapse the boundary between past and present—between Sinai and the synagogue. Through the refrain of the poem (an unusual feature in his corpus), he also extends the truth of the Torah, as embodied in its recitation, into the endless future. The repeated utterances of "Forever, let it be said"—twenty-two times in all—serve to weave the congregation into the span of sacred history. In reciting the refrain, they speak alongside their ancestors at the mountain as the Torah is given by God to Moses, and they speak in the present as well, anticipating a future that will be marked by scripture's endurance. In a fundamental way, just as "This is his great writing," so too is the people eternal and unchanging. That is, by joining themselves to the Torah and participating in the Sinai event in all its iterations, the congregation becomes as timeless as their Torah. Implicit in the refrain "Forever let it be said" is another wish: "Forever let us say it"—an eternal God, an everlasting writing, and an enduring people, each interconnected to the others.

Said on the sixth Sabbath between Passover and Shavuot.

Preface
Who can speak of
The greatness of the one who spoke the truth?
His master sanctified him at the hour when he spoke with him:
The gift from the giver of life,
5   The light that reveals the greatness of his God,

edition of the hymn; his text includes the preface and sixteen of the twenty-two stanzas of the acrostic; the remainder are supplied from Cowley, *SL*, and are marked by asterisks in the line numbering.

The source of his joy as he leads us[161] to peace,
The master of the wholly faithful,
He hastened[162] them toward his words.
The great voice sounds before him, saying:
10   Greatness belongs to the great one, who gave it.[163]
Who is like you, enduring?
For thus you revealed to us this utterance:

א   This is his great writing,
Which the great king extends
15   To his trusted prophet.
This is that for which
The standing ones descended,[164]
The deity and all his creatures with him;
Israel accepted it faithfully
20   And will execute [its] decrees.
        Forever, let it be said!

ב   By the right hand of the singular one was it given;
By the arm of him who bears the world
On the summit of Mount Sinai
25   Was the prophet standing
And offering praise
To his master, at the moment he came
To receive life for all generations.[165]
        Forever, let it be said!

30   ג   His might flashes forth mysteries,
And all his revelations cause quaking,
Frightening [the inhabitants of] the land with their sounds;
They are fearful when the singular one speaks.
The great sign appeared upon him:
35   What an utterance went forth from the flaming fire!
And who has ever heard an utterance like this?
        Forever, let it be said!

---

161. The translation adopts Ben-Hayyim's tentative emendation (*RPH*, 228) of לון ("them")
to לן ("us").
162. Lit., "advanced them," with the sense of "led them."
163. I.e., God, who gave the Torah.
164. The "standing ones" (קעימין) are angels.
165. *SL*, 53, reads: "To receive writings from the right hand of God."

ד A voice from the heavens was heard by his prophet;
He ascended and received the tablets
40 That have eternal life within them.
The radiance of Moses his prophet wearing a beam of light,
Trembling—there was no other like him, and would never be
    again;
God, a consuming fire, was speaking,
And even those not there trembled.
45   *Forever, let it be said!*

ה Your speech is eternally new;
You brought forth everything from nothing: "Let there be . . ."
God called—without being heard—
To every creation, and they came, hearing.[166]
50 Who is worthy to praise you?
Who is fit to learn from you?
Trusted is the prophet who brought you[167] to us,
It is enough for us that we are called yours.
For he is our life, and that which is between us [endures].
55   *Forever, let it be said!*

ו The mighty one of the world,
Whose hosts are with him above
And for whose sake the heralds call out—
His shofar sounds and inspires fear,
60 The proclamation of the king before him;
And the hidden one speaks truth,
And his congregation trembles at the sound of the living beings.[168]
And trusted is the prophet to whom it was said,
"Hear, and speak to us!" [Exod 20:19].[169]
65   *Forever, let it be said!*

ז Fearsomely hard shaking
That caused rumbling upon Mount Sinai—
The assembly of standing ones was above,
And the assembly of mortals was below.

166. Ben-Hayyim translates as "bowed down" (*RPH*, 232).
167. The underlying verb, אנדיך, is from the root דני.
168. A term for angels.
169. An allusion to the words of the people to Moses.

70   And God was the reader,
        And Moses was the hearer,
        And all the congregation of Israel
        Saw the flashes of fire
        And the mountain aflame.
75   *Forever, let it be said!*

1*   ה   The great power stirred,
        And his glory descended upon them,
        And the sound of the shofar was heard
        Within the flame of fire,
5*   And lightning illumined
        Moses, his trusted one,
        Who trod within the fire to come
        And receive the writings
        From the right hand of God.
10*   *Forever, let it be said!*[170]

76   ט   The good one stirred and descended;
        Mount Sinai trembled on his account.
        His children [Israel] gathered
        To hear the voice of God,
80   For he [Moses] was an exceedingly good scribe,
        Teaching them lest they sin.
        And he would speak with them
        Through the mouth of their master:
        "There shall be no other gods for you except me [Exod 20:3],
85   [For] I am enduring."
            Forever, let it be said!

      י   Splendid was his schoolhouse,
        Which was equal to hearing the voice of God.[171]
        Splendid was Moses,
90   And how seemly to hear him—
        The holy one is among his beloveds:
        "I stir [myself] and descend
        So that the people may hear me
        When I speak with you,

170. This stanza is present in *SL* but not in *RPH.*
171. On the image of Torah as a schoolhouse, see the discussion in the note to Ninna 1, l. 68.

95   So that your greatness may be recounted
     To all the generations of the world."
          Forever, let it be said!

כ   The glory stirred and descended;
     Mount Sinai trembled on his account.
100   The shofar resounded before him;
     Thunder and lightning went forth,
     And flashes of fire illuminated [it all].
     And the creatures descend,
     And the primordial ones gather together,[172]
105   And God speaks from within the flame of fire,
     And all Israel hears and trembles
     Out of fear of [their] Creator.
          Forever, let it be said!

ל   The heart of the heavens opened,
110   And the eternal king arose;
     Darkness, cloud, and thick fog
     Descended with him upon Mount Sinai.
     And he spoke with all Israel
     From within the flame of fire,
115   And his lightning illuminated Moses, his trusted one
     And all the people trembled upon hearing his voice;
     Then they said to the prophet,
     "We are not able to hear all this utterance."
          Forever, let it be said!

120   מ   From his heavenly dwelling, sublime, it is given;
     By the holy one, it is spoken;
     From Mount Sinai, it is heard,
     From a splendid cloud,
     From within a flame of fire.
125   And Mount Sinai trembled, as it is said:
     "All the mountain trembled mightily" [Exod 19:18].
     God, a consuming fire, speaks,
     And those who were not there felt terror.
          Forever, let it be said!

172. The terms "creatures" (בוראיה) and "primordial ones" (יסדיה) refer to kinds of angels.

130 ‬ The awesome one is the enduring king,
     For the good one lowered himself before all this,
     Speaking with dust[173]
     From within flaming fire;
     Luminous was Moses
135 And he was worthy to hear him.
     He trod within the flame of fire,
     And he dwells among the standing ones,
     And he had faith in the concealed and the revealed.
     And he was fit to be clothed in his name
140 Through which he created the world
       Forever, let it be said![174]

1** ס The good book spoke with them from
     Within the flame of fire;
     his book, which kindles the light,
     Its voice was heard there.
5** And Moses, who was called "God" [Exod 4:16],
     Stood in his glory, and a multitude, six hundred thousand,
     Were at the base of Mount Sinai, seeing the torches;
     And the mountain was aflame.
       Forever, let it be said!

10** ח The mighty one to whom all belongs, speaks words of life,
     How he is eternal, forever,
     He whose writings are eternal.
     A mighty one is his great prophet,[175]
     Who wrapped himself in five books and stood between two
       assemblies:
15** Between standing ones and mortals[176]—
     And they stood because of his standing to speak with all of them,
     These and those, who hear and tremble.
       Forever, let it be said!

     פ The mouth of the living one spoke words of life to his followers,
20** Speech from the source of life,

---

173. I.e., mortals.
174. The next five stanzas are present in *SL* but not in *RPH*. *SL* does not consistently include the refrain, however.
175. Moses is here classified among the angels.
176. The terms here (בין קעימין ובין מאתין) might also be translated "the living and the dead."

He who is heard but unseen;

And crowds of his mighty ones were trembling

Because of his might, and crowds of mortals were hearing and
  fearing.

And the eternal one was speaking audibly to all of them,

25** To these and those, hearing and fearing.

  Forever, let it be said!

צ [It was] a nigh impossible assembly that trembled upon Mount
  Sinai:[177]

Assemblies of standing ones and assemblies of mortals,

And God, who since **"in the beginning"** [Gen 1:1],

30** Is within their eternal assemblies;

And God, whom man resembles,

Is between the two assemblies,

And God stands to teach his prophet,

And his prophet hears and teaches his followers.

35** *Forever, let it be said!*

ק The voice of God speaks and says, "You shall have no gods
  besides me [Exod 20:3].

I am he who created the world, by myself, and not with another.

My words were my works and my deeds

And they are my handiwork.

40** Who could create [anything] like my creations?

I created great and mighty worlds

that do not need nourishing[178] from the knowledge of another."[179]

43** *Forever, let it be said!*

142 ר Great was the trembling

That shook Mount Sinai;

The exalted one, immeasurable, upon the mountain

145 Descended, and it did not tremble.

And his voice and the voice of the shofar

---

177. This translation understands אזדוע as a form of the root זוז. The phrase rendered "nigh
impossible" is קשי מותר (lit., "exceedingly difficult, extremely hard"). The sense is that for angels
and humans to be so close to the divine was physically and existentially overwhelming.

178. Taking מהרין as a participle from the root מור (*DSA*, 457, s.v. מור).

179. It is not clear here whether "another" refers simply to knowledge from outside of the
Torah and its traditions or rejects a more specific notion, such as the idea that God was assisted by
a demiurge during creation.

And a splendid cloud was upon his mountain,
And a flame of fire [burned] far as the heart of heaven;
And the son of Yocheved was treading
150   Within it and was unharmed.
Forever, let it be said!

י   The Great Name[180] who created the world
Makes his voice heard among the multitude.
And Moses, who was called "God" [Exod 4:16],
155   Stood among the many multitudes,
And six hundred thousand
Were on the slopes of Mount Sinai.
And all the people trembled upon hearing his voice;
There they said to the prophet,
160   **"You draw near and listen"** [Deut 5:24].
Forever, let it be said!

ח   His might, by which he created the [angelic] hosts
And the [terrestrial] creatures, bears witness to his greatness:
He descended, and a multitude of the holy ones were with him,
165   And he spoke with all Israel,
An utterance that was never repeated.[181]
Yea, O congregation, do not forget this, his utterance!
Keep God's commandments, which he has taught in truth;
He who keeps it,
170   *Lo, his life is kept [safe]!*
Forever, let it be said!

17 "Come in Peace, O Day of Fasting" (*SL*, 62–63 [ll. 1–36], 666 [ll. 37–44]; *RPH*, 238–41)

If we assume that this poem originally embedded a complete alphabetical acrostic, then the second half of this hymn of atonement is missing; what survives is an acrostic that embeds the first half of the alphabet (א through כ) and concludes

---

180. The text spells out the Tetragram (lit., "the great YHWH") at the beginning of this stanza, where a word beginning with ש is expected; this indicates how thoroughly the circumlocution שמא ("the Name," equivalent to Hebrew *ha-Shem*) had been adopted by this time. See *RPH*, 237, and also Marqe 5, l. 81, where this same use of the Tetragram occurs.

181. The utterance that was never repeated is the revelation of the Decalogue during the theophany on Sinai.

with the final letter of the alphabet, ת. The abbreviated א-to-ת structure conveys a sense of completeness despite the missing ten stanzas; it may be that performative custom "trimmed" the length of the work or an editor chose to shorten it.[182] Regardless, the extant half of the poem provides worthwhile material for reflection.

While the hymn explicitly addresses the "day of fasting"—the Day of Atonement—and Marqe consciously grounds his language and imagery in Lev 16, which provides the biblical source for the dramatic ritual of the scapegoat, the tone of the poem is confident and even joyful. (The opening phrase, "Come in peace," echoes two hymns by Ninna, both of which bid the Sabbath farewell, beginning with the words "Go in peace" [Ninna 1 and 2]; the present poem of welcome addresses "the Sabbath of Sabbaths" [l. 37].) While the poet asserts that those who violate the fast and neglect its prayers will suffer, those who keep the fast and utter their prayers have every reason to celebrate. Indeed, while the first half of the extant poem juxtaposes those who observe the fast and those who transgress it, the second half focuses on the joy that keeping the fast brings: it is a jubilee, no day is better, and "happy is the congregation that is worthy of it" (l. 34).

This poem's understanding of the fast of the Day of Atonement is not entirely exceptional, as the conclusion of m. Taʿanit 4:8 suggests: "Rabbi Simeon ben Gamaliel said: Never were there more joyous festivals in Israel than the fifteenth of Av and the Day of Atonement." But whereas the Mishnah suggests the joy derives from the custom of matchmaking while in a state of purity, in this poem, the fast itself seems to be the cause of joy. Marqe certainly regards Israel's understanding of the fast as distinctive; he writes:

All nations observe fast-days,
But none resemble this one;
All those of the nations are like nighttime,
But this one, of Israel, is sunshine! (ll. 41–44)

In short, it is not the act of fasting that distinguishes Marqe's community, but the joy the community experiences when it fasts. In the final lines, the poet urges the community to "lift your faces to the abode" (l. 46) and ask God's forgiveness. This day is marked not by self-abasement, fear, or anxiety, but by the joyful confidence of looking up to God and feeling the sun on one's face.

---

182. The genre of classical Hebrew *piyyut* known as the *qedushta*, which postdates Marqe by several centuries, contains a ten-line unit that runs from *alef* to *yod* and is known as the *'asiriyyah*. The *'asiriyyah* does not conclude with the letter *tav*, however, and likely developed independently.

Said on the Preparatory Feast (צמות) of the Festival of Booths[183] and from the new moon of the seventh month[184] until the Day of Atonement.[185]

א Come in peace, O day of fasting,
On which two goats for sin-offerings
Are offered on the heights:
One for Azazel and one for YHWH.

5   ב On the tenth of the month, it is said:
"You shall afflict your souls" [Lev 16:31].
A Hebrew, abstaining from food,
Denies himself on account of his sin.

ג Praises [accrue] to the one who fasts on it,
10   And great disgrace upon the one who violates it.
They will depart, empty, from all goodness,
These [Hebrews] who abstain from fasting on it.

ד A remembrance that shall never be nullified,
A remembrance of a day of fasting for [all] generations,
15   O choicest[186] of the nations, O Israel:
[You] fast upon it, and he grants forgiveness.

ה Indeed, any soul that does not fast
Shall be cut off from the midst of its people,
A commandment uttered by God—
20   Who could neglect it?

ו Woe to them!—To these who are not fasting,
Or are fasting, but not praying—
For they are like a blind man in the dark,
Wounding themselves, day and night.

---

183. In Samaritan tradition, both Passover and the Festival of Booths are preceded by feast days (which always fall on Sabbath), each known as a צמות (lit., "meeting, conjunction"). The special Sabbath falls seven weeks prior to the festival. See Pummer, "Samaritan Rituals," 689.

184. I.e., the Festival of the Seventh Month.

185. See Zsengellér, "Day of Atonement."

186. The term דמע can mean both "offering" (תרומה) and "choicest, best," which creates a resonant double meaning here: Israel is the best of the nations. but through fasting, it also makes an offering of itself.

25 ז The moon and the sun bear witness
        To the nature of this day of forgiveness,
        A holy convocation in the name of the holy one:
        For the holy congregation—there is none like it!

        ה Lo, a jubilee[187] comes at this very moment,
30   Once a year for [all] Israel;
        If one fasts upon it and repents,
        Then he merits redemption.

        ט Who has seen a day better than the day of fasting?
        Happy is the congregation that is worthy of it;
35   The dew of forgiveness
        Glistens over all who fast upon it.

        י The day upon which a Sabbath of Sabbaths is observed,
        The day of forgiveness for Israel,
        Let them fast upon it in repentance,
40   These who are petitioning their master.

        כ All nations observe fast-days,[188]
        But none resemble this one.
        All those of the nations are like nighttime,
        But this one, of Israel, is sunshine![189]

45 ת *Be repeating the day, O fasters.*[190]
        Lift your faces to the abode
        And say: Forgive your people Israel
        Whom you redeemed, O YHWH!

18 "O Good One, in Whom the One Who Hopes" (*SL*, 85; *RPH*, 241–45; *D*, 244–45)

Although Ben-Hayyim attributes this poem to Marqe, it is formally quite unlike most of Marqe's works and Ben-Hayyim notes that a tradition recorded

---

187. "Jubilee" here seems to refer to the Day of Atonement, "the Sabbath of Sabbaths" in l. 37. The Day of Atonement is a "jubilee" that comes every year.

188. This line offers an unusual acknowledgment of non-Samaritan Israelite religious practice.

189. Lit., "daylight."

190. Language of a liturgical formula, with a plural verbal form (תנים) in Hebrew (see *SL*, 435).

in one manuscript assigns it to Marqe's son, Ninna; it usually follows Ninna's "Go Forth in Peace" in the service.

Ben-Hayyim observes that the poem lacks formal elements that clearly establish its poetic structure; Brown, in fact, published it as prose. The present translation takes Ben-Hayyim's division of the text into poetic lines as a starting point but alters some of his line divisions and stanza breaks. Although there are no signs of an acrostic arrangement or any clear indications of line breaks, the poem does include a substantial insertion of Hebrew liturgical language and several repetitive passages in Aramaic. The repetitions strongly suggest some form of congregational participation in the performance of the poem.[191]

The distinctive formal elements of this poem are matched by its unusual perspective: the poet speaks in the first-person singular throughout. Marqe writes here in his own voice (as "I" and "mine") rather than in a communal voice ("we" and "ours"). To be sure, the use of the first-person singular is a conceit, not a window on the poet's own emotional interiority. But as a poetic device, it creates a sense of intimacy, even as each individual listener is implicitly invited to identify with the speaker's voice, and indeed, if the congregation recited part or all of the prayer during liturgy, then they joined their voices to his. In either case, the poet's words are experienced by all who say them.

The themes and imagery of this poem highlight the role that context can play in literary interpretation. Most commonly, this hymn would be performed, and thus heard, at the close of the Sabbath. In such a framework, as the day of rest closes and the week of work resumes, the poem's images of gates remaining open, prayers still being heard, and human activity being rewarded (or forgiven, as the case may be) acquire particular resonance. The day of rest is ending, but not the sense of communion with the deity. Throughout the week, humans may continue to pray and petition, and God will respond and forgive. When the prayer is recited in the context of the Day of Atonement, these routine elements are amplified and the language of repentance and forgiveness acquires particular force. When read in the context of the Paschal offering, however, its resonances with the language of Exodus—particularly Exod 3 and 15—echo more forcefully, and the references to doorways stand out. Expressions of repentance and forgiveness, alongside assurances of rescue, redemption, and eternal fidelity, imbue the offering with elements of atonement alongside thanksgiving, expressing gratitude for salvation in the past and an implicit petition for restoration to come.

---

191. For a more detailed analysis of the performative elements in this work and its use of Hebrew, see Lieber, "No Translation Needed."

Recited at the end of the Sabbath, at the opening of the prayers of the Passover sacrifice, and in the service for the evening of the Day of Atonement.[192]

O good one, in whom the one who hopes in your goodness finds no disappointment,

And beside whom there is no other who may be sought out,

And whose Gate of Mercy never shuts in the face of one who seeks refuge,

And [by whom] the poor man is not rejected when he comes seeking repentance,[193]

5 Your fearsomeness, O my master, is like a consuming fire [cf. Deut 4:24; 9:3].

But your mercifulness is like water extinguishing every flame.

Your proclamation concerning your greatness—that you are merciful and gracious—

It is the medicine that heals all the sick.

O rescuer, you who are the refuge of all living beings,

10 O [you] who are found by all who cry out, beseeching

[you] to favor your servants for the labors of their forefathers[194]

And [the merit] of those who cried out, "**Who is like you, splendid in holiness?**" [Exod 15:11].

O good one, whose goodness fills all the world

Forgive the wickedness of my deeds

15 And move me to return to your hand, and accept me;

On the great day of judgment, O my master, in your mercifulness have mercy upon me and forgive me!

And do not repay me according to the wickedness of my deeds,

For you are YHWH, a God merciful and gracious forever and ever, unendingly so.

"**I am that I am**" [Exod 3:14] is my master: Have mercy!

20 And extend comfort, for such is your faithfulness, O my master YHWH.

---

192. See Zsengellér, "Day of Atonement."

193. The translation here is uncertain and relies on construing לשובה as a cognate of the Hebrew verb שוב rather than the expected Aramaic lexeme תוב.

194. Lit., "foundations."

**Blessed are you, O YHWH our God! Your petitioner does not
  return empty-handed.**
And the doorway of your mercy is not shut against him![195]
And your faithfulness is forever and ever;
Blessed is your holy name forever![196]

There is no God but one, the One!
There is no God but one, the One![197]
There is no God but one!

25 Praise belongs to you alone;
      Your servant prays to you,
    O giver of goodness and faithfulness.
      May your shade shelter us,
    You who possess divinity;
      Eternal life is yours[198]

O giver of gifts: gratitude to you for your greatness!
O giver of gifts: gratitude to you for your greatness!
30 *O giver of gifts: gratitude to you for your greatness!*

Oh, my master is YHWH always!

19 "You Are the One Who Created the World" (*SL*, 67–68; *RPH*, 244–47; *D*, 161–62)

This poem is unique among Marqe's compositions, for it embeds an acrostic (as is typical for him) but the stanzas are very brief. Rhetorically, the poem is quite forceful: every line addresses the deity, often employing imperatives as the poet implores God to act, and almost every line includes the community as a participant in the liturgical dialogue. The poet, mediating between the "you" whom he addresses and the "we" with whom he stands, enacts a kind of rhetorical-liturgical duet, not through voice—God never speaks—but through intellectual and rhetorical force of will. In all likelihood, congregational voices added their

---

195. *RPH* treats this stich along with the following one as l. 22.
196. *RPH* treats this stich along with the following one as l. 23.
197. *RPH* treats this stich along with the following one as l. 24.
198. The lineation here departs from *RPH* by placing each stich of ll. 25–27 on a separate line.

weight to his words in the refrain.[199] Marqe's counterpoint in this dialogue is present, however, and the poem's conclusion (ll. 22–27) orients the congregation toward God, whom they petition to reciprocate and complement their performance (repentance) with his own (forgiveness). As complete as the poem is (and the fivefold repetition of the letter *tav* in the conclusion rounds it off firmly), the conversation between God and Israel seems to continue, as the intensive litany of imperatives in the main lines and the refrains awaits a response.

> *Said on festivals.*

א You are the one who created the world, without companion:
> *Accept our prayers from us, O merciful one.*

ב O Creator who created all and gives life to all:
> *Accept our prayers from us, O merciful one.*

ג The powerful one, the awesome one, the mighty one:
> *Accept our prayers from us, O merciful one.*

5 ד Whose power is praised and exalted:
> *Accept our prayers from us, O merciful one.*

ה Just as you stood by our ancestors, stand by us:
> *Accept our prayers from us, O merciful one.*

ו Woe to the one who does not feel[200] fear of you nor cry out and say:
> *Accept our prayers from us, O merciful one.*

ז Small and great alike say unto you:
> *Accept our prayers from us, O merciful one.*

ח Your great might, O my master, is a shield about us:
> *Accept our prayers from us, merciful one.*

10 ט Best of the good, O our master, hear our voice:
> *Accept our prayers from us, O merciful one.*

י May your great right hand lift anger away from us:
> *Accept our prayers from us, O merciful one.*

כ We all cry out before you, O our master, rescue [us]!
> *Accept our prayers from us, O merciful one.*

ל Not because we are worthy, but because you are merciful:
> *Accept our prayers from us, O merciful one.*

מ It is enough for us that you honored us by choosing us:
> *Accept our prayers from us, O merciful one.*

15 נ At ease are we, for your goodness exceeds our evil:

---

199. In *RPH*, the refrain is given only after the first line of the acrostic. The translation repeats the refrain after every line but retains *RPH*'s line numbering.

200. Lit., "bear, carry."

> *Accept our prayers from us, O merciful one.*

    ס Forgive the descendants of those who loved you in your great
        goodness:

> *Accept our prayers from us, O merciful one.*

    ע Show us that you are merciful and thus shall always be:

> *Accept our prayers from us, O merciful one.*

    פ Open the storehouse of your goodness; lock it not, O master of all:

> *Accept our prayers from us, O merciful one.*

    צ Our plea is before you, O my master; far be it from you to reject our
        prayers:

> *Accept our prayers from us, O merciful one.*

20 ק Forget not your covenants with our ancestors, for such is our balm:

> *Accept our prayers from us, O merciful one.*

    ר You are the merciful one, and thus we find you extending your
        mercy unto us:

> *Accept our prayers from us, O merciful one.*

    ש We beseech you, stay your judgment, for you are merciful:

> *Accept our prayers from us, O merciful one.*

    ת Praise [is yours] from heart and soul, O master of all!

> *Accept our prayers from us, O merciful one.*

    ת Return to us and forgive our sins!

> *Accept our prayers from us, O merciful one.*

25 ת Lift anger away from us and spread your mercy over us!

> *Accept our prayers from us, O merciful one.*

    ת Accept our repentance and forgive our sins!

> *Accept our prayers from us, O merciful one.*

    ת The Gate of Your Mercy, my master, shut not in our faces!

> *O God of Abraham, Isaac, and Jacob,*
> *Hear our voice and have mercy on us in your mercifulness!*

20 "You Are the Great Writing" (*SL*, 55–56; *RPH*, 247–50; *D*, 280–82)

The most striking aspect of this poem is that the entire work speaks directly to the Torah. Every stanza—indeed, almost every line—is addressed to the writing, while the refrain exclaims twenty-two times, "And there is no writing as great as you!"[201] This is not simply a hymn about the Torah; it is a paean

---

201. In *RPH*, the refrain is given only after the first stanza of the acrostic. The translation repeats the refrain after every stanza but retains *RPH*'s line numbering.

sung explicitly to it. The Torah is personified, and with an insistent boldness that blurs the boundaries between the text and the author. The potency of this conflation reflects the fact that, for Marqe's community, the Torah mediates the divine presence, and their sense of God's power and understanding of his might derives from the scroll that is physically in their midst. Marqe ultimately maintains a distinction between the Torah and its author, as he concludes the work with a call to praise "the one who gave you" (l. 45). And yet, lines such as "all healing comes through you" (l. 23) and descriptions of the Torah as a heavenly intercessor nonetheless suggest a transformation here of the Torah into a kind of Logos.

The form of this poem is almost as striking as its rhetorical stance. It is a graceful lyric, composed of brief, two-stich stanzas, each followed by the refrain. An alphabetical acrostic structures the work, as is customary for Marqe, but the individual stanzas are much briefer than usual. The performative effect of this hymn could have been almost ecstatic, with the intense, punchy repetitions of the refrain augmenting the springy energy of the individual stanzas. It is, in short, a rapturous hymn to the sacred item that stands at the heart of the synagogue ritual and Samaritan identity.

Said on holy days.

א You are the great writing
Before whom we have come to bow,
And there is no writing as great as you![202]

ב In devotion and with reverence
5 We stand before you,
And there is no writing as great as you!

ג Our hymns are your praise,
For you were written by the finger of God,
And there is no writing as great as you!

ד We are in awe, and we tremble,
For the Great Name[203] is written upon you,
And there is no writing as great as you!

10 ה We are like slaves before you,

202. Subsequent repetitions of the refrain are not included in the line count.
203. Lit., "the Great YHWH."

Abased before your greatness,
And there is no writing as great as you!

ו   Woe to the one who swears falsely by you and sins,
For you were written by the finger of God,
And there is no writing as great as you!

ז   You nourish those who hear you with life,
15   And you crown those who recite you with loyalty,
And there is no writing as great as you!

ע   Our maker and our Creator,
Teach us awe before you,
And there is no writing as great as you!

ט   Happy is the one who rises from his sleep
And hastens to seek your support,[204]
And there is no writing as great as you!

20 י   The great right hand extended you,
The great prophet received you,
And there is no writing as great as you!

כ   You calm any great anger,
And all healing comes through you,
And there is no writing as great as you!

ל   The heavenly household trembled
25   At the moment that the prophet received you,
And there is no writing as great as you!

מ   From the abode on high you descended,
From within the great fire you were revealed,
And there is no writing as great as you!

נ   The prophet was crowned with light,
For he was chosen to receive you,

---

204. This translation follows Ben-Hayyim (*RPH*, 248); the unemended text is difficult but could be rendered as "and who merits to greet you, your well-being." Brown renders: "Happy is he that arises from sleep and is deserving to greet thee" (*D*, 281).

And there is no writing as great as you!

30 ס Forgiveness and mercy
      We seek from your giver,
         And there is no writing as great as you!

    ע We saw all that preceded you,
      And we hearkened [to] all that came after you,[205]
         And there is no writing as great as you!

    פ The great rescuer that entreats[206]
35   On behalf of sinners, lest they be lost,
         And there is no writing as great as you!

    צ The vessel of manna and the staff[207]
      And the cherubim surround[208] you,
         And there is no writing as great as you!

    ק The voice of Moses was heard,
      Along with the voice of the shofar,
         And there is no writing as great as you!

40 ר The mountain was trembling terribly
      At the moment when your prophet received you,
         And there is no writing as great as you!

    ש The nations gave praise when they heard [cf. Exod 15:14–16]
      Your commanding words,
         And there is no writing as great as you!

    ת Praises and hymns
45   Let us utter with devotion to the one who gave you!
         And there is no writing as great as you!

---

205. This line interweaves the sensory experience of revelation and its aftermath (seeing, hearing) with its existential consequences (witnessing, obeying).

206. This line casts the Torah in the role of intercessor.

207. Of Aaron.

208. The text reads "(are) thy work" (פעלתך), but the present translation follows Ben-Hayyim (*RPH*, 250) in deriving the form from the root פלה (see *DSA*, 683, s.v. פלחה, "surrounding"). The stanza describes the physical environs of the tabernacle, with the tablets of the covenant enclosed within the ark on which the cherubim are mounted.

21 "Lo, the Radiant and Holy Writing" (*SL*, 56–58; *RPH*, 250–53 [ll. 1–41]; *D*, 282–86)

Marqe 20 stands out for its lyrical personification of Torah and its vision of the Torah as a mediator between God and community, which seems on the verge of conflating the Torah with its divine author. This poem advances a similar identification but heightens the ambiguity even more.[209] In this hymn, Marqe blurs the distinctions between God (author), Torah (text), and Moses (mediator) in ways that suggest some of these distinctions may be, in practical terms, without difference.[210] To highlight just how entwined these figures are, ambiguities in the Aramaic text arising from pronouns whose antecedents are unclear are indicated by square brackets in the translation. The simple fact is that translation requires a resolution of uncertainty that the original text can maintain. On the other hand, some phrases are startlingly bold and unequivocal: the image of sitting "at the hand of the writing" (l. 96*), for example, offers an image both visually clear and theologically striking. Torah heads the table as if it were God.

The ambiguity may strike readers as troubling and unexpected in a tradition that so strongly emphasizes God's singular uniqueness. But the blurriness does not trouble Marqe, apparently, and we may hypothesize that this is simply because the Torah, given to Israel through Moses, remains the tangible sign of God's presence and ongoing relationship with Israel. To know God, study God's writing; to love God, show devotion to his Torah; to praise God, discern the magnitude of his greatness in his revelation. As Marqe writes:

> A book, like no other,
> A book that casts a ladder to its beloveds;
> Exalted, they ascend upon it to their God.
> His witnesses are heaven and earth. (ll. 49*–52*)

God is unique, and his Torah is unique, and by means of the Torah, God is connected to his people, who in turn bear witness to his singularity. God's writing, unlike any other text, has agency, even a kind of personhood. In short, God's words become God's Word: Torah becomes Logos.

Said on holy days.

ה   Lo, the radiant and holy writing,

---

209. Here, as in Marqe 15, *RPH* includes only the initial portion of the hymn, which is still recited in the contemporary liturgy; *SL* provides an edition of the complete composition. Here asterisked line numbers indicate the stanzas taken from *SL*.

210. See MacDonald, "Samaritan Doctrine of Moses." These poems make clear that, within the world of the liturgy, an equally evocative and dramatic understanding of the Torah emerges.

That which the God of Gods gave to his trusted one,[211]
That which God proclaimed he should teach to his servants
So that they might give thanks for its [his?] holiness,
5   Because he chose them for himself as a holy nation.

ב   Written on two tablets,
Expounded in five books,
On Mount Sinai its roots are fixed;
In the Valley of Moab[212] are its branches.
10   Its words came forth from a flaming fire;
Heaven and earth began within it.

ג   It reveals the one who made the world;
Its enduring decrees,
He [it] revealed [them] to his [its] lovers.
15   To God are praises fitting;
To God we offer praise,[213]
When we recount his [its] wisdom.

ד   The prophet became afraid;
Fearfully he received the tablets.
20   For God passed before him;
His [its] form resembled fire,
When the entire congregation saw him[214]
And were afraid to draw near to his hand,[215]

ה   He [it] is the healing of the living.
25   He [it] purifies the spirits.
He [it] sanctifies the souls.
He [it] nourishes the hearts.
He [it] is what shows to all Hebrews
He who created them and leads them.

211. I.e., Moses.

212. The Torah here becomes a kind of landscape or map, with points marked at Sinai (Exodus) and Moab (Deuteronomy). Sinai and Moab constitute the place where revelation occurred and was then recollected, or acted and reenacted; furthermore, Sinai is where the Torah was given to Moses, and Moab (as in Deut 11:18–20) is where Moses instructs all the Israelites to write "these words" and where Moses writes "this Torah" (Deut 31:24) for transmission to the elders and priests.

213. Or "To God are (the) praises (that) we offer." Ben-Hayyim translates: "To God we are praise" (*RPH*, 252).

214. I.e., Moses.

215. In this stanza, Moses's radiance—a sign of divinity—may be implied. Moses has "caught" the divine splendor, as it were.

30   ו   And there is no writing as great as it,
         And no prophet like its writer,
         And no congregation as holy as the one that keeps it,
         And no dwelling like this one within it.[216]
         And no world can prosper unless it is fulfilled,
35   Unless it [he[217]] is utterly revered.

     ז   Sacred assemblies are within it,
         Summoned by the hand of the Living God.
         The just walk in his [its] ways;
         We, their offspring, inherit it[218]
40   So long as we do not cease to read from it
         And magnify God, the one who gave it.[219]

1*   ח   Loyalty crowns those who read it;
         Joy fills those who hearken unto it.
         Wisdom it gives to those who seek it;
         Life it gives to those who keep it,
5*   Might and triumph.
         And we bless the mighty one who gave it,
         He who gives recompense.[220]

     ט   Beneficent dews[221] fall upon the Hebrews;
         When they are gathered around[222] the writing,
10*   He pours forth goodness over their visages,
         Dew in their mouths.
         [He was] a pupil attending to his teacher;[223]
         Mercy is at hand
         For each who gazes upon it.[224]

---

216. This may refer to the tabernacle (for which the Torah provides a blueprint), although it also suggests the temple atop Mount Gerizim and the Torah shrine in which scrolls are kept. The ambiguity is resonant.

217. Ben-Hayyim observes: "Here it is difficult to discern if the antecedent of the pronoun is God or the writing" (*RPH*, 253).

218. Lit., "are its inheritors."

219. *RPH*'s text concludes here; the remaining translation follows the text published in *SL*.

220. Lit., "wages."

221. The words of Torah are here compared to dew, as in Deut 32:2.

222. Lit., "at the hand of, nearby."

223. Cf. *TM* I §5 (5א, p. 43): "The angel of YHWH was proclaiming and he (Moses) listened to him like a pupil who listens to the words of his teacher."

224. Lit., "mercy is through each who gazes upon it."

15*   ’   His great right hand extended,
         A great day was made for its sake.
         Israel promised[225] its master:
         It would keep his words and his covenant;
         Praises would be uttered to its giver,
20*   Who has granted goodness
         By giving us his handwriting.

      כ   The hands of our master concealed Moses
         When he received it at his hands.
         His throne of mercy concealed him;
25*   Cherubim kept watch over him.
         His priests proclaim his decrees;
         All the house of Israel keeps it.

      ל   We shall hearken only to his writing;
         Nothing else can compare to it.
30*   On high, the king is his[226] master;
         He is exalted over all other prophets.
         He is its scribe
         Forever [let it be said]:
         "There is no God but the one!"
35*   *Let us recite to its giver [this] praise.*

      מ   Who could create such a world?
         Who could bring about[227] such rites?
         Who could descend as God descended?
         Who could ascend as Moses ascended?
40*   Who could be as trustworthy as the trusted one,
         Entrusted with the words of his master?

      נ   A lamp, unchanging and undimmed,
         Is his writing for those who sustain it,
         A light, complete;
45*   Its speaker is
         The most radiant of mortals;
         Through it shall be glorified his enlightened ones,

225. Lit., "covenanted, made an agreement."
226. I.e., God is Moses's master; alternatively, God is "its" master—the master of Torah.
227. From נדי (*DSA*, 503).

Who serve his [its] words.

כ A book, like no other,
50*   A book that casts a ladder to its beloveds;[228]
       Exalted, they ascend upon it to their God.
       His witnesses are heaven and earth,
       But who has the ability
       To articulate his greatness?

55* ע A dowry[229] in which unchanging
       Rites and decrees are written;
       When we obey [them],
       His compassion is ours forever.
       The world was given in complete perfection;
60*   No flaw can be found within it.

פ A sliver of life, unlike any other,
       It transmits wisdom into the world,
       A sliver of life eternal.
       And this is from Eden,
65*   Which was opened by God;
       It sustains all its generations,
       And all are prolonged by its light.

צ It was a good morning upon Mount Sinai
       When the master descended bearing it.
70*   The prophet fasted and entreated
       And sanctified himself
       Before he received it—
       A form that resembled fire—
       As he stretched forth his hand from Sinai.

75* ק Holiness [comes] from his holy abode.
       The holy of holies is his writing.

---

228. According to Gen 28:12, Jacob dreamed of a ladder rising up to the heavens, but this line reverses the image by describing a ladder lowered from on high.

229. Lit., "something taken up," but the meaning "dowry" was current in Aramaic at that time (see *CAL*, s.v. *'llh*). Alternatively, it could be translated as "crop" or "harvest of grain" (either of which may have in and of themselves constituted elements of a dowry). Whether understood as dowry or harvest, each element within the collection (money, possessions, grain, etc.) is the subject of a distinct law, rite, or decree included in the Torah.

He hallowed Mount Sinai for its sake;
He, himself, descended,
And it was in his hand.

80*   Holy is the congregation of Israel
That is faithful to its teaching.

ר   The chief of the gods gave it,[230]
And the chief of the prophets received it.
The most exalted of congregations keeps it;

85*   The most exalted of prophets wrote it.
Forever [*let it be said*]:
"There is no God but he!"
Let us magnify our praise of its giver.

ש   The name of the Creator is written within.

90*   It bears witness: there is no God but the one.
It teaches the path of repentance
To the one who reads and acts.
Praise the name of its giver
And trust in his prophet who received it.

95*   ת   Three are they that set you free
When you sit at the hand of the writing:
Covenant, ancestors, and the righteous,[231]
[But] the love of God suffices.[232]
Lift your faces to his abode,

100*   For the master who is on high is merciful!

22 "This Is the Great Writing" (*SL*, 56; *RPII*, 254)

The manuscripts that include this brief hymn place it before or after Marqe 21.
It is not associated with any regular liturgical occasion, but in just a few lines it
weaves together essential elements of Samaritan belief. It begins by praising the

230. The underlying text is ריש אלהיה יהבה.
231. Brown translates as "Taheb" (*D*, 286), i.e., the quasi-messianic figure in Samaritan tradition; if Brown is correct, this is the only mention of the Taheb in Marqe's poetry. This catalogue is
reminiscent of similar catalogues of three essential items in rabbinic literature: Torah, worship, and
fidelity (m. Avot 1:2); justice, truth, and peace (m. Avot 1:18); and—perhaps most evocatively—
prayer, repentance, and charity (from the late antique Jewish High Holy Day poem *Unetaneh Tokef*).
232. Lit., "is full" or "fulfilled."

Torah as a kind of perfect object, perhaps to cue a gesture toward the ark where the scrolls were kept (if the word "this" is understood in performative terms). The Torah is intrinsically precious. The next stanza connects it to its divine author, the Creator of the world. The Torah is valuable not only because of what it contains but also because it was revealed. In the third stanza, the poet—speaking from within the community in the first-person plural ("all of us")—connects the unity of God with the unique revelation of Torah. The Torah was given not simply as a symbol but as a means by which the God who created life also sustains it. Torah is not only truth, but life. Following these carefully interwoven observations, the poet calls his community to offer praise.

> This is the great writing
> That is entirely meritorious;[233] truth is within it.
>
> This is what was revealed by God,
> He who drew forth the world by himself.
>
> 5 All of us shall give thanks to his oneness,
> For he gave it to sustain our lives.
>
> May God be praised!

23 "Continue to Bless the Name" (*SL*, 59; *RPH*, 254–55)

This work, to a degree unusual among Marqe's output, contains a substantial admixture of Hebrew phrases in its Aramaic text. In addition to this linguistic distinction, its stichometry is also highly irregular; indeed, no poetic format is preserved in the manuscript consulted by Ben-Hayyim, who followed his own sense of the work in dividing it into stanzas and lines. Likewise, this composition lacks any obvious structural device, such as an acrostic. Ben-Hayyim conjectured that it may not be the work of a single author but was unwilling to reject the traditional attribution of this work to Marqe, insofar as the Aramaic portions of the poem are in keeping with his style. (This hymn most resembles Marqe 25, which likewise may bear the imprint of multiple hands.)

The most intriguing aspect of the poem is the interlocking, mosaic aesthetic of its composition. The repetition of key words and phrases ("blessing," "life," "writing," "Ten Utterances," and the root קום, with meanings that include

---

233. The term זכותה connotes merit and justice but may also have the nuance of something obligatory and covenantal.

"standing," "presence," and "covenant") lends the poem a sense of unity, weaving the poem's potentially disjointed bilingualism into a thematically, if not linguistically or formally, unified whole.

Said on the sixth Sabbath between Passover and Shavuot.

Continue **to bless the Name**:[234]
The honored and awesome one!
For it is good for us to bless
Our God; **may he be blessed!**
All of us hasten to say:
5   "May the writing be praised with peace!"[235]

For forty days the prophet stood, fasting,
Upon the mountain: **he ate no bread**;
No water did he drink [Exod 34:28].

In order to learn and to teach
10   The children [of Israel] the words of the covenant,
The Ten Utterances.

"The writing was the writing of God" [Exod 32:16],
His words of life and blessing.

From the highest of heavens did God descend
15   Upon Mount Sinai, to proclaim in the presence of
His prophet the Ten Utterances.

Happy are we on account of what we heard,
For it is our life!

24 "Receive the Word of the Living One" (*SL*, 58–59; *RPH*, 256–58)

While Marqe wrote a number of poems extolling the Torah and dramatizing its revelation, this poem is his most lyrical offering—a quick, almost rough sketch

---

234. *Ha-Shem* (Hebrew השם rather than Aramaic שמא). This stich and the following one appear as a single line in *RPH*.

235. Ben-Hayyim (*RPH*, 255) suggests reading משלם ("fully, perfectly") instead of בשלם.

of fleeting images and ideas. Its lines are brief, and the stanzas irregular; most (but not all) stanzas divide into six lines, but no acrostic structures the poem and confirms the stichometry. The repetition of certain phrases suggests a refrain in the opening three stanzas, but the repetitions do not carry through the rest of the work. Nor does Marqe address the audience throughout the hymn: in the first stanza, he addresses the congregation, in the second he speaks to God as "you" and the congregation as "they," and in the third stanza, he inserts himself within the community ("we") and speaks of God in the third person.

Despite these irregularities, which keep listeners engaged by confounding their expectations, Marqe keeps his key elements in constant focus, even if the rhetorical relationships among them combine kaleidoscopically: God, Torah, and Israel. God is defined here primarily as the Torah giver, whose act of beneficence earns ongoing praise and thanksgiving. Torah is described in terms of its radiance and purity, and its splendor inspires reverence for its giver even as it displays some agency of its own. The people, in turn, bask in the light of the Torah and revere both its words and its source. The Torah offers a very tangible stand-in for the deity, as in the twice-repeated exclamation "When the great writing is opened / We hasten to bow down before its giver!" (ll. 15–16, 27–28). Reverence for the Torah expresses reverence for God.

In this poem, Marqe extols the Torah not because of its contents but because of its origins. While he describes the Torah as being opened and read, he does not mention laws or statutes, obedience or faithfulness. Everything is secondary to the communion between God and Israel as facilitated by the Torah. Even Moses goes unnamed, referred to simply as "the prophet." The relationship between deity and people, sealed and symbolized by the Torah, inspires ever-expanding circles of praise. Moses "multiplied hymns and praises" (l. 23) while he waited atop Sinai for God to extend the Torah to him. The congregation likewise bows and reveres the Torah and God. And this poem itself offers a script for such worship, concluding with the liturgical cue "May God be praised!" This cue comes in response to the line "God extended and the great prophet received" (l. 38). The Torah, as unique as its author, inspires the very words of this poem. In this lyric Marqe, invisible behind his words, stands as an heir to Moses, transmitting words that inspire praise.

Said on the Sabbath in the afternoon and on holy days.

Receive the word of the living one
Extended by the hand of God,
To whom eternal life belongs:
    Praise the great king
5   Who so enlightens the Hebrews

With writings, all of them illuminating.[236]

This is the Torah
That you gave to the children of Israel
So they might read in it and say:
10   Praise the great king ... [237]

Let all the Hebrews bow down
Before the holy writing,
And let them praise the one who gave it and say:
     Praise the great king;
15   *When the great writing is opened*
      We hasten to bow down before its giver!

It does not resemble the luminaries,
For they are concealed and then revealed every day,
But the great writing that is in our midst
20   Enlightens both day and night ... [238]

For forty days the prophet stood
Fasting atop the mountain, for its sake,[239]
Multiplying hymns and praises
      On account of the greatness of its utterance.
25   He received it from the eternal one
      And teaches it to mortals.

When the great writing is opened,
We hasten to bow before its giver
For it is the great and pure and holy writing,
30   That descended from the highest heavens;
      Just as there is no God like its giver,
      So, too, there is no writing as great as it.

The powers and the mighty ones were seen[240]
On the day when the Torah descended.

236. The word underlying this translation (נהר) connotes both light and wisdom.
237. Two stichs missing?
238. Two stichs missing?
239. I.e., for the sake of the writing.
240. The terms here are חילין and גבוראן ("powers" and "mighty ones"); i.e., the invisible angels became visible.

35 The great and glorious fire,
        And the cloud, and the voice of the shofar—
        Standing ones and mortals trembled;
        God extended and the great prophet received.

May God be praised!

25 "Germon, the Roman Official" (*SL*, 846; *RPH*, 258–62)

This poem celebrates the entry of a male child into the covenant through the ritual of circumcision.[241] The composition is not only attributed to Marqe but "signed" by means of a name acrostic—the only *piyyut* by Marqe that bears his signature. The very uniqueness of this feature in Marqe's corpus may cast doubt on the authenticity of authorship, but nothing in the poem's language or form intrinsically indicates a date after the fourth century CE. The name acrostic may, in fact, reflect the custom of bestowing a name on an infant boy at circumcision: on the occasion of naming, the poet cleverly tells us his name.[242]

The poem seems to be knit together from four diverse units: a four-stanza acrostic that constitutes a complete unit defined by the signature; a five-stanza narrative unit that speaks in philosophical and historical terms about the value of circumcision; a three-stanza ritual unit defined by its refrain, which anticipates the immediate performance of the rite; and the concluding stanza recited after the circumcision, with its enigmatic historical reference.[243] We can hypothesize various compositional histories to account for these formal differences within the poem, but as the language is consistently true to the Samaritan Aramaic of late antiquity, there is no need to posit that any of the four units postdate Marqe. Instead, the internal diversity of the hymn may reflect its function in a liturgy for the ritual of circumcision, with the different units corresponding to distinct elements of the ceremony.

The infant to be circumcised is explicitly present in the poem. In the second stanza, the poet refers to the great goodness "that we see here," referring to both the gathered witnesses and the two "good things" that are present, the infant and the mitzvah about to be fulfilled. Stanzas 8 through 10 (ll. 29–40) speak of "[this] boy who approaches" (l. 37)—a phrasing that emphasizes the child's agency (although he is brought by his father)—and seek for him divine protection and

---

241. For an in-depth study of this poem, see Lieber, "Good Christian."

242. On name acrostics, see Krueger, *Writing and Holiness*, 159–88.

243. It is possible to read the final four hemistichs as a single line, especially given their relative brevity compared to the hemistichs that constitute other stanzas.

a long life. The repetitive structure suggests that others, perhaps the assembled community, speak to the boy directly. And the final stanza (stanza 13) speaks directly to "this little boy" (l. 49).

The final stanza is conspicuous not only because of its direct, tender reference to the infant being circumcised but also because of its "aggadic" or historical allusion. In the last two stichs, Marqe singles out for blessing the "good Germon / the Roman official." While this reference probably eludes most modern readers, it refers to a key tradition in early Samaritan history. Germanus ("Germon" in Marqe's Aramaic) was a Byzantine official, perhaps the bishop of Neopolis/Nablus.[244] He is honored here because he refused to enforce Emperor Decius's short-lived ban on circumcision;[245] indeed, he is even credited with facilitating the circumcision of the infant Baba Rabba, the great Samaritan reformer (and the leader with whom Amram Dare was affiliated). While the story of Baba Rabba's circumcision may be a legend, if this poem is the work of Marqe then the memory of anticircumcision legislation would have been fresh. The infant being brought forward for circumcision, along with his family and the community, may well have been understood to be participating in something not only existentially significant for the child and his family but also communally heroic.

This poem is said when a newborn boy is brought into the covenant of Abraham, when the boy's name is given.

Master of the divine beings,[246]
You to whom greatness belongs,
Such manifold honors
Befit this one, who is worthy to don [it].[247]

5   Exceedingly great is
That which we see here,
The precious image[248]
Planned by the hand of God.

---

244. The common root גרם has the meaning of "bone, self" in Aramaic (parallel to Hebrew עצם); see *DSA*, 158, s.v. גרם. It may be that the derived qualities of "strength" and "fortitude" colored how this Latin name was heard by Marqe's audience.

245. The ban lasted from 250 to 251 CE. On the Decian persecution—remembered primarily for its anti-Christian elements—see Rives, "Decree of Decius."

246. Lit., "deities, gods."

247. I.e., to receive in his flesh the sign of the covenant, which he will wear all his life.

248. A reference to the baby, who is made in the divine image.

He himself is the one who planned it
10   With great tenderness,
A gift from God,
Eternal life.[249]

Lo, such a joyous vision,
So overwhelming![250]
15   May God be magnified
For doing thus!

Happy are the fathers
When they behold this [scene]:
A son donning
20   His covenant.[251]

And happy is the boy
Who dons it, [his] first [commandment],[252]
For it is a purifying immersion,
But without water.

25   It is a powerful ordeal[253]
Without a ritual bath[254]—
It is an eternal covenant
That shall not be nullified.

Abraham donned it first, and his sons,
30   And all the members of his household,
And he commanded those who would come afterward
To don it [too].

249. This may suggest the idea of "intergenerational eternity," the idea that one generation lives on through the next.

250. Lit., "greatly strong, powerful."

251. Lit., "clothes himself in [or wears] his cutting/commandment." The translation attempts to acknowledge the infant's lack of physical agency while also rendering the important theme word גזרה consistently throughout the work. The term combines the meaning of "cutting" as the physical act of circumcision with that of "decree" and is thus suggestive of the covenant.

252. I.e., the sign of the covenant in his flesh. As Ben-Hayyim notes, the poet seems to celebrate the circumcision as the first commandment a Samaritan boy fulfills (RPH, 260).

253. This stanza puns on the consonant sounds /b-r/, which appear in "ordeal" (בחור) and "covenant" (בריה) while evoking the essential word "son" (בר).

254. Lit., "cistern."

And one who does not don it himself
On the eighth day,
35 He is not one of the Hebrews,
And he is not holy.

[*This*] *boy who approaches*
To don his circumcision:
   May God protect him—
40   He who lifts up the heavens.

[*This*] *boy who approaches*
To don his circumcision:
   May he be pleasing, and may he grow,
   And may he reach a ripe old age.[255]

45 [*This*] *boy who approaches*
To don his circumcision:
   May he stand firm and live long
   On account of his donning [of the sign of] the Almighty.[256]

[The circumcision takes place.]

Lo, may this little boy
50 Grow into a man.[257]
Remember for good Germon,[258]
The Roman official!

255. Lit., "may he arrive at the stage of old age."

256. The term חיולה (lit., "the strong, mighty one") is here taken as a divine epithet. Alternatively, it could be taken as an adjective modifying "donning," yielding the translation "on account of his powerful (act of) donning (the sign of the covenant)."

257. Lit., "become a big one." This stanza (unusually) employs two Greek words: κόρος ("boy") and μέγιστος ("very large," i.e., a grown man). A third word (מקסקס) is difficult and may be corrupt; Ben-Hayyim suggests that it may derive from the Greek μέγας ("big") or υἱός ("son"), and he hypothesizes that this entire stanza was originally written in Greek (*RPH*, 262). Tal summarizes Ben-Hayyim's proposal and translates the phrase as "this little son shall be a great one" (*DSA*, 484, s.v. מקסקס). The phrase strongly echoes the language of the Jewish circumcision ritual, which expresses the wish זה הקטן גדול יהיה: "May this little one become a great one!"

258. Germon, probably a shortened form of the Latin name Germanus, was a Byzantine official or perhaps a bishop in Nablus/Neopolis. Medieval chronicles remember Germanus positively for not enforcing the ban on circumcision proclaimed in the Edict of Decius. See Stenhouse, "Germanus."

Ninna ben Marqe

NINNA IS THE THIRD AND last of the classical Samaritan poets. He was, according to tradition, the son of Marqe and grandson of Amram, and he lived in the fourth century CE. The origin of his name has been debated. Cowley derived it from the Latin Nonus (in keeping with the Latinate names of his grandfather, Amram-Tute [Titus], and his father, Marqe [Marcus]). Ze'ev Ben-Hayyim, however, regarded it as the Samaritan variant of the Hebrew name Nannus/Nanna— itself a diminutive or abbreviated form of Hananiah or Haninah—attested in Tannaitic and Amoraic sources from the Land of Israel.[1]

Either Ninna was not as prolific as his father and grandfather, or fewer of his works were incorporated into and preserved in the Samaritan liturgy. Only one poem is ascribed to him with certainty, the first one translated below; another, also translated below, is dubious; a third is attributed either to Ninna or to Marqe (see Marqe 18). The two poems included here are quite different: the first one is lengthy and in terms of its form resembles Marqe 18; the second is, by contrast, a short lyric. While Ninna wrote in the same Samaritan Aramaic as Amram and Marqe, there is no substantial body of work or style of writing that is distinctly "Ninnan." Ninna left behind no equivalent to his grandfather's *Durran*, nor any conventional hymn form akin to that of his father, Marqe.

While Ninna's few compositions do not share a common form, they do share a common focus. His works are associated with a particular liturgical station: the end of the Sabbath. The first poem translated here bids the Sabbath farewell, while the second speaks to the worshippers as they reenter the workaday world. Marqe 18, while it does not explicitly address the conclusion of the Sabbath,

---

1. On the derivation of the name, see *RPH*, 16. In the Mishnah, Rabbi Shimon b. Nannus appears on multiple occasions (m. Bikkurim 3:9; m. Shabbat 16:5; m. Eruvin 10:15; m. Ketubbot 10:5; m. Gittin 8:10; m. Baba Batra 7:3; 10:8; m. Shevu'ot 7:5; m. Menahot 4:3). In other sources, he is referred to as "Ben Nannus." The Hebrew name Hanani(ah) is also common in the Jewish Bible, but not in the Torah; it appears in 1 Kgs 16; Jer 28; 36; 37; Dan 1; Ezra 10; Neh 1; 3; 7; 8; 10; 12; 1 Chr 3; 8; 25; 2 Chr 16; 19; 20; 26.

is conventionally read in that context. Ninna's first poem in particular provides a rich description of the rituals of the Sabbath and an evocative sense of its meaningfulness, particularly as the Sabbath relates to the creation narrative of Gen 1.

1 "Go in Peace, O Sabbath Day" (*SL*, 15–16; *RPH*, 263–74; *D*, 238–42)

This lengthy hymn, the only poem ascribed to Ninna with confidence, celebrates a liturgical moment that was embroidered upon by Amram Dare and Marqe: the conclusion of the Sabbath day. The Sabbath, which enters as the sun sets on Friday evening, departs with the sunset on Saturday, and these poems embellish the liturgy of farewell. Thus, this hymn constitutes a kind of bookend to the poems by Ninna's father and grandfather that welcome the Sabbath as it begins.[2]

Ninna weaves together themes that include praise for the Sabbath as it leaves, couched in terms of how the human community observes the Sabbath rites; praise for creation, which includes the creation of rest; and praise for the Torah and for Torah study, which transpires in the heavens as well as on earth and integrates Sabbath and creation into a singular, scripturalized whole. The Sabbath offers a moment to celebrate creation and Torah: creation bequeaths the Sabbath, as is recorded in scripture, while scripture contains within it the wonders of creation, in which humans and angels alike can immerse themselves on the Sabbath. It is a moment when the pillars of religious life, both terrestrial and heavenly, find balance, resonance, and harmony. And as Ninna notes, it is a respite and gift that comes after six days of "servitude," freeing the observant Israelite from the oppression of tedium and offering him sanctuary in the holy "schoolhouse" of Torah.

In the opening stanza, the poet speaks to both the personified Sabbath and the congregation: he bids the Sabbath farewell—"Go in peace!" (l. 1)—and describes it as bedecking Israel like a royal, protective crown. Israel's choice to embrace the Sabbath ornaments it, while a decision to cast it aside would incur harm. Throughout most of the rest of the poem, however, the poet speaks from within the congregation ("we") as they offer praise and thanks to God, whom he addresses directly as "you." But as much as the conversation of the poem creates a sense of intimacy and relationship within the prayer, the most fascinating element of the poem may be its imagery and its sense of motion, its kinesthetics. The dialogue does not conjure a sense of restful stillness but rather a vision

---

2. Brown translates this composition as prose (*D*, 238–42).

of tremendous activity swirling around the divine object of the poet's address. Respite is active: the Sabbath rescues a person from the hand of oppression that would seize him. Prayer is physical: worshippers bow down, sing, and turn to one another. Worship is musical: the congregation offers up melody, song, and praise. Even holiness moves: having descended to earth for the Sabbath, when the Sabbath concludes holiness ascends back to its supernal home, where it is honored and kept for the other six days of the week. The poem is an energetic tapestry depicting the motions of bodies both familiar (the ritual acts of the congregation) and purely conceptual.

The final section of the poem, which begins with the words "For this schoolhouse is lovely" (l. 68), takes us simultaneously up to the heavens and into the Torah. The heavenly bodies and angelic beings are depicted as diligent students. The Sun "dawns every day, [rising early] like an obedient youth" (l. 71), acting like a diligent pupil who arrives early to open the classroom doors in eager anticipation of a day of learning. The poet depicts God's action using similarly humble imagery. The creation of the world, which the poet identifies with the creation of the Torah, is described as God's "drawing it forth" from the wellspring of the "very good," and he likewise makes the angels by pulling them forth out of the "cistern of water" (ll. 75–81). Creation here is not simply an act of speech, but a muscular effort of the most familiar kind. Creation was work, so the Creator created rest.

As a poem that bids farewell to the Sabbath, it has as its backdrop the division between the week of work and the rest of Sabbath; performatively, it marks that liminal moment that divides sacred and profane time, in a fashion akin to rabbinic rituals of *havdalah* (literally "division").[3] As the poet writes:

(Now) you have brought us to nightfall, and to the border of (the day
    of) rest;
And we see how [you] work the transformation
And [keep] the borders untransgressed.
Unto you we render praises, for thus is a portion of your wisdom.
    (ll. 33–36)

The evening is arriving as the sun departs, and the boundary of the day of rest approaches. The transformation that takes place now, the boundary that will be respected, is the boundary of the workaday world. Recognizing this transition from rest back to work, the poet celebrates the hum of sacred activity that is the Sabbath even as he articulates his wonder at the created world that awaits.

---

3. For an overview of *havdalah* in rabbinic Judaism, see Lavee, "Literary Canonization."

Recited after the conclusion of the Sabbath [motzei Shabbat], *except for the Sabbaths that fall during festivals.*

Go in peace, O Sabbath day,
Great crown of Israel!
When you are bedecked by it, you are a king;
When you cast it aside, you are greatly afflicted.[4]

5   A slave's freedom comes after six years,
But Israel's [comes] every six days.
And were it not for the Sabbath, which comes
And relieves the affliction of Israel,
A person would be seized by the hand of oppression,
10   Which overwhelms him so greatly;
But instead, he ceases [from work] and rests,
And gives thanks, and praises God.

Lo, who would pass[5] the holy day
In anything but melody and praises and glory?
15   Let us bow down, all of us, this one with that one, to sanctify him,
He who gave it to us and filled it with all of his riches
And crowned it with all good.
Those who bow down to him sing and utter praises:
        Happy are those who bow down, for they are joined with you;
20   *Lo, the holy day: a gift from God to all!*

The holiness of the Sabbath turns away from the world below
And ascends to the uppermost heights,
[Returning] to the place sanctified by the master from the first,
Where it is guarded among the secrets
25   And honored among the revelations;
Above and below it arrives
At the appointed time, and its greatness comes after.
        Happy are those who bow down, for they are joined with you;
        Lo, the holy day: a gift from God to all!

---

4. The root translated here as "afflicted" (דוש) has very physical connotations of crushing, trampling, and threshing.

5. The underlying word (געו) connotes "to pass by" but also "to transgress." To pass the time in any way but proper observance is to violate it.

30 O merciful one, O good one, O leader-unto-life,
    Who has designated us[6] to pass the length of its day in peace
    Out of your great goodness,
    [Now] you have brought us to nightfall,[7] and to the border of [the day
      of] rest;
    And we see how [you] work the transformation
35 And [keep] the borders untransgressed.
    Unto you we render praises, for thus is a portion of your wisdom.[8]

    My master, you who stand with us today,
    And support us through the nighttime,[9]
    And watch over us, unseen:
40 *We arise after our sleep*
    And sing[10] *songs unto you,*
    And [offer] thanksgiving and praises,
    For you, O our master, are good, merciful, and gracious.

    O Creator of all,
45 God of all generations,
    Before you created humanity
    You foresaw[11] the weakness of humankind,
    And so you fashioned rest to follow weariness,
    So there would be respite from all affliction and weariness.
50 You created the day for the doing of all handiwork
    And the night for sleep and rest,
    And for both, it is incumbent upon us to praise you.

    My master, you who stand with us today,
    And support us through the nighttime,
55 *And watch over us, unseen:*
    We arise after our sleep
    And utter[12] *songs unto you.*
    And [offer] thanksgiving and praises,
    For you, O our master, are good, merciful, and gracious.

6. Lit., "bestowed upon us" or "decreed for us."
7. Lit., "darkness," referring to the period after sunset, when the Sabbath has gone out.
8. I.e., our perception of the workings of the natural world reflects a glimpse into the divine wisdom undergirding all creation.
9. Lit., "portion of the night."
10. Lit., "say."
11. Lit., "saw."
12. Lit., "say."

60 Come, let us open that of "**in the beginning**" [Gen 1:1],[13]
And let us read within it, and [find] what is found from the first;[14]
Come, let us bow down before it.
Indeed, we find "**wilderness and waste**" [Gen 1:2],
A wellspring of water,[15] and God,
65 The craftsman who apportioned from it life—
His words he would send into the waters of "**wilderness and waste**"
   [Gen 1:2].
They would return, laden with creatures.

For this schoolhouse[16] is lovely,
The schoolhouse of "**in the beginning**" [Gen 1:1].[17]
70 The youths who are within it? heaven and earth!
Light dawns every day, [rising early] like an obedient youth
Who enters the schoolhouse, morning and evening:
He opens it and locks it, and afterward none may object.[18]
Affliction comes upon those who say: "There is another beside him."[19]

75 This is a beautiful realm, the realm of "**in the beginning**" [Gen 1:1].
And every creature within it is holy, like its Fashioner,
The holiest one,[20] may he be praised, for he created it,
And it was drawn forth by his hand from the wellspring of "**very
   good**" [Gen 1:31].
Its footings are strength-angels, its foundations are creature-angels,[21]
80 And the craftsman, who fashioned it, rooted it well:
Praise the craftsman, who created the cistern of water!

13. I.e., the Torah; the opening word of Genesis is here given in Hebrew (בראשית) rather than in Aramaic.

14. A reference to the creation narratives of Gen 1–2.

15. The "wilderness and waste" of Gen 1:2 seems to be understood here as a primordial sea or pool.

16. The phrase "schoolhouse" (lit., "house of the book") is used in Samaritan Aramaic as an epithet for the Torah (see *DSA*, 88, s.v. בות); in the earliest stratum of *Tibat Marqe*, for example, God calls the Torah "the schoolhouse" and describes Moses as "its teacher" (*TM* 1 §30 [20א, p. 65]). Here, however, the term seems to refer to a heavenly house of study, analogous to the earthly structure. For a detailed analysis of the image of the schoolhouse in late antiquity, see Fine, "For This Schoolhouse Is Beautiful."

17. Signifying both Torah and creation; as in l. 60, the poem uses the Hebrew phrase.

18. Or perhaps "none may knock" (seeking belated entry).

19. The translation follows Ben-Hayyim (*RPH*, 271), against Fine, who translates it as "anyone but us" ("For This Schoolhouse is Beautiful," 69).

20. Lit., "the holy of holies," but here a reference to God rather than the inner sanctum.

21. The translation treats these two categories of beings as angels; alternatively, the terms may be translated as "angels" (חיליו) and "mortals" (בריאו).

And he drew forth from it strength-angels and creature-angels,
And he made day and night, and organized them with his word:
And he called the darkness "night" and the light "day,"
85   And he entrusted to them their tasks,
And thus they are forever.
We proclaim to him with devotion:
Great is God, who has done thus!
And we entreat you, O God who sustains life,[22]
90   Pity us in your goodness, and rescue us in your loyalty.
We know, O our master, that our sins are many,
But your mercy is boundless and your compassion eternal.

My master, forgive us, and pardon us, and redeem us, and release us;
Your goodness is our rescue at every moment.
95   Remember them—the three good men:
Abraham and Isaac and Jacob, the pure one,
To whom you swore upon yourself;
You swore to them by yourself.
Their covenant will not be broken for all the generations of the world.
100 The praise of our master shall not be interrupted;
In the evening and in the morning, all of us, we say it,
Just as Moses said at the sea, so we say:
"O awesome one, O praised one, O worker of wonders!"
All of you respond: "And they said:
105   All that YHWH spoke to Moses,
Let us hear and let us do!" [cf. Exod 24:7].[23]

May God be praised!
There is no God but the one!

2 "Go Forth in Peace" (*SL*, 410, 442; *RPH*, 371; *D*, 246)

This brief hymn, though attributed to Ninna, quite probably postdates him. Ben-Hayyim draws attention to features of its language that bespeak a date several

22. Alternatively, "God of life."
23. Near quotation of Exod 24:7 in Aramaic; it is close to but not identical with the rendering of the SamT (the poem has דמלל where the targum has אד מלל), and "to Moses" (למשה) does not appear in the SamP, the SamT, or the MT. In regard to the final stich, the poet presents the words in the same order as does the SamT, a noteworthy difference from the tradition in the MT and the SamP: "We will do and we will hear" (נעשה ונשמע). The SamT may have been influenced by Deut 5:27, which offers the more logical order. Cf. the note on Marqe 14, ll. 111–12.

centuries after Ninna's lifetime.[24] The fact that the poem specifically references Ninna's great hymn "Go in Peace" (Ninna 1) certainly places this poem in a position of dependence on that composition.

And yet, despite its dubious attribution, this composition provides a lyrical example of Samaritan poetry with which to close this volume. Its spare and elegant language is richly suggestive of antiphonal recitation that draws the congregation into the liturgical experience of the work; the fluidity with which the composition shifts between first, second, and third person puts the listener in the position of subject, object, and audience, and it suggestively blurs the boundaries between revealer and revelation. This hymn weaves together phrases from the Torah, Marqe, and Ninna, and whereas Ninna's hymn bids the Sabbath farewell, this hymn addresses the community, as it too sets forth from the sanctuary into the workaday world.

> *Said at the end of the Sabbath that follows Shavuot and after Shemini Atzeret, and with minor differences, at the end of the Sabbath that precedes the new moon of the first month and the new moon of the seventh month.*[25]

Go forth[26] in peace,
    O congregation of Hebrews.

From [this] prayer,[27] "Go in peace";[28]
    It is the prayer of the first ones.

5   Its utterance upon the heart
    Is like "**dripping dew**" [Deut 32:2].

A treasure-house full of wisdom,
    Happy is the one who seeks it.[29]

---

24. Ben-Hayyim dated this poem after the Muslim conquest, citing phrases that seem to reflect the influence of Arabic, and placed it in his section of "Anonymous Hymns" (*RPH*, 371). Cowley includes two versions of the hymn; the new moon version (*SL*, 410) differs slightly from the text translated here (*SL*, 442). Brown treats the hymn as a prose composition, and his division of the text into phrases and clauses differs significantly from the stichometry in *SL* and *RPH* (*D*, 246).

25. The first day of the seventh month is known to the Samaritans not as Rosh Hashanah (as is the case in Judaism) but as the Feast of the Seventh Month (Powels, "Samaritan Calendar," 730–31).

26. In Cowley's new moon version (*SL*, 410), the text reads אקדמו, which could be translated as "set forth."

27. In Cowley's new moon version (*SL*, 410), the text reads על צלות, "upon (this) prayer."

28. The poet refers to the previous poem by Ninna, "Go in Peace."

29. The text is ambiguous: it can be translated, "seeks it" (i.e., Torah) or "seeks Him" (i.e., God).

May God accept from me, for your sake,
10   My request and my entreaty.

Let your assembly conclude,
And you, in response to my joy and my happiness,
Respond to my utterance and say:

Remember the first ones,
15 *And forget not the last ones!*[30]

---

30. The final lines of the hymn quote a poem by Marqe (2, ll. 61–62).

BIBLIOGRAPHY

A. B. Institute of Samaritan Studies. *The Samaritan Survival: To Whom It May Concern*. Pamphlet. Holon, Israel, 1995.

Anderson, Robert T. "Mount Gerizim." Pages 99–103 in Crown, Pummer, and Tal, *Companion to Samaritan Studies*.

Anderson, Robert T., and Terry Giles. *Tradition Kept: The Literature of the Samaritans*. Ada, MI: Baker Academic, 2005.

Beckwith, Roger T. "Formation of the Hebrew Bible." Pages 39–86 in *Mikra: Text, Translation, Reading, and Interpretation of the Hebrew Bible in Ancient Judaism and Early Christianity*. Edited by Martin Jan Mulder and Harry Sysling. Compendia Rerum Iudaicarum ad Novum Testamentum. Assen: Van Gorcum; Philadelphia: Fortress, 1988. Reprint, Grand Rapids, MI: Baker Academic, 2004.

Ben-Hayyim, Ze'ev, ed. *The Recitation of Prayers and Hymns*. Vol. 3, part 2, of *The Literary and Oral Tradition of Hebrew and Aramaic Amongst the Samaritans* [Hebrew]. 5 vols. Jerusalem: Academy of the Hebrew Language, 1957–77.

———. *Tibat Marqe: A Collection of Samaritan Midrashim* [Hebrew]. Jerusalem: Israel Academy of Sciences and Humanities, 1988.

Bowman, John. "Early Samaritan Eschatology." *Journal of Jewish Studies* 6, no. 2 (1955): 63–72.

———. *Samaritan Documents Relating to Their History, Religion, and Life*. Pittsburgh: Pickwick, 1977.

Broadie, Alexander. *A Samaritan Philosophy: A Study of the Hellenistic Cultural Ethos of the "Memar Marqah."* Leiden: Brill, 1987.

Brown, Solomon. "A Critical Edition and Translation of the Ancient Samaritan *Defter* (i.e., Liturgy) and a Comparison of It with Early Jewish Liturgy." PhD diss., University of Leeds, 1955. http://etheses.whiterose.ac.uk/id/eprint/2196.

Bull, Robert J. "Ras, Tell er-." Pages 407–9 in vol. 4 of *The Oxford Encyclopedia of Archaeology in the Near East*. Edited by Eric M. Meyers. New York: Oxford University Press, 1997.

Campbell, Edward F., Jr. "Shechem—Tel Balâtah." Pages 1345–54 in vol. 4 of *The New Encyclopedia of Archaeological Excavation in the Holy Land*. Edited by Ephraim Stern. Jerusalem: Israel Exploration Society, 1993.

Chazon, Esther G. "Human and Angelic Prayer in Light of the Dead Sea Scrolls." Pages 35–47 in *Liturgical Perspectives: Prayer and Poetry in Light of the Dead Sea*

Scrolls; Proceedings of the Fifth International Symposium of the Orion Center, 19–23 January 2000. Edited by Esther G. Chazon. Leiden: Brill, 2003.

Collins, Marilyn F. "The Hidden Vessels in Samaritan Tradition." *Journal for the Study of Judaism* 3, no. 2 (1972): 97–116.

Comprehensive Aramaic Lexicon. http://cal.huc.edu.

Cowley, Arthur E. *The Samaritan Liturgy*. 2 vols. Oxford: Clarendon, 1909. Vol. 1, https://archive.org/details/samaritanliturgy01cowluoft; vol. 2, https://archive.org /details/thesamaritanlitu02cowluoft.

Crown, Alan D. "The Samaritan Diaspora." Pages 195–217 in Crown, *Samaritans*, 195–217.

———, ed. *The Samaritans*. Tübingen: J. C. B. Mohr (Paul Siebeck), 1989.

Crown, Alan D., and Reinhard Pummer. *A Bibliography of the Samaritans*. 3rd ed. Lanham, MD: Scarecrow, 2005.

Crown, Alan D., Reinhard Pummer, and Abraham Tal, eds. *A Companion to Samaritan Studies*. Tübingen: Mohr Siebeck, 1993.

Dar, Shimon. "Archaeological Aspects of Samaritan Research in Israel." Pages 189–98 in *Religious Diversity in Late Antiquity*. Edited by David Gwynn and Susanne Bangert. Leiden: Brill, 2010.

Davidson, Israel. *Thesaurus of Mediaeval Hebrew Poetry* [Hebrew]. 4 vols. New York: Jewish Theological Seminary of America, 1924–33.

Dexinger, Ferdinand. "Samaritan Eschatology." Pages 262–92 in Crown, *Samaritans*.

Di Segni, Leah. "The Church of Mary Theotokos on Mount Gerizim: The Inscriptions." Pages 343–50 in *Christian Archaeology in the Holy Land: New Discoveries. Essays in Honour of Virgilio C. Corbo*. Edited by Giovanni Claudio Bottini, Leah Di Segni, and Eugenio Alliata. Jerusalem: Franciscan Printing Press, 1990.

———. "Samaritan Revolts in Byzantine Palestine" [Hebrew]. Pages 454–80 in *The Samaritans*. Edited by Ephraim Stern and Hanan Eshel. Jerusalem: Yad Yitzhak ben Zvi, 2002.

Doyle, Chris. *Honorius: The Fight for the Roman West, AD 395–423*. New York: Routledge, 2019.

Dušek, Jan, ed. *The Samaritans in Historical, Cultural and Linguistic Perspectives*. Berlin: de Gruyter, 2018.

Fine, Steven. "'For This Schoolhouse Is Beautiful': A Note on Samaritan 'Schools' in Late Antique Palestine." Pages 65–75 in *Shoshannat Yaakov: Studies in Honor of Professor Yaakov Elman*. Edited by Shai Secunda and Steven Fine. Leiden: Brill, 2012.

Florentin, Moshe. *Late Samaritan Hebrew: A Linguistic Analysis of Its Different Types*. Leiden: Brill, 2005.

———. *Samaritan Elegies: A Collection of Lamentations, Admonitions, and Poems of Praising God* [Hebrew]. Jerusalem: Bialik, 2012.

———. *Tulida: A Samaritan Chronicle* [Hebrew]. Jerusalem: Yad Yitzhak Ben-Zvi, 1999.

Gaster, Moses. *The Samaritans: Their History, Doctrines and Literature*. Schweich Lectures 1923. London: Oxford University Press, 1925.

Hall, Bruce. "From John Hyrcanus to Baba Rabbah." Pages 32–54 in Crown, *Samaritans*.

Hjelm, Ingrid. "Samaritans: History and Tradition in Relationship to Jews, Christians, and Muslims: Problems in Writing a Monograph." Pages 173–85 in Zsengellér, *Samaria, Samarians, Samaritans*.

Israelite Samaritan Information Institute. "Population." https://www.israelite
-samaritans.com/about-israelite-samaritans/population-survey.

Jacobus, Helen R. *Zodiac Calendars in the Dead Sea Scrolls and Their Reception: Ancient Astronomy and Astrology in Early Judaism.* Leiden: Brill, 2015.

Jacoby, Ruth. "The Four Species in Jewish and Samaritan Tradition" [Hebrew]. *Eretz Israel* 25 (1996): 404–9; English summary, p. 103*. English translation: "The Four Species in Jewish and Samaritan Traditions." Pages 225–30 in *From Dura to Sepphoris: Studies in Jewish Art and Society in Late Antiquity.* Edited by Lee I. Levine and Zeev Weiss. Portsmouth, RI: Journal of Roman Archaeology, 2000.

Josephus, Flavius. *Jewish Antiquities.* Vol. 7, *Books 18–19.* Translated by Louis H. Feldman. Cambridge: Harvard University Press, 1965.

Kalimi, Isaac, and James D. Purvis. "The Hiding of the Temple Vessels in Jewish and Samaritan Literature." *Catholic Biblical Quarterly* 56, no. 4 (1994): 679–85.

Kartveit, Magnar. "The Origin of the Jews and Samaritans According to the Samaritan Chronicles." Pages 283–97 in *"Through Thy Word All Things Were Made!" Second International Conference of Mandaic and Samaritan Studies.* Edited by Rainer Voigt. Wiesbaden: Harrassowitz, 2013.

———. *The Origins of the Samaritans.* Leiden: Brill, 2009.

Kaufman, Stephen A. "The Dialectology of Late Jewish Literary Aramaic." *Aramaic Studies* 11, no. 2 (2013): 145–48.

Knoppers, Gary N. *Jews and Samaritans: The Origins and History of Their Early Relations.* New York: Oxford University Press, 2013.

Koester, Craig R. "'The Savior of the World' (John 4:42)." *Journal of Biblical Literature* 109, no. 4 (1990): 665–80.

Krueger, Derek. *Writing and Holiness: The Practice of Authorship in the Early Christian East.* Philadelphia: University of Pennsylvania Press, 2004.

Kugel, James L. *A Walk Through "Jubilees": Studies in the "Book of Jubilees" and the World of Its Creation.* Leiden: Brill, 2012.

Kutscher, E. Y. *Studies in Galilean Aramaic.* Translated by Michael Sokoloff. Ramat Gan: Bar-Ilan University Press, 1976.

Langer, Ruth. "From Study of Scripture to Reenactment of Sinai." *Worship* 72, no. 1 (1998): 43–67.

Lavee, Moshe. "Literary Canonization at Work: The Authority of Aggadic Midrash and the Evolution of Havdalah Poetry in the Genizah." *AJS Review* 37, no. 2 (2013): 285–313.

Lehnardt, Andreas. "'If a Cuthean Comes and Forces You into Military Service' (*Pesiqta de-Rav Kahana, Ha-Hodesh, pisqa* 5): Anti-Samaritan Polemics in a Homiletic Midrash." Pages 75–90 in Dušek, *Samaritans.*

———. "The Samaritans (*Kutim*) in the Talmud Yerushalmi: Constructs of 'Rabbinic Mind' or Reflections of Social Reality?" Pages 139–60 in *The Talmud Yerushalmi and Graeco-Roman Culture, III.* Edited by Peter Schäfer. Tübingen: Mohr Siebeck, 2002.

———. "Die Taube auf dem Garizim: Zur antisamaritanischen Polemik in der rabbinischen Literatur." Pages 285–302 in *Die Samaritaner und die Bibel: Historische und literarische Wechselwirkungen zwischen biblischen und samaritanischen Traditionen.* Edited by Jörg Frey, Ursula Schattner-Reiser, and Konrad Schmid. Berlin: de Gruyter, 2012.

Levine, Lee I. *The Ancient Synagogue: The First Thousand Years.* 2nd ed. New Haven: Yale University Press, 2005.

Lieber, Laura S. "Forever Let It Be Said: Issues of Authorial Multivocality in a Samaritan Hymn." *Journal of Ancient Judaism* 7 (2016): 113–32.

———. "The Good Christian: A Classical Samaritan Circumcision Poem." In *Genesis in Late Antique Poetry*. Edited by Andrew Faulkner, Jeffrey Wickes, and Cillian O'Hogan. Washington, DC: Catholic University of America Press, forthcoming.

———. *Jewish Palestinian Aramaic Poetry from Late Antiquity*. Cambridge Genizah Studies 8. Leiden: Brill, 2018.

———. "No Translation Needed: Hebrew in Two Samaritan Aramaic Hymns." Pages 161–82 in *The Poet and the World: Festschrift for Wout van Bekkum on the Occasion of His Sixty-Fifth Birthday*. Edited by Joachim Yeshaya, Elisabeth Hollender, and Naoya Katsumata. Berlin: de Gruyter, 2019.

———. "The Rhetoric of Participation: Experiential Elements of Early Hebrew Liturgical Poetry." *Journal of Religion* 90, no. 2 (2010): 119–47.

———. "Scripture Personified: Torah as Character in the Hymns of Marqah." *Jewish Studies Quarterly* 24, no. 2 (2017): 195–217.

———. "Shabbat in the Garden of Eden: Two Samaritan Hymns for Sukkot." In *Avirat Eretz Israel Mahkimah: Land and Spirituality in Rabbinic Literature*. Edited by Shana Schick and Steven Fine. Eugene, OR: Wipf and Stock, forthcoming.

———. "With One Voice: Elements of Acclamation in Early Jewish Liturgical Poetry." *Harvard Theological Review* 111, no. 3 (2018): 401–24.

———. "'You Have Been Skirting This Hill Long Enough': The Tension Between History and Rhetoric in a Byzantine Piyyut." *Hebrew Union College Annual* 80 (2009): 63–114.

Lightstone, Jack N. "My Rival, My Fellow: Conceptual and Methodological Prolegomena to Mapping Inter-Religious Relations in 2nd- and 3rd-Century CE Levantine Society Using the Evidence of Early Rabbinic Texts." Pages 85–108 in *Religious Rivalries in the Early Roman Empire and the Rise of Christianity*. Edited by Leif E. Vagge. Waterloo, ON: Wilfrid Laurier University Press, 2006.

MacDonald, John. *Memar Marqah: The Teachings of Marqah*. 2 vols. Berlin: Töpelmann, 1963.

———. "The Samaritan Doctrine of Moses." *Scottish Journal of Theology* 13, no. 2 (1960): 149–62.

Magen, Yitzhak. "The Areas of Samaritan Settlement in the Roman-Byzantine Period" [Hebrew]. Pages 382–443 in *The Samaritans*. Edited by Ephraim Stern and Hanan Eshel. Jerusalem: Yad Yitzhak ben Zvi, 2002.

———. "Gerizim, Mount." Pages 484–92 in vol. 2 of *The New Encyclopedia of Archaeological Excavations in the Holy Land*. Edited by Ephraim Stern. Jerusalem: Israel Exploration Society, 1993.

———. *Mount Gerizim Excavations: A Temple City*. Edited by Michal Haber and Noga Carmin. Jerusalem: Israel Antiquities Authority, 2008.

———. *The Samaritans and the Good Samaritan*. Edited by Noga Carmin. Translated by Edward Levin. Jerusalem: Israel Antiquities Authority, 2008.

Marcone, Arnaldo. "A Long Late Antiquity? Considerations on a Controversial Periodization." *Journal of Late Antiquity* 1, no. 1 (2008): 4–19.

Mirsky, Aharon. *Yosse ben Yosse: Poems* [Hebrew]. 2nd ed. Jerusalem: Bialik, 1991.

"Newly-Discovered 1,600-Year-Old Mosaic Sheds Light on Ancient Judaism." *UNC University Communications*, July 1, 2019. https://uncnews.unc.edu/2019/07/01/newly-discovered-1600-year-old-mosaic-sheds-light-on-ancient-judaism.

Nitzan, Bilhah. "Prayers for Peace in the Dead Sea Scrolls and the Traditional Jewish Liturgy." Pages 113–32 in *Liturgical Perspectives: Prayer and Poetry in Light of the Dead Sea Scrolls*. Edited by Esther G. Chazon with the collaboration of Ruth A. Clements and Avital Pinnick. Leiden: Brill, 2003.

———. *Qumran Prayer and Religious Poetry*. Translated by Jonathan Chipman. Leiden: Brill, 1994.

Novick, Tzvi. *Piyyut and Midrash: Form, Genre, and History*. Journal of Ancient Judaism Supplements 30. Göttingen: Vandenhoeck & Ruprecht, 2019.

Patrich, Joseph. "Urban Space in Caesarea Maritima, Israel." Pages 77–110 in *Urban Centers and Rural Contexts in Late Antiquity*. Edited by Thomas S. Burns and John W. Eadie. East Lansing: Michigan State University Press, 2001.

Powels, Sylvia. "The Samaritan Calendar and the Roots of Samaritan Chronology." Pages 691–742 in Crown, *Samaritans*.

Pummer, Reinhard. *Early Christian Authors on Samaritans and Samaritanism: Texts, Translations, and Commentary*. Tübingen: Mohr Siebeck, 2002.

———. "Inscriptions." Pages 190–94 in Crown, *Samaritans*.

———. "Samaria/Samaritans." *Oxford Bibliographies Online*. doi:10.1093/obo /9780195393361-017.

———. "Samaritan Material Remains." Pages 135–77 in Crown, *Samaritans*.

———. "Samaritan Rituals and Customs." Pages 650–90 in Crown, *Samaritans*.

———. *The Samaritans: A Profile*. Grand Rapids, MI: Eerdmans, 2016.

———. "Samaritan Synagogues and Jewish Synagogues: Similarities and Differences." Pages 118–60 in *Jews, Christians, and Polytheists in the Ancient Synagogue*. Edited by Steven Fine. London: Routledge, 1999.

———. "Synagogues—Samaritan and Jewish: A New Look at their Differentiating Characteristics." Pages 51–74 in Dušek, *Samaritans*.

Rives, James B. "The Decree of Decius and the Religion of Empire." *Journal of Roman Studies* 89 (1999): 135–54.

Rodrigues Pereira, A. S. *Studies in Aramaic Poetry (c. 100 B.C.E.–c. 600 C.E.): Selected Jewish, Christian and Samaritan Poems*. Leiden: Brill, 1997.

Rutgers, L. V. *The Hidden Heritage of Diaspora Judaism*. Leuven: Peeters, 1998.

Schiffman, Lawrence H. "The Samaritans in Tannaitic Halakhah." *Jewish Quarterly Review* 75, no. 4 (1985): 323–50.

Schorch, Stefan, ed., with Evelyn Burkhardt and Ramona Fändrich. *Leviticus*. Vol. 3 of *The Samaritan Pentateuch*. Berlin: de Gruyter, 2018.

Schreiber, Monika. *The Comfort of Kin: Samaritan Community, Kinship and Marriage*. Leiden: Brill, 2014.

Shepardson, Christine. *Anti-Judaism and Christian Orthodoxy: Ephrem's Hymns in Fourth-Century Syria*. Washington, DC: Catholic University of America Press, 2008.

Sivan, Hagith. *Palestine in Late Antiquity*. Oxford: Oxford University Press, 2008.

Sixdenier, Guy Dominique. "Elements of Samaritan Numismatics." Pages 178–89 in Crown, *Samaritans*.

Stausberg, Michael, Yuhan Sohrab-Dinshaw Vevaina, and Anna Tessmann, eds. *The Wiley Blackwell Companion to Zoroastrianism*. Hoboken, NJ: John Wiley, 2015.

Stenhouse, Paul. "The Chronicle of Abu 'l-Fatḥ and Samaritan Origins: 2 Kings, 2 Chronicles and Ezra-Nehemiah Viewed Through the Prism of Samaritan

Tradition." Pages 303–21 in *Die Samaritaner und die Bibel: Historische und litera-rische Wechselwirkungen zwischen biblischen und samaritanischen Traditionen.* Edited by Jörg Frey, Ursula Schattner-Rieser, and Konrad Schmid. Berlin: de Gruyter, 2012.

———. "Germanus." Page 103 in Crown, Pummer, and Tal, *Companion to Samaritan Studies.*

———. *The Kitāb al-tarīkh of Abū 'l-Fatḥ: Translated into English with Notes.* Sydney: Mandelbaum, 1985.

Swartz, Michael D. "*'Alay le-shabbeaḥ*: A Liturgical Prayer in *Ma'aśeh Merkabah.*" *Jewish Quarterly Review* 77 (1986): 179–90.

Tal, Abraham. *A Dictionary of Samaritan Aramaic.* 2 vols. Leiden: Brill, 2000.

———. "Mârqe." Pages 152–53 in Crown, Pummer, and Tal, *Companion to Samaritan Studies.*

———, ed. *The Samaritan Pentateuch, edited according to MS 6 (C) of the Shekhem Synagogue.* Tel Aviv: Tel Aviv University Press, 1994.

———. "The Samaritan Targum of the Pentateuch." Pages 189–216 in *Mikra: Text, Translation, Reading, and Interpretation of the Hebrew Bible in Ancient Judaism and Early Christianity.* Edited by Martin Jan Mulder and Harry Sysling. Compendia Rerum Iudaicarum ad Novum Testamentum. Assen: Van Gorcum; Philadelphia: Fortress, 1988. Reprint, Grand Rapids, MI: Baker Academic, 2004.

———, ed. *The Samaritan Targum of the Pentateuch: A Critical Edition.* 3 vols. Tel Aviv: Tel Aviv University Press, 1980–83.

Tal, Oren. "A Bilingual Greek-Samaritan Inscription from Apollonia-Arsuf/Sozousa: Yet More Evidence of the Use of ΕΙΣ ΘΕΟΣ ΜΟΝΟΣ Formula Inscriptions Among the Samaritans." *Zeitschrift für Papyrologie und Epigraphik* 194 (2015): 169–75.

Theodor, Yehuda, and Chanoch Albeck, eds. *Midrash Bereshit Rabbah.* 3 vols. Berlin: Itskovski, 1903.

Tsedaka, Benyamim. *Understanding the Israelite-Samaritans, from Ancient to Modern: An Introductory Atlas.* Jerusalem: Carta Jerusalem, 2017.

Tsedaka, Benyamim, and Sharon Sullivan, eds. *The Israelite Samaritan Version of the Torah: First English Translation Compared with the Masoretic Version.* Grand Rapids, MI: Eerdmans, 2013.

Visotsky, Burton L. "Leaning Literary, Reading Rabbinics." *Prooftexts* 28 (2008): 85–99.

Weiss, Herold. "The Sabbath Among the Samaritans." *Journal for the Study of Judaism* 25, no. 2 (1994): 252–73.

Williams, Alan, Sarah Stewart, and Almut Hintze, eds. *The Zoroastrian Flame: Exploring Religion, History and Tradition.* London: I. B. Tauris, 2016.

Yahalom, Joseph, and Michael Sokoloff. *Shirat Bene Ma'arava: Jewish Palestinian Aramaic Poetry from Late Antiquity* [Hebrew]. Jerusalem: Israel Academy of Sciences and Humanities, 1999.

Zsengellér, József. "The Day of Atonement Among the Samaritans." Pages 139–61 in *The Day of Atonement: Its Interpretations in Early Jewish and Christian Traditions.* Edited by Thomas Heike and Tobias Nicklas. Leiden: Brill, 2012.

———, ed. *Samaria, Samarians, Samaritans: Studies on Bible, History and Linguistics.* Berlin: de Gruyter, 2011.

———. "The Samaritan Diaspora in Antiquity." *Acta Antiqua Academiae Scientiarum Hungaricae* 56, no. 2 (2016): 157–75.

SUBJECT INDEX

ANCIENT SOURCE INDEX